Post-Conflict
Central American Literature

Post-Conflict Central American Literature

Searching for Home and Longing to Belong

Yvette Aparicio

Lewisburg
BUCKNELL UNIVERSITY PRESS

Published by Bucknell University Press
Copublished with Rowman & Littlefield
4501 Forbes Boulevard, Suite 200, Lanham, Maryland 20706
www.rowman.com

10 Thornbury Road, Plymouth PL6 7PP, United Kingdom

Copyright © 2014 by Yvette Aparicio

All rights reserved. No part of this book may be reproduced in any form or by any electronic or mechanical means, including information storage and retrieval systems, without written permission from the publisher, except by a reviewer who may quote passages in a review.

British Library Cataloguing in Publication Information Available

Library of Congress Cataloging-in-Publication Data

Library of Congress Cataloging-in-Publication Data Available

ISBN 978-1-61148-547-9 (cloth : alk. paper)

∞™ The paper used in this publication meets the minimum requirements of American National Standard for Information Sciences Permanence of Paper for Printed Library Materials, ANSI/NISO Z39.48-1992.

Printed in the United States of America

To Jamie,
For building a home away from home with me.

Contents

Acknowledgments		ix
Introduction		1
1	Central America in Pieces: Dismembering the Isthmus	23
2	(Re)membering Central America	49
3	The Stench of Belonging	77
4	Touring the Homeland	101
5	Almost Home: Central America in a Virtual World	121
Conclusion		141
Bibliography		153
Index		163
About the Author		169

Acknowledgments

This book is the result of many years of contemplating the meaning of home and homesickness. It began with U.S. texts but quickly migrated south to post-conflict Central America. As it is, it begins and ends with films about Latin America by directors and actors from the North. It is a book that attempts to remain erect astride different geographies of home and belonging.

Fittingly, I owe thanks to people here in the United States and there on the isthmus. I thank Bucknell University Press for backing this book project; and, the editorial staff at Bucknell UP and Rowman & Littlefield for answering my many questions. Grinnell College generously granted me research leaves and summer funding to both conduct research in El Salvador, Nicaragua, and Costa Rica and to write. Richard Fyffe, librarian of the Grinnell College Libraries, repeatedly approved my requests for a library faculty study. The rest of the library staff, including librarians, Interlibrary Loan, Circulation, Acquisitions, and the Media Room always graciously answered my seemingly random questions and fulfilled many requests. I am also thankful for the help I have received from Patty Dale in Academic Support at Grinnell. In Central America, I also benefitted from libraries and research facilities, including the libraries of the Universidad Centroamericana (UCA) in San Salvador and Managua, the Instituto de Historia de Nicaragua y Centroamérica (IHNCA) at UCA-Managua, and the Centro de Investigación e Identidad y Cultura Latinoamericanas (CIICLA) at the Universidad de Costa Rica. At the CIICLA, I am particularly grateful to the late Elvia Ramírez who helped me find many materials and made me feel at home with many cups of coffee.

I am also grateful to the poets and writers who met with me and often gave me copies of their, and others', difficult-to-find books. This list of people to thank is long and incomplete: in Costa Rica—Adriano Corrales Arias, Luis Chaves, Jacinta Escudos, Ana Istarú, Osvaldo Sauma; in El Salvador—Salvador Canjura, Carmen González-Huguet, Claudia Hernández, Osvaldo Hernández, Silvia Ethel Matus, María Cristina Orantes, Eva Ortiz, Silvia Elena Regalado, Susana Reyes, Eleazar Rivera; in Nicaragua—Claribel Alegría, Marta Leonor González, María del Carmen Pérez Cuadra, Helena Ramos, Eunice Shade, Juan Sobalvarro. I also want to thank colleagues and friends who generously shared their time and Central American contacts with me, especially, Mary Addis, Leonel Delgado Aburto, Erin Finzer, Julia Medina, and Sonia Ticas.

This book also benefitted enormously from kind readers, anonymous as well as from the writing group into which John V. Waldron generously invited me. It also profited from incisive questions colleagues posed when I presented chapter drafts at academic conferences. And, without the work of fellow Central Americanists in the United States and on the isthmus this project would not have been possible.

Additionally, I am grateful to friends and colleagues at Grinnell who supported me throughout the research and writing of this book. I name a few. Thanks to Valérie Benoist for her solidarity and especially to Monessa Cummins for working feverishly alongside me at the library, and to Dennis and Jean Perri for their warmth and many amazing meals and conversations.

Finally, I am thankful to my family for a lifetime of sustenance. Ruth Ann and Chuck Leonard treated me as family from the start; as did Kevin, Kris, Scott Leonard and their families. Without my mother, Frances S. Aparicio, and late paternal grandmother, Elena Valdés de Aparicio, El Salvador and the rest of Central America would not be more than a tiny wrinkle on a map. I am eternally grateful to my mother and brothers, Moses and Michael Aparicio, for always keeping a space for me at home, no matter how long I am away.

This book would not have been researched or written without Jamie Leonard's unending supply of love and patience. Our long conversations about literature, Central America, and writing as well as his many insights are threaded throughout this book. Jamie has fueled this project with fantastic meals and encouragement. I cannot thank him enough.

I sincerely and gratefully acknowledge poets and publishers for permission to reprint copyrighted poetic extracts from the following poetry collections:

- from Roque Dalton, *Taberna y otros lugares*, San Salvador: UCA Editores, 1995. Reprinted by permission of Herederos de Roque Dalton [Heirs of Roque Dalton];
- from Ernesto Cardenal, *Antología*, Managua: Nueva Nicaragua-Monimbó, 1983. Reprinted by permission of Ernesto Cardenal;
- from Ernesto Cardenal, translated by Donald D. Walsh, *Zero Hour and Other Documentary Poems*, copyright ©1980 by Ernesto Cardenal. Reprinted by permission of New Directions Publishing Corp.;
- from Leonel Rugama, "The Earth is a Satellite of the Moon," from *Poetry Like Bread*, ed. Martín Espada. Williamantic: Curbstone Press, ©2000 by Curbstone Press/Northwestern University Press. New and Expanded edition published in 2000 by Curbstone Books. First edition published in 1994 by Curbstone Books. All rights reserved;
- from Claribel Alegría, *Esto soy: Antología poética*, San Salvador: Dirección de Publicaciones e Impresos (DPI), 2004. Reprinted by permission of DPI;

- from Marta Leonor González, *Casa de fuego*, Managua: 400 Elefantes, 2008, and *Huérfana embravecida*, Managua: Ediciones de Bolsillo 400 Elefantes, 1999. Reprinted by permission of 400 Elefantes and Marta Leonor González;
- from Susana Reyes, *Historia de los espejos*, San Salvador: Dirección de Publicaciones e Impresos (DPI), 2004. Reprinted by permission of DPI;
- from María Cristina Orantes, *Paso leve que el polvo avanza*, San Salvador: Alkimia Libros, 2005. Reprinted by permission of María Cristina Orantes;
- from Juan Sobalvarro, *Agenda del desempleado*, Managua: 400 Elefantes, 2007 and *Unánime*, Managua: Nuevo Signo INC, 1999. Reprinted by permission of 400 Elefantes and Juan Sobalvarro;
- and from Luis Chaves, *Asfalto: un road poem*, San Jose: Ediciones Perro Azul, 2006 and *Chan Marshall*, Madrid: Visor Libros, 2005, and *Historias Polaroid*, San Jose: Ediciones Perro Azul, 2000. Reprinted by permission of Luis Chaves.

All translations are my own unless otherwise noted.

Introduction

País mío vení
papaíto país solo con tu sol
todo el frío del mundo me ha tocado a mí
y tú sudando amor amor amor.

[Come, country of mine
papaíto country alone with your sun
I got all the cold in the world
and you sweat love, love, love.]
—Roque Dalton, "Temores"

Bananas, Woody Allen's 1971 farce, opens with famed sportscaster Howard Cosell calling the assassination of the president of San Marcos. Though San Marcos is a fictitious Latin American country, the usual markers of tropical Latin America are accounted for in the opening scenes: palm trees, colonial buildings, crowds of agitated people and military men (not to mention the brown faces), and "colorful hats" and "flags."[1] Cosell's presence at this "live assassination" intimates the role of the United States in Latin American coups and other political crises, additional markers of so-called Banana Republics. Cosell's filming of the soon-to-be dead president and of the "traditional bombing of the American embassy," and later his cameo calling the play-by-play of the Mellishes' honeymoon night, brings attention to the idea of Latin American politics as a U.S. sport, as well as the intrusion of U.S. television into every aspect of daily life.

Allen's character, Fielding Mellish, is lured to San Marcos by Nancy, a college student dabbling in political activism, and kept there by corrupt politicians and Cuban-like revolutionaries who see in Mellish the opportunity to attain power. Before ending up living with San Marcos guerrillas, Mellish lives alone in New York City. He is an inept product tester, too embarrassed to be seen buying pornographic magazines. When Nancy knocks on his door asking him to sign a political petition, Mellish, attempting to sound like an intellectual, clumsily initiates a senseless conversation. It is clear in the exchange that, like Mellish, Nancy does not understand the philosophers and jargon she interjects. The two date for a while, but Nancy is dissatisfied with the relationship and finally breaks it off. It is this breakup, and not political commitment, that incites Mellish to travel to San Marcos, one of Nancy's pet political interests. Upon Mellish's arrival in Latin America, *Bananas* focuses on a hapless Mellish in (mis)adventures with the guerrillas as they struggle for political power. Eventually Mellish, dressed in fatigues and sporting a fake Castro-inspired beard, returns to the United States as a rebel leader and is prosecuted for his subversive activities. After court scenes that lampoon U.S. political figures and current events, Mellish is freed on the condition he does not move into the judge's neighborhood. At the end of the film Nancy unenthusiastically marries Mellish.

The film is populated throughout with parodies of Latin American governments and their armed opposition as well as of overzealous but ineffective U.S. activists who dream of effecting change in "backward" foreign countries. Its portrayal of revolutionaries recalls Cuba and its revolution of the late 1950s against Fulgencio Batista and Fidel Castro's subsequent regime. But its images also prefigure Central American armed conflicts of the 1970s through the 1990s. In Allen's film the vicissitudes of these conflicts are fodder for jokes and slapstick comedy. Here the whole of Latin America is replete with a wacky abundance of people who have "gone bananas."

Why begin a discussion of contemporary Central American literature with one of Woody Allen's early, minor films? Why begin with visions of Latin America from without instead of from within?

What *Bananas* offers is a concise and comical presentation of Central American reality.[2] The revolutions that shook the region from the 1950s through the 1990s are reflected in the idealism of Allen's revolutionaries, dictatorial governments' corruption and abuses, and the film's mockery of malleable ideology. What can one do but laugh at the governmental edicts ordering citizens to change their underwear every half hour and to wear it on top of their clothes to make it easy for the security forces to check for compliance? Or with the decision to make Swedish the official language of a clearly un-Scandinavian country? Or even more outrageous, the guerrillas' election of Fielding Mellish, a bumbling American tourist, as their leader? While the parody is obvious, it is not difficult to find underlying truths or half-truths in the depiction of politics in Latin America. What is also clear is that, for some foreigners, viewing the region's political crises approximates watching a sporting event. In addition to comparing the excitement surrounding the assassination to that around the first Clay (Ali)-Liston match (Miami, 1964), Howard Cosell's narration follows the pattern of calling boxing matches. He announces "El presidente's" entrance into the plaza, or boxing ring, outside the presidential palace as if he were the reigning champ. The camera then focuses on the revolver, or boxing glove, that knocks the president down. At this point, Cosell bullies his way through the crowd—using his authority as a U.S. television sportscaster[3]—to get the "champ's" reaction to being knocked out. Ultimately Cosell gets his way and gets his television network a shot of the dying president and of his last words, "Fascist dictator," as well as a short interview with the new "champ," the dictator General Vargas. In the interview, Vargas enumerates the rights he'll curtail in order to destroy the rebels as though he were proclaiming future sports victories to come. The scene of Cosell pushing through the "mob" of onlookers is easily read as a representation of the tactics the United States uses to force Latin Americans to submit to its political and economic will. Further, the film reminds us of Latin America's history of repressive regimes and of U.S. support of many of those regimes.

As in Allen's farce, much of U.S. policy toward Central America in the 1980s required the reader and viewer to suspend disbelief. As Joan Didion puts it in her acerbic 1983 reportage on El Salvador[4] early in its civil war (1980–1992),

> [The Land-to-the-Tiller program[5]] had been one of many occasions when the American effort in El Salvador seemed based on auto-suggestion, a dreamwork devised to obscure any intelligence that might trouble the dreamer. (92)
> It occurred to me that we were talking exclusively about the appearance of things, about how the situation might be made to look better. (93)

Not unlike *Bananas*, Didion's *Salvador* confronts the non-Salvadoran U.S. reader with a place that is "ineffable" (61, 64, 74, 96) and that can only be apprehended if its surface, its appearance, is seen as its entire substance. Didion's cast of characters maneuvers through their stays in "Salvador" by accepting a dream undisturbed by troubling "intelligence," or inside information. Didion's own time in El Salvador, mostly spent among other U.S. journalists, embassy workers, and high-ranking Salvadoran soldiers, leads her to characterize her experiences there—not to mention the place—as one of "pointless confrontation with aimless authority" (104) and where "any situation can turn to terror" (105).[6] The paperback cover of Didion's book (1983) is plastered with rave reviews of her journalistic report. One in particular grabs my attention, "THE SUBJECT IS FEAR.... Hot places, opaque people and events whose edges shimmer into hallucination.... Didion has produced an account that evokes García Márquez at his best" (*Washington Post Book World*). The review—written by Joanne Omang, a *Washington Post* foreign correspondent stationed in Latin America—highlights Didion's ability to render the place and the terror it elicits without bogging down the text with facts.[7] Didion, unfettered from the responsibility of having to report "straight" facts, produces a "mood piece to break molds."[8] She can also soak up El Salvador's hallucinatory effects at her leisure. For Omang, the narration of historical events edged with details that may seem fantastical to some readers links Didion to Gabriel García Márquez's magical realism. As evidence, she cites Didion's assertion that García Márquez is really a social realist (Didion, *Salvador*, 59). Thus Omang draws attention to *Salvador*'s reliance on the author's constant re-creation of the excesses of violence and fear and the resulting paranoia born of the Salvadoran civil war and of her hosts' and wealthy interviewees' acceptance of paranoia as normal. The veneer of normalcy in Salvadoran daily life is clear in Didion's retelling of her trip to Metrocentro, "Central America's Largest Shopping Mall" (35). As she strolls through the mall, Didion takes notes on the merchandise for sale and the human background, "young matrons in tight Sergio Valente jeans, trailing maids and babies behind them" (36). In and of itself the image of Didion strolling through an impoverished, warring country's modern monument to modernity and consumerism is jarring. But what is more jarring is the juxtaposition of this "commonplace" image for the U.S. reader with one of normalcy, or not anomalousness, for El Salvador, that of the military's arrest of a young man in front of Metrocentro. Didion's freedom to portray the mall shoppers in a sarcastic way but to avert her eyes from the arrest is not unlike the "dreamwork" (92) required of the United States to continue funding El Salvador's leaders. The mall, an example of Western normality and modernity, is one illustration of the parody of El Salvador's "development" that made it eligible to continue receiving U.S. aid and allowed the Reagan administration to announce "progress" in the early 1980s even as Salvadorans were disappeared and U.S. journalists were harassed. In short, using different mediums, both *Salvador* and *Bananas* present aesthetic visions of Latin America. One reduces the irreducible Salvadoran experience to fear and the other pokes fun at the region's history of demagoguery and concomitant violence.

The satirizing and critique of political and historical processes as well as the heavy presence of the media (in the form of journalists and sportscasters) that we see in Didion and Allen serve as tools to begin thinking about the current state of a post-conflict, globalizing Central America and its literature. The representation of Latin America's political instability and cultural peculiarities by outsiders—foreigners like Didion and Allen and his cast of characters—animates texts written by Central Americans about their homelands. Central American texts depicting the isthmus's dire straits frequently use humor, parody, and irony. Despite the low odds of success, many such texts hold out an element of hope for and a degree of belief in the possibility of change. In these texts, Central America is a place of habitation (or home) and of origin and nationality (homeland) that exists both intangibly and yet tangibly. In examinations of quotidian reality, by Central Americans as well as by outsiders such as Allen and Didion, this place cannot be more evident. It cannot be more *there*. It is a presence palpable but also foreign, hallucinatory in its extreme violence, almost too *there* for its inhabitants and visitors. Its ubiquity, or *there-ness*, is difficult to assimilate but impossible to ignore. In Didion's words,

These were not people much given to solutions, to abstracts: their lives were grounded in the specific. (47)

Actual information was hard to come by in El Salvador, perhaps because this is not a culture in which high value is placed on the definite. (61)

The first quote narrates a day trip to San Francisco Gotera, the capital of Morazán province, an area highly disputed by the Salvadoran army and the guerrillas. Didion describes the attitudes of the local church's foreign Franciscan priests and nuns toward the violence and privations to which they and the local citizens are subjected. The second quote reflects on Salvadorans' apparent inability to use numbers scientifically or to give concrete information. One example she uses is of the varied readings published in the press to describe the strength of the 1982 San Salvador earthquake (61). In these observations the author seems to contradict herself in her analysis of Salvadoran reality: its daily difficulties are too much to allow for abstract musings, but at the same time this reality cannot be defined, or described in "definite" terms. But, for me, Didion's interpretation attests to the importance of place in experience. The existence of the place she calls "Salvador" cannot be denied. It is *there*. Yet it also cannot be grasped definitely. Didion's short volume is an example of the definite and indefinite in the experience of place. While her experience differs from that of Central Americans who contemplate their home and homeland at home, they too cope with the weight of the isthmus's presence in daily life.

The preponderance of Central America's *here-ness*, or its weight on the mind of many of its poets and writers, is plain in varied contemporary texts. This chapter's epigraph, a stanza from "Temores," published in Roque Dalton's award-winning poetry collection *Taberna y otros lugares*[9] (Casa de las Américas[10] Prize in Poetry, 1969), is a case in point. Dalton (1935–1975) was and is well-known as a Salvadoran urban guerrilla, leftist polemicist, and poet.[11] Like Allen's Mellish and Didion, Dalton's poetic speakers confess to being afraid in the humid "tropics," of being overwhelmed by its geography, its climate, its way of life. But, unlike Didion and Allen, Dalton also finds home in that place, home that is too present for comfort. The epigraph's poetic I yearns for and calls out to his home, his "papaíto país" (18). In this, the poem's final stanza, Dalton imagines a country that is endearing and seems so full of familial love that in the tropical heat it even sweats "love, love, love" (20). And the poetic speaker reveals his love for, and intimacy with, his *patria* (homeland) by addressing it as *papaíto*, a term of endearment used between parents and children. The poetic I, away from his *papaíto*, laments his physical distance and frigid, sleepless nights (16), while in the meantime his homeland withstands unpredictable environmental changes (snow) and political change (military men) (1, 6, 8). Through it all, Dalton's *papaíto* maintains its heat. Away from El Salvador, the poetic I freezes and misses its hot climate and the home it represents for him (17, 18). In "Temores," as is the homeland's warmth, Dalton's cold is both literal and figurative: he is away from home, cold and fearing for his homeland's future. The sweltering sun under which the *papaíto país* sweats provokes a distinctly different reaction from Dalton's poetic speaker than from Didion's narrator and Allen's reluctant revolutionary. While Dalton's poetic speaker yearns for the sun's warmth and perceives love in sweat, Didion's sweaty hands "kept blurring" her attempts to write,[12] and she eventually simply has to acquiesce to El Salvador's harsh heat and conditions. Her text repeatedly notes the impossibility of describing the country of El Salvador and its inhabitants, of describing the numbing fear being there causes her and her companions. In Didion's reportage El Salvador is the terrifying heart of darkness (highlighted by *Salvador*'s epigraph[13]) that cannot be defined. That same indefinable place that Didion rushes out of and where people seem unable to provide her with hard data[14] is the same place that Dalton and other Central American poets and writers call home. Surely the homeland is not always *papaíto país*, and its heat is not always love; however, the homeland is—to those who live in it, write about it, and long for it—the *here*, present even when its name goes unspoken.

Home and homeland are different from the nation, particularly for the purposes of this book. Home and homeland are belonging; they are more like *patria*. Home represents the ties that bind us to a local place. The homeland is that place that contains and grounds home and gives us a home identity, a nationality, to carry beyond the local home. Home is a sentimental, psychological place to inhabit, to defend, to love. To be sure, as is nation, it is a place people will die to defend, as during the Central American internal conflicts when both the right and left fought for the nation's seat of power and for an imagined homeland. But home, rather than nation, is belonging. It is an image of community, a feeling carried in and away from it and represented by its "authentic" foods, its national symbols (e.g., flags, birds, mottos, nicknames, heroes), and its geography. It is also the place defended, no matter what, during *fútbol* contests.[15] The affective ties that compel soccer fans to continue to cheer for their home countries even when they have emigrated elsewhere exemplify the importance of home identity in a global world.[16] In examples of Mexican and Latin American fans cheering Mexico, for instance, in a soccer match against the United States, or waving their home countries' flags while chanting proimmigrant slogans in immigrant rights protests, fans and protesters do not see a disconnect between their actions and their daily life in the United States. In short, here the pull of the *patria* does not give way to notions of more flexible global identities even when globalization efforts, through Free Trade agreements such as CAFTA-DR (Dominican Republic–Central America Free Trade Agreement), have resulted in immigrants' departures from home. Even in a globalized world, speaking against the homeland is akin to cursing another's mother. It is to "mentar la madre." Or in Puerto Rican Calle 13's "Latinoamérica," not loving one's homeland means not loving one's mother.[17] The subject of this book, then, is homeland as place of origin and, most importantly, of home as belonging, a "feeling" that is palpable yet undefinable; of being part of a flexible, changeable yet constant *we*.

National borders define and assign a nationality to *us*. For this book, home as the feeling of belonging is not a political call to nationalist sentiments.[18] Benedict Anderson highlights the *political* nature of the nation in his seminal text on nationalism and nation-formation: "Indeed, nationness is the most universally legitimate value in the political life of our time."[19] Anderson's nation is delimited by set borders, by sovereignty, and imagined as a shared space with other like-citizens (7).[20] Most important to this study's conception of belonging to a place, called home and homeland, is Anderson's contention that the imaginary connection between compatriots is made possible through mass-produced books and newspapers and their separate but simultaneous consumption by (national) readers. He posits that as one reads the morning paper, the reader "is continually reassured that the imagined world is visibly rooted in everyday life" (35–36). The newspaper thus grounds the reader in the local, her/his everyday, and demonstrates "remarkable confidence in community in anonymity" (36). While Anderson's text, originally published in 1983 and expanded in 1991, predates the explosion of Internet communication, his concept of an "imagined community" fed and kept alive by citizens' simultaneous consumption of language (text and image), "building in effect *particular solidarities*," maintains its validity (133; italics in the original). For Anderson, what changes in society and consciousness, and solidarity with compatriots, cannot explain about nationhood are the intangible "attachments," the affection that people feel for their imagined communities, or "inventions of their imaginations" (141, 154). It is these attachments and "fond imaginings" that my book considers (154).

The fondness residents feel for the place they inhabit is clearly related to nationalism and national identity, but again it is not limited to politics and/or nationalist movements. Sociologist Craig Calhoun, in his 1997 study of nationalism, presents the formation of solidarity among citizens as important to a sense of national identity.[21] He posits that seeing the nation as a home is a "powerful facilitator" of nationalist programs that impels citizens to mobilize with their compatriots;[22] again, though, that solidarity does not automatically equate to political action. Further, "membership in the category 'nation' locates people in a complex, globally integrated world" whereas it is a "web of interpersonal relationships [that] locates a person locally."[23] For me, Calhoun's "web" that links compatriots together at a local level is home. And it is also this extensive linking of anonymous citizens that places home inside the *patria*, or homeland.

In a similar line of thought that also draws a connection between the homeland and sentiment, Carlos Monsiváis's essay on Mexican nationalism in a post-9/11 globalized era reflects on what he terms "un sentimiento nacionalista cambiante" [a changing nationalist sentiment].[24] Monsiváis characterizes nationalism and national identity, in a society dominated by mass media and consumption, as sentiments that reflect class divisions (32). The social and economic hierarchy that splits Mexican society between the wealthy elite and the poor masses, or "los de Abajo" [the underdogs], determines the scope of their purchasing power and also their access to Mexican-ness.[25] For Monsiváis, the masses have appropriated national identity from the elite classes and politicians, whereas "traditional" nationalism was paternalistic and multiclass (32, 36).[26] Monsiváis's alternative mass-controlled "post-traditional" nationalism retains its historical symbology—flags, statuary, commemorations of national anniversaries (36)—and is, in summary,

> casi exclusivamente popular, rijoso, obsceno, desconfiado, desencantado, cínico, admirador de la tecnología, *centrado no en la unidad política sino en el traslado casi íntegro de la nación a la esfera de la vida cotidiana tal y como la expresa el habla* [almost exclusively popular, libidinous, obscene, distrustful, disenchanted, cynical, admirer of technology, *focused not on political unity but rather on the almost complete transfer of the nation to the sphere of daily life as it is expressed in speech*]. (36; italics in original)

The cleaving of the sentiment of nationalism from "la unidad política" and its incorporation into quotidian living divests nationalism of its more institutional trappings. It also places national belonging in marginal communities. In fact, Monsiváis likens this nationalism to a condensing of Mexican-ness into a jingle (e.g., "Mexicano tú puedes" [Mexican, you can]) (36), as any other product in consumer society.[27] It also represents a gradual separation from politics and from a sense of communal obligations among compatriots (43). In short, Monsiváis's nationalism is a disembodied nationalism, a sentiment that relies on representations of the nation but is disconnected from its institutions, its formal workings, and citizenship practices. But it still bespeaks the sense of belonging to a *patria*. Monsiváis's is akin to social psychologist Michael Billig's "banal nationalism." In their review of theories of nationalism, Graham Day and Andrew Thompson note that "banal nationalism" is focused on "symbolic markings of nations," in other words, on the rhetoric of national identity or a conception of "national belonging."[28] As Billig writes in his study, unlike conventional conceptions of nationalism, "banal nationalism" is reproduced as "ideological habits" through which the nation is "indicated, or 'flagged,' in the lives of its citizenry."[29] This constant "flagging" of the nation and its characteristics, and of the national identity it entails, is a nationalism that "far from being an intermittent mood" of extremist politics is constant.[30] Following Billig, Day and Thompson posit that this "multidimensional" national identity allows us to see that "national" characteristics "provide a background hum within which a particular identity is constituted."[31]

This constant "hum" of national identity constructs markers of home and homeland, the ambient music of daily life, in contemporary Central American texts and is what concerns this book. This "hum" is not the pounding sound of a patriotic anthem played on Independence Day or at official commemorations of national feats. Rather the homeland and home reverberate more quietly in the daily life of its citizens, in the foods that are labeled *típicas* (typical) or *criollas* (creole), in regionalisms, in telltale accents, in sports affiliations, in the home objects for which the immigrant and the exile yearn. It is the place of belonging, like it or not. In the texts I read in this book, acknowledging belonging does not mean uncritically celebrating home or idealizing it. It may mean rejecting it vociferously but staying put. Home is a presence, a thrum, a pulsing *here-ness* that exists amid the mass media images of the placeless-ness trumpeted by globalization.

The place that thrums in this book, contemporary Central America, is a place whose very definition, as a geographic and cultural and political entity, has been historically debated and questioned. Such debates about the definition of Central America aptly demonstrate both the region's marginality—does it exist?—and its importance in international relations at distinct historic moments (e.g., the construction of an interoceanic canal[32] or the Cold War). Historian Héctor Pérez-Brignoli, for instance, begins *A Brief History of Central America* (1989) by asserting that, depending on how the isthmus is read, it can include the Yucatan Peninsula, Belize, and Panama, as he and Carolyn Hall read it in the coauthored 2003 *Historical Atlas of Central America*, or be limited to the five countries that formed the United Provinces of Central America in 1821 after declaring independence from Spain.[33] *A Brief History* defines Central America as Costa Rica, El Salvador, Guatemala, Honduras, and Nicaragua "on the basis of a common history in the economic, social, political and cultural senses."[34] Other well-known historical studies, including *Central America: A Nation Divided* and *Understanding Central America: Global Forces, Rebellion, and Change*, delimit Central America to the same five countries.[35] Due to their different histories of colonialism and nation-ness, Panama and Belize are not often incorporated into isthmian studies. Central American historians explain that Belize's and Panama's histories diverge from those of the other five nations: Belize did not gain independence from Great Britain until 1981.[36] Panama was not an active participant in the region's politics "up until the Torrijos regime (1968–1981)."[37] In both of the cited examples, Belizean and Panamanian history is explored only when it directly impacts its neighbors. As such, in this project I do not include Belize and Panama.

Nor do I include Guatemala or Honduras, even though they share important cultural, social, historical, and economic characteristics with El Salvador, Nicaragua, and Costa Rica. Each of these countries cultivates its own history and culture, and the resultant (dis)unity has oftentimes manifested itself through a type of sibling rivalry as, for example, in Honduras's and El Salvador's senseless Soccer War (1969);[38] Costa Rica's and Nicaragua's continued disputes over the San Juan River;[39] and, the recent CAFTA-DR negotiations in which each country attempted to gain an edge over the others but to which the five Central American countries eventually acquiesced.[40] However, although its decades-long war between right-wing government forces and leftist guerrillas shares similarities with the Nicaraguan and Salvadoran armed conflicts of the 1970s and 1980s, Guatemala's civil war turned out to be much more protracted, beginning years prior to its neighbors' and not ending until the mid-1990s. It also followed a decade of reform (1944–1954). Yet what most distances Guatemala from my exploration of its neighbors' contemplation of the meanings of home and homeland is its government's destruction of ancestral homelands and genocide of the Guatemalan Maya.[41] Honduras, on the other hand, did not endure an internal armed conflict during the time period under discussion. Thus, in the context of ideologically driven civil wars and a neoliberal post-conflict era, and due to the representativeness and particularity of their national and literary histories, Nicaragua and El Salvador (and Costa Rica as a counterpoint) engage in a distinctly productive dialogue on the poetic construction and deconstruction of notions of home, homeland (*patria*), and belonging.

The selection of these three countries is both for their literary, cultural, and historical similarities as well as for their differences. Both Nicaragua and El Salvador experienced revolutionary struggles in the 1970s and 1980s, respectively, with different outcomes. While the Sandinistas were able to topple Anastasio (Tachito) Debayle Somoza[42] in 1979 and maintain power until Daniel Ortega's 1990 electoral loss to Violeta Chamorro, El Salvador's twelve-year civil war ended in a military stalemate and the subsequent signing of a peace treaty (Chapultepec Accords, 1992). The Sandinistas (Sandinista National Liberation Front—FSLN), unlike El Salvador's FMLN (Farabundo Martí National Liberation Front), were able to foment popular uprisings across the country against the Somoza regime. In the two years prior to Somoza's overthrow, the FSLN garnered the support of the Group of Twelve, which included well-respected intellectuals and business people, the Nicaraguan Catholic Church, and Latin American leaders. In addition, key events in 1978 catapulted the FSLN toward success: the mass mobilization that followed the assassination of Pedro Joaquín Chamorro, the owner and editor of Nicaragua's main daily, *La Prensa*, and the capture of the National Palace by FSLN commander

Edén Pastora. The Somoza regime's response was to increase repression of the opposition. Eventually, the OAS (Organization of American States) condemned the government's tactics, and the United States stopped sending military aid. The FSLN's victory, though, was not unanimously celebrated at home or internationally. By the early 1980s the Sandinistas were fighting a counterrevolutionary war against different Contra groups, including those supported by the United States. As the Contra War dragged on, funding for the FSLN's reforms in education and health languished, international pressure to negotiate mounted, and the revolutionary government was obliged to hold elections. Ortega lost to Chamorro, the widow of Pedro Joaquín Chamorro.[43]

The civil war in El Salvador was also punctuated by key moments, but these did not culminate in unified mass mobilization. In the 1970s, repressive military dictators and military-civilian juntas ruled El Salvador. In the fall of 1979, politically progressive military officers overthrew dictator Humberto Romero. The coup leaders formed a military-civilian junta and established a government program that included agrarian and financial reforms as well as the dissolution of the official paramilitary organization, ORDEN (Democratic Nationalist Organization). Both ends of the political spectrum resoundingly rejected these government initiatives, and a new junta with U.S. backing was formed. Its leader, José Napoleón Duarte, would lead El Salvador for the rest of the decade. Importantly, Duarte's junta supported the continued use of repressive counterinsurgency against the armed opposition.[44] While human rights abuses were par for the course in 1980s El Salvador, as I note earlier in my discussion of *Salvador*, three events temporarily galvanized public opinion against the Salvadoran government but did not lead to spontaneous uprisings or an end to the conflict: the March 1980 assassination of Archbishop Óscar Arnulfo Romero during Mass; the December 1980 rape and murder of three U.S. nuns and a laywoman; and the November 1989 assassination of six Jesuit professors, their housekeeper, and her daughter at the Universidad Centroamericana (UCA) in San Salvador. Similarly, the FMLN's inaptly named "final" offensive (1981) and "general" offensive (1989), in which the FMLN attacked simultaneously across El Salvador, failed to inspire the mass uprisings seen in Nicaragua. Between 1990 and 1992, under the auspices of the United Nations and the OAS, the FMLN and Salvadoran government negotiated an end to the war.[45] An estimated 70,000 people died, approximately 80 percent at the hands of military, police, and ORDEN.[46]

While the political ideologies, strategies, and practices of Nicaragua's and El Salvador's revolutionary movements can be compared and contrasted at many levels ad nauseam, regardless they shared a fundamental goal: to create a new homeland to replace the current homeland. That is to say, in both cases, revolutionaries fought to replace entrenched military-dictatorial regimes with left-inspired, imaginary visions of their countries' possible futures. Costa Rica, on the other hand, served as a safe haven for exiled leftists and upended the war image of its neighbors with its own representation of a peaceful Central American homeland. In the 1970s and 1980s, Costa Rica also faced popular manifestations protesting, among other things, worsening living conditions, but it did not face armed opposition. *Understanding Central America* contends that Costa Rica's political and social stability "resulted from elites' decisions in the 1970s and 1980s to alleviate some of the erosion of popular living standards and to avoid brutal political repression."[47] In other words, Costa Ricans shared their Nicaraguan and Salvadoran neighbors' economic, social, and political concerns; but, their government's response was specifically not to use violence to repress opposition. Rather, the Costa Rican government enacted changes to cushion the lower classes from the worst everyday living difficulties.[48] Costa Rica's years of peace[49] and its status as a place of sociopolitical and economic refuge allow it to serve as a counterpoint to 1970s and 1980s Nicaragua and El Salvador.

The conception of home in Central America continues to be contested. The debate surrounding the approval of CAFTA-DR is a case in point.[50] The treaty received prompt approval in all legislatures except Costa Rica's, where eventually the country's citizenry narrowly passed the treaty by referendum. The campaigns for approval and rejection of the free trade agreement mobilized a frenzy of political advertisements presenting opposing visions of Costa Rican-ness.[51] Advocates promoted images of economic development, abundant employment, and modernization to convince citizens to vote yes and warned that a no vote would retard Costa Rica's economic growth and void its exceptionalism. Meanwhile, opponents recalled Costa Rica's historical differences and advantages— its public health and education systems as well as its public assistance programs. In short, both sides presented a partisan vision of the homeland in order to "save" it from the disaster that the rejection or approval of the treaty would bring. Similar calls to citizens' concern for the *patria*'s wellness are heard in the news media as El Salvador and Nicaragua struggle with dire poverty, under- and unemployment, *maras* (gangs), drug trafficking, human rights abuses, and the like. Costa Rica maintains its neoliberal economic path amid current economic crises and while reducing its commitment to the country's welfare state.[52] Drug and sex trafficking and domestic issues, largely immigration from Nicaragua, Panama, and Colombia, precipitate ongoing debates on the homeland's changing demographics.[53]

The current debates on the fate of twenty-first century Central America have not reproduced politicized literature that would echo the production of the 1970s through the 1990s.[54] In El Salvador and Nicaragua, literary production during the war periods as well as the first Sandinista regime[55] present similarities in the predominance both of politicized poetry and testimonial narratives.[56] Both countries share a tradition of politically committed poetry written by well-known figures such as Roque Dalton (1935–1975), Claribel Alegría (1924), Ernesto Cardenal (1925), and Gioconda Belli (1948), among others. Many of these figures also participate(d) in the region's political movements either as combatants or as supporters. This new politicized poetry by poet-combatants, poet-activists, and poet-fellow travelers denounced the injustices and oppression suffered by the poor majority and by reformers at the hands of repressive governments. Stylistically this poetry was "conversational,"[57] colloquial, often direct though not devoid of metaphor and, importantly, "urgent." In other words, it was the poetic counterpart of the era's popular testimonial narratives. The many anonymous "guerrilla" poems, prison poems, Cardenal's epic retelling of Central American history, Sandinista workshop poetry, and revolutionary erotic poetry by women, for instance, attracted many politically committed literary scholars to the region during the late 1970s and through the early 1990s. Their scholarly research resulted in many journal articles and collections of essays, as well as poetry anthologies and translations.[58] Unfortunately, however, only one book-length study problematized the entire region's poetry. In 1990 John Beverley and Marc Zimmerman published their influential *Literature and Politics in the Central American Revolutions*.[59] In the post-war period (early to mid-1990s), however, Central American poetry lost its luster for both publishers of creative works and for literature scholars. Unlike studies of poetry, studies of narrative production as well as narrative texts have appeared steadily in the last ten to fifteen years.[60] Recent narrative studies include those by Arturo Arias and Ana Patricia Rodríguez.

Arturo Arias closes his "inconclusive conclusion" to *Taking Their Word: Literature and the Signs of Central America* with the contention that *afectividad* (sensitivity or affection) is an instrument that Central Americans can wield against the globalization that "threaten[s] to obscure them," and that with *afectividad* Central Americans can "rework their singular identities."[61] In her reading of Central American fictional and other cultural productions, *Dividing the Isthmus: Central American Transnational Histories, Literatures, and Cultures*, Ana Patricia Rodríguez also reflects upon the detrimental effects of globalization and neocolonialism on the isthmus's inhabitants and their nations. She examines the isthmus as a "trespassed" "intermediary zone of crossings" that Central Americans continually reimagine and "reterritorialize."[62] The following project's exploration of the meaning and constitution of home and homeland, of the sense of belonging, responds to Arias's and Rodríguez's calls for critical attention to Central Americans' "many affections"[63] and impassioned appeals against the isthmus's consumption and destruction[64] by oppressive global processes.

In addition, this project diversifies literary and cultural studies of Central America by focusing on poetry and its intersections with the short story, and by calling attention to young poets and writers. Contemporary poets in Central America have had to come to terms with the poetic and political legacies of committed poetic production. The poetry of the post-conflict, globalized era has begun to turn away from the tone of political outrage and protest that preceded, and popularized, it. It has also turned inward to become more intimate, less enmeshed in its social environs. At the same time, its cultural referents have become less local and more global. It is also a poetry that tests contemporary generic boundaries in form as well as content. For instance, one poet studied here produces classic sonnets written in colloquial Spanish critiquing the state of post-conflict peace. Others write nostalgic "postcard" or "Polaroid" poems, while another narrates a road trip in short prose poems and calls the book-length text a "road poem." The experimentation with form can be read as a response to the tradition of the socially committed poetry of the past and to the digital globalized present. The inclusion of select contemporaneous short fiction alongside poetry plays a role similar to that of Costa Rica as counterpoint to El Salvador and Nicaragua. It highlights poems' poetics as well as their push into prose. The stories I weave into the analyses of poetry share thematic and formal concerns. They, too, make ample use of metaphor and offer the reader indirect, perhaps fuzzy snapshots of protagonists and their settings. They help to amplify poets' representations of Central American homes and homelands. Narrative poems and poetic short stories dialogue with each other and create a dynamic vision of the isthmus. While the short story writers I include have received some critical attention, this book is the first to seriously critique the works of up-and-coming Salvadoran, Nicaraguan, and Costa Rican poets such as Susana Reyes, Juan Sobalvarro, and Luis Chaves. All of the writers I study in this book have published in respected regional presses including the DPI (San Salvador), 400 Elefantes (Managua), and Perro Azul (San José); in international venues (Visor, La Garúa); and, in print and Internet journals.

Against the backdrop of the many challenges faced by the globalizing isthmus, this book explores conceptions of home after the end of revolutionary experiments and of the waning of the dominance of politicized, militant literature. I trace the changes in the ways in which contemporary Salvadoran, Nicaraguan, and Costa Rican poets and short story writers interpret and inhabit their homelands. It is an interdisciplinary study of the meanings of home (those feelings of belonging to a place) and the homeland (a place that contains an individual's original home and which provides individuals a home identity) in post-conflict, globalized, and neoliberal El Salvador, Nicaragua, and Costa Rica. It analyzes literary representations of and reflections on the current conditions as well as the recent pasts of Central American homelands. It is literary in that it highlights poets' and writers' aesthetic renditions of home. Yet it also engages with, and is grounded by, other disciplines' explorations of contemporary Central American cultures, politics, and societies. In effect, this book contests the hegemonic and apparently commonsense view that globalization produces a mode of global citizenship and globalized experiences that transcend the significance and function of local citizenship and daily life. It details the ways by which contemporary Central American writers are imagining and finding home.

This book begins with the study of revolutionary poets' visions of the homeland and its future. In this first chapter I research the function of the representation of martyred heroes' bodies as well as of monuments to memorialize the national past in Latin America. I then examine the metaphorical dismemberment of the homeland in 1960s and 1970s works by Ernesto Cardenal (Nicaragua, 1925), Leonel Rugama (Nicaragua, 1949–1970), and Roque Dalton (El Salvador, 1935–1975) and also analyze the contemporary short fiction of Claudia Hernández (El Salvador, 1975). In these varied texts, writers engage official, hegemonic constructions of the homeland to debunk them and present their own versions of home. I demonstrate strategies employed by some well-known radicalized writers who create poetic monuments that attempt to supplant official monuments in order to establish new national identities and an alternative understanding of what national monuments signify. In an effort to build a new homeland, Central American poets and writers imagine more inclusive imaginary homes. In short, this chapter includes texts that envision revolutionary homelands that ideally would replace the existing, repressive ones. It also begins to explore post-conflict homelands in Hernández's short story, which ironizes the significance bestowed on martyrdom by Central American revolutionaries.

Chapter 2 is a study of texts written after the failure of the national refounding projects conceived by the armed left during the 1960s through the early 1990s. It briefly reflects on the massive migration of Central Americans to the United States and their continued relationship with their nonmigrating compatriots. It then proceeds to focus on and inquire into the nostalgia and homesickness felt by those who have remained home on the isthmus. These younger writers deal with dismembered, post-conflict homelands. They still cling to the remnants of their memories of home. They feel homesick for what was before the war and even what was before post-war "modernization." In these texts, by poets such as Susana Reyes (El Salvador, 1971), there is an often nostalgic longing for homes that have disappeared because of physical, economic, political, emotional, and/or familial transformations. The texts I study in this chapter reveal that individuals keep souvenirs from and create meanings in the places they inhabit or have inhabited and to which they still feel tied despite the sense that, in a world reconfigured by globalization, talking about the homeland is antiquated or outdated.[65] Therefore, while it is more difficult to identify who "we" are (Salvadorans, Nicaraguans or Costa Ricans) and where home is, individuals maintain their ties to what they feel to be their place(s). As in the previous chapter, these writers are inclusive in their re-creations of home; however, they do not propose revolutionary action.

While the young writers I consider in chapter 2 may suffer from homesickness, those in chapter 3 cannot contain their disdain for and disappointment with their homelands. They express their sentiments through scathing sarcasm and unflinching reviews of their homelands' deterioration—increasing levels of extreme poverty, pollution, and violence. In contrast to the writers described above, writers like Juan Sobalvarro (Nicaragua, 1968) and Marta Leonor González (Nicaragua, 1972) perceive only gangrenous homeless people and a lake brimming with human scat. The attempts of Central American governments to modernize capital cities and globalize their economies are nothing more than superficial makeovers masking the rot lying beneath. Even as they figuratively spit at their homelands, though, these writers acknowledge a sense of belonging. Their poetic speakers and narrators continue to strive to survive in their places as they are. Unlike the texts of the first two chapters, the texts of chapter 3 dwell on the fetid present without finding respite in an idealized future or a nostalgic past.

The fourth chapter examines a dramatically different experience of being at home in Central America. Gone are chapter 3's visceral reactions to everyday-ness. Instead, narrators and poetic speakers are physically at home and yet simultaneously at a great emotional distance from it. They, too, inhabit decomposing homelands, but they contemplate those homelands from afar as if tourists faced with exotic foreign realities that belong to someone else. Thus they are impelled to search for a home-like *elsewhere*, be it physical or metaphorical, in which they can belong. In texts such as Luis Chaves's (Costa Rica, 1969), the poetic speakers accept their everyday angst as they live at home as tourists. But in "El vaho," by Salvador Canjura (El Salvador, 1968), the narrator attempts to deal with the dense fog that has enveloped his city, making it not just unrecognizable but also unnavigable, by calmly gouging out his eyes.[66] The self-mutilation of Canjura's protagonist illustrates the quiet desperation caused by displacement and the constancy of the desire for home.

Finally, in the fifth chapter, I analyze literary works that leave home for a globalized, intangible world, one where belonging depends less on origin and more on ties to globality as constructed by or seen in the mass media. In these works home is virtual, with few concrete connections to Central American aesthetics and sociopolitics. Whereas in chapter 4 Central American homelands are still visible to local eyes, albeit through a fog, in the fifth chapter home is manufactured by way of globally produced, mediated images. For the poetic speakers and narrators of these texts, lived experiences are less real than those generated by television, film, and computer screens. In fact, they voluntarily lose their national identities in favor of an ambiguous, amorphous attachment to a nebulous global identity. Ironically, however, the writers I discuss in chapter 5 continue to identify themselves, if not their characters, with their homelands. These homelands may be less than desirable or even detestable but yet are present locally, not wholly supplanted by globality.

The constant "hum" of the loved and/or hated *papaíto país* punctuates poets' and writers' meditations on the meaning of belonging to the places they inhabit. Many of them may agree with Didion's assessment of El Salvador, "[t]error is the given of the place,"[67] and conclude that even now in the post-conflict era their homelands are comprehensible only as representations of terror, even if that terror is economic or social. They may also see in Fielding Mellish, a man playing at political commitment and without clear ideological beliefs, the possibility of stumbling blindly through the everyday to survive. And they may manage to come to terms with their surroundings and interact with their compatriots, their invented and imagined communities. And, finally, they may come to agree that they are at home in the homeland and that it may very well be that home is the place where they will always have to be taken in.

NOTES

1. Legendary boxing announcer Don Dunphy, introducing viewers to the event they are about to witness, describes the rowdy, "colorful" inhabitants of San Marcos. Dunphy is also the lead-in to Howard Cosell's report on the president's assassination.

2. For a commentary on *Bananas'* politics and critique of U.S. politics, see Richard A. Schwartz's *Woody, From Antz to Zelig: A Reference Guide to Woody Allen's Creative Work, 1964–1998* (Westport, CT: Greenwood Press, 2000), 30–37.

3. Schwartz posits that, with Cosell's cameos, Allen makes the viewers aware of television's growing influence and transformation of political and private events into "entertainment for passive consumers" (35). Besides appearing in the opening scenes, Cosell returns at the end of the film to announce the Mellishes' honeymoon night.

4. Joan Didion, *Salvador* (New York: Washington Square Press, 1983).

5. Richard A. Hagerty, ed., *El Salvador: A Country Study*, Federal Research Division. (Washington, D.C.: U.S. G.P.O, 1990). This U.S.-funded program was being implemented during Álvaro Magaña's presidency (1982–1984) when Didion visited El Salvador. The program, though, was decreed in 1980 (42) and was open to applicants until mid-1984 (150); implementation was "slow and difficult" (88). The Land-to-the-Tiller program granted land titles to the land they tilled to renters and sharecroppers. Peasants could not seek ownership of more than seven hectares, but by 1987 most grantees had received less than two hectares (88). As Didion mentions, Roy Prosterman from the American Institute for Free Labor Development was "the architect of the Land-to-the-Tiller programs in both El Salvador and Vietnam" (94).

6. Needless to say that in *Bananas* acts of violence and fear are played for laughs. One example of this is the guerrilla's execution of traitors. Mellish is responsible for blindfolding the prisoners. His fingers get stuck in the blindfold, but the execution is not halted. He ends up jumping around in a hilarious effort to avoid the firing squad's bullets.

7. Joanne Omang, "El Salvador and the Topography of Terror," Review of *Salvador*, *Washington Post*, March 13, 1983, final ed., Book World sec.: 1, *Newsbank, Inc.* Web. (accessed March 21, 2011).

8. Ibid.

9. Roque Dalton, *Taberna y otros lugares* (San Salvador: UCA Editores, 1995).

10. Casa de las Américas in Havana is a cultural institute, publishes a culture-literature journal, *Cultura*, and awards annual prizes in various genres, including poetry, essay and fiction. See http://www.casa.cult.cu.

11. Dalton's role in debates in El Salvador and Latin America about leftist ideologies and guerrilla tactics is significant. In chapter 1, I will further discuss the controversy surrounding Dalton's execution by his own guerrilla group, the ERP (Ejército Revolucionario del Pueblo [Revolutionary Army of the People]). Salvadorans continue to debate what led to his trial and death. A recent reappraisal of this controversy can be found at elfaro.net: Efren Lemus, "La prueba en el asesinato de Dalton que la justicia salvadoreña se niega a analizar," March 26, 2012, http://elfaro.net/es/201203/noticias/7562/.

12. Didion, *Salvador*, 42.

13. The epigraph ends as follows, "It was very simple, and at the end of that moving appeal [by Kurtz] to every altruistic sentiment it blazed at you, luminous and terrifying, like a flash of lightning in a serene sky: 'Exterminate all the brutes!'"

14. Didion, *Salvador*, 61, 62.

15. Manipulating soccer fans' fervor in order for governments to act against other nations and to cover up for governmental missteps, abuses, and corruption, for instance, is not discounted here. A regional example of such use of soccer is the 1969 Soccer War between El Salvador and Honduras. For a cruelly humorous exposition of El Salvador's and Honduras's motives in warring with each other, see Roque Dalton's collage-poem "La guerra es la continuación de la política por otros medios y la política es solamente la economía quintaesenciada: (materiales para un poema)" ["War Is the Continuation of Politics by Other Means and Politics Is Simply Pure Economics: (Materials for a Poem)"] in *Las historias prohibidas del Pulgarcito* [*Tom Thumb's Forbidden Histories*] (1974).

16. Here I take into account many Latin American immigrants' shared lower-class origins and/or class status in the U.S. Robinson posits that in a transnationalized Central America it is social class that links the poor and the elite to their class peers across the isthmus and around the globe. William I. Robinson, *Transnational Conflicts: Central America, Social Change, and Globalization* (New York: Verso, 2003).

17. "Latinoamérica," Calle 13, *Entren los que quieran*, Sony BMG US Latin, 2010. As does Carlos Monsiváis in a later discussion in this chapter, Calle 13's lyrics here and elsewhere privilege the poor and disenfranchised. They directly address the lower classes as representatives of Latin America. In this album, see, for instance, "El baile de los pobres"; also "Pa'l norte" in 2007's *Residente o Visitante*.

18. For a postcolonial feminist reading of home and the homeland, see Susan Strehle, *Transnational Women's Fiction: Unsettling Home and Homeland* (Basingstoke, UK: Palgrave Macmillan, 2008).

19. Benedict Anderson, *Imagined Communities: Reflections on the Origin and Spread of Nationalism*, rev. ed. (London: Verso, 1991), 3.

20. Anderson also notes the power of this fraternity to impel citizens to die and kill for their nation (7).

21. Calhoun, *Nationalism* (Minneapolis: University of Minnesota Press, 1997).

22. Ibid., 19.

23. Ibid., 7.

24. Carlos Monsiváis, "De la sociedad tradicional a la sociedad postradicional," in *Imaginarios de nación: Pensar en medio de la tormenta. Cuadernos de nación*, coord. Jesús Martín-Barbero (Bogota: Ministerio de Colombia, 2001), 35.

25. Using William I. Robinson's concept of the formation of transnational social classes in which "domestic classes tend to become globalized, pre-globalization classes such as peasantries and artisans tend to disappear, and new classes and class fractions linked to the global economy emerge and become dominant" (*Transnational Conflicts*, 61), one could expand Monsiváis reading of Mexican-ness from below to posit that in

Central America, too, home identities lie within the grasp of the "underdogs," the "preglobalized."

26. Monsiváis writes, "Ante el sistema que los excluye, las masas se declaran de mil maneras la única nación real, opuesta a la ficticia o inaccesible de políticos y burgueses" [Faced with a system that excludes them, the masses declare themselves in myriad ways the only real nation, the opposite of the fictional or inaccessible one of politicians and the bourgeoisie] (32).

27. Monsiváis asserts, "[S]obre todo, se instala la reverencia por el Mercado que es la patria irrefutable de los consumidores" [Above all, reverence for the Market, undeniably consumers' homeland, is established] (33).

28. Graham Day and Andrew Thompson, *Theorizing Nationalism*, edited by Jo Campling (Basingstoke, UK: Palgrave Macmillan, 2004), 99.

29. Michael Billig, *Banal Nationalism* (London: Sage Publications, 1995), 6.

30. Ibid.

31. Day and Thompson, *Theorizing Nationalism*, 100.

32. Héctor Pérez-Brignoli, *A Brief History of Central America*, trans. Richard B. Sawrey and Susan Stettri de Sawrey (Berkeley: University of California Press, 1989). U.S. interest in the construction of an interoceanic canal in the isthmus intensified in the mid-nineteenth century with the 1848 California Gold Rush. At this time the fastest routes from the east coast were via the San Juan River and Lake Nicaragua to the Pacific or via railroad in Panama: "Between 1848 and 1868 [before the 1869 opening of the U.S.' transcontinental railroad], some 68,000 travelers had crossed Nicaragua on their way to California while about 57,000 returned by the same route" (81). In 1903 Panama became independent of Colombia and signed the Canal Treaty with the United States. The United States built the canal and also acquired the right of intervention and territorial rights in the canal zone (24, 123).

33. Carolyn Hall and Héctor Pérez Brignoli, *Historical Atlas of Central America*, cartographer John V. Cotter (Norman: University of Oklahoma Press, 2003), 4–5; Pérez-Brignoli, *A Brief History of Central America*, xi–xii.

34. Pérez-Brignoli, *A Brief History of Central America*, xii.

35. Ralph Lee Woodward, Jr., *Central America: A Nation Divided*, 2nd ed. (New York: Oxford University Press, 1985); John A Booth, Christine J. Wade, and Thomas W. Walker, *Understanding Central America: Global Forces, Rebellion and Change*, 5th ed. (Boulder: Westview Press, 2010). Some Central American literature specialists, such as Ana Patricia Rodríguez, do include Panamanian texts in their literary studies of the isthmus.

36. Booth, et al., *Understanding Central America*, 5.

37. Pérez-Brignoli, *A Brief History*, xii.

38. The so-called Soccer War originated in a long boundary dispute between the two countries and large-scale Salvadoran migration to Honduras. The July 1969 war exploded after Honduras passed and implemented Article 68 of the Agrarian Reform Law. This law prohibited non-Honduras-born residents from using state lands. The war's moniker derived from the violence that had erupted between Hondurans and Salvadorans during the elimination rounds of the World Cup in June 1969. An armistice was signed in 1970, but a peace agreement was not signed until 1980. The boundary dispute itself was not resolved until 1992 (Arbitration Award, International Court of Justice) (Hall and Pérez Brignoli, *Historical Atlas*, 49, 260).

39. Hall and Pérez-Brignoli, *A Historical Atlas*, 48, 277 note 27. Nicaragua and Costa Rica negotiated the Cañas-Jérez treaty in 1858 by which Costa Rica retained Guanacaste and Nicaragua retained a boundary south of the San Juan and, thus, control over a "potential canal route." Costa Rica also received navigation rights and control over the river's right-bank tributaries. Nicaragua also agreed to consult with Costa Rica if a canal route were negotiated. After continued disputes, the 1888 Cleveland Award upheld the 1858 treaty.

More recent conflicts include Costa Rica's attempts to transport arms to its police posts (2005) and Nicaragua's dredging of the San Juan (2011). See Delilah Catalan, "San Juan

River Dispute Between Costa Rica and Nicaragua Could Undermine Economic Development for Both Countries," *Center for International Development and Finance, University of Iowa College of Law* (blog), February 24, 2011, http://uicifd.blogspot.com/2011/02/san-juan-river-dispute-between-costa.html

40. One example being the Honduran delegation's 2003 challenge of El Salvador's claim that *pupusas*, as an "autochthonous food," should be protected from import duties in the United States. Honduras also claimed ownership of this food. Ultimately, *pupusas* did not receive special treatment. In any case, in a 2005 response, the Salvadoran legislature decreed the second Sunday of November a day to celebrate *pupusas*' Salvadoran origins, *"El día de la pupusa"* (Legislative Decree 655). See Orsy Campos, "La pupusa tiene su día," "Hablemos Online," *El diario de hoy*, November 6, 2005, http://www.elsalvador.com/hablemos/2005/061105/061105-4.htm; and, "Principales Beneficios del TLC con Estados Unidos," OAS Foreign Trade Information System, n.d., accessed February 27, 2012, http://www.sice.oas.org/TPD/USA_CAFTA/Studies/BenefTLC_SLV.pdf.

41. For an in-depth analysis of the Guatemalan government's 1970s–1980s genocidal policies against the Mayan people and their homelands and of the United Nation's CEH's (Comisión de Esclarecimento Histórico [Commission for Historical Clarification]) report, *Guatemala: Memoria del silencio Tz'inil na 'tab'al*, see Victoria Sanford, *Buried Secrets: Truth and Human Rights in Guatemala* (New York: Palgrave Macmillan, 2003).

42. Tachito was preceded in the Nicaraguan presidency by his father, Anastasio (Tacho) Somoza García, who ruled between 1937–56, and his brother, Luis Somoza Debayle, who ruled until 1967. In addition to the presidency, the Somozas also controlled the National Guard (Booth, et al., *Understanding Central America*).

43. Hall and Pérez Brignoli, *A Historical Atlas*, 264–65. Also, see Booth et al., *Understanding Central America*, for a more detailed overview of the Sandinista revolution and regime.

44. Hall and Pérez Brignoli, *A Historical Atlas*, 266.

45. Hall and Pérez Brignoli, *A Historical Atlas*, 266–67. For a more detailed overview of the Salvadoran civil war, see Booth et al., *Understanding Central America*.

46. Booth et al., *Understanding Central America*, 124.

47. Ibid., 65.

48. Ibid.

49. In 1983, Costa Rica declared itself neutral in its neighbors' conflicts (Pérez-Brignoli, *A Brief History*, 174).

50. "The agreement entered into force for the United States and El Salvador, Guatemala, Honduras, and Nicaragua during 2006, for the Dominican Republic on March 1, 2007, and for Costa Rica on January 1, 2009. With the addition of Costa Rica, the CAFTA-DR is in force for all six countries that signed the agreement." "CAFTA-DR (Dominican Republic-Central America) FTA," Office of the U.S. Trade Representative, http://www.ustr.gov/trade-agreements/free-trade-agreements/cafta-dr-dominican-republic-central-america-fta. Also see, Booth et al., *Understanding Central America*; and, William I. Robinson, *Latin America and Global Capitalism: A Critical Globalization Perspective* (Baltimore: Johns Hopkins University Press, 2008).

51. A few advertisements from 2007 are still posted on youtube.com. Search for "Sí al TLC" and "Corazón del No al TLC." Also see Booth et al, *Understanding Central America*; and Robinson, *Latin America and Global Capitalism*.

52. Booth et al. *Understanding Central America*, 76.

53. The recent elections of leftist presidents in Nicaragua and El Salvador further illustrate the rhetorical struggles in creating post-conflict homelands. They exemplify the political schisms and corruption that continue to plague the region. In Nicaragua, Daniel Ortega and Rosario Murillo's brand of "Christian" Sandinismo battles against the more "authentic" brand, Movimiento de Renovación Sandinista (MRS), of the regime's former allies and officials (e.g., Sergio Ramírez, Dora María Tellez, the Mejía Godoys, etc.). Ortega, who won the presidential elections in 2006, has been dogged by

allegations of corruption and manipulation of the Nicaraguan political system, namely for rewarding supporters with state aid and for *el pacto*, his 1999 power sharing agreement with former president Arnoldo Alemán of the Partido Liberal Constitucional (Liberal Constitutional Party). And in El Salvador, the celebrated 2009 election of Mauricio Funes, of the guerrilla coalition-turned-political party FMLN against the ARENA (Nationalist Republican Alliance) candidate, has given way to disillusionment as Funes has veered right in attempts to gain conservatives' support. Lastly, in 2010 Costa Rica elected Laura Chinchilla, its first female president, who is confronting rising crime in what has been considered a Central American Switzerland. She has disappointed those who expected her to follow the path set forth by Óscar Arias.

See the Council for Hemispheric Affairs' (COHA) succinct review of Nicaragua's current institutional crisis: Brendan Riley, "This Ongoing Institutional Crisis Brought to You By Nicaragua's Daniel Ortega," COHA, June 16, 2012, http://www.coha.org/this-ongoing-institutional-crisis-brought-to-you-by-nicaragua's-daniel-ortega.

54. Here I am not taking into account protest literature written during the recent political upheaval surrounding the CAFTA-DR referendum vote (2007) in Costa Rica and the pro-Zelaya, anti-coup opposition movements (2009-present) in Honduras.

55. Daniel Ortega regained the Nicaraguan presidency in 2006 and was re-elected for a second term in 2011. See note 53, also.

56. For analyses and critiques of *testimonio* narratives in Central America, see Arturo Arias, ed. *The Rigoberta Menchú Controversy* (Minneapolis: University of Minnesota Press, 2001); John Beverley, *Testimonio: On the Politics of Truth* (Minneapolis: University of Minnesota Press, 2004); and, Linda Craft, *Novels of Testimony and Resistance from Central America* (Gainesville: University Press of Florida, 1997), to name a few.

57. Roberto Fernández Retamar, *Para una teoría de la literatura hispanoamericana*, rev. ed. (Havana: Editorial Pueblo y Educación, 1984).

58. Examples include Carolyn Forché's translation of Alegría, *Flowers from the Volcano* (Pittsburgh: University of Pittsburgh, 1982); Alegría's and Flakoll's *On the Frontline: Guerrilla Poems of El Salvador* (Willamantic, CT: Curbstone Press, 1995); and Curbstone Press's translations of the poetry of Otto René Castillo, *Let's Go* (1995) and Leonel Rugama, *The Earth Is a Satellite of the Moon* (1995).

59. In addition, in 1993, Greg Dawes published his book on Nicaraguan poetry written during the Sandinista regime, *Aesthetics and Revolution: Nicaraguan Poetry, 1979-1990* (Minneapolis: University of Minnesota Press); and, in 1994 James Iffland published *Ensayos sobre la poesía revolucionaria de Centroamérica* (San Jose: EDUCA), a book of essays on revolutionary poetry in Costa Rica.

60. Authors of book-length studies focused on Central American fiction include Arturo Arias, *Gestos ceremoniales, narrativa centroamericana, 1960–1990* (Guatemala City: Artemis-Edinter, 1998); Laura Barbas-Rhoden, *Writing Women in Central America: Gender and the Fictionalization of History* (Athens: Ohio State University Press, 2003); Beatriz Cortez, *Estética del cinismo: Pasión y desencanto en la literatura centroamericana de posguerra* (Guatemala City: F & G Editores, 2010); and, Ileana Rodríguez, *Women, Guerrillas, and Love: Understanding War in Central America* (Minneapolis: University of Minnesota Press, 1996), among others.

61. Arturo Arias, *Taking Their Word: Literature and the Signs of Central America* (Minneapolis: University of Minnesota Press, 2007), 226.

62. Ana Patricia Rodríguez, *Dividing the Isthmus: Central American Transnational Histories, Literatures and Cultures* (Austin: University of Texas Press, 2009), 234.

63. Arias, *Taking Their Word*, xix.

64. Rodríguez, *Dividing the Isthmus*, 234.

65. See, for instance, Thomas Friedman's *The World is Flat* (New York: Farrar, Strauss, & Giroux, 2005); or, Pico Iyer's *The Global Soul: Jet Lag, Shopping Malls, and the Search for Home* (New York: Knopf, 2000), among others.

66. Salvador Canjura, *Prohibido vivir* (San Salvador: Istmo Editores, 2000).

67. Didion, *Salvador*, 14.

ONE

Central America in Pieces

Dismembering the Isthmus

Noches tropicales de Centroamérica,
con lagunas y volcanes bajo la luna
y luces de palacios presidenciales,
cuarteles y tristes toques de queda.
"Muchas veces fumando un cigarrillo
he decidido la muerte de un hombre",
dice Ubico fumando un cigarrillo…
En su palacio como un queque rosado
Ubico está resfriado. Afuera el pueblo
fue dispersado con bombas de fósforo.
San Salvador bajo la noche y espionaje
con cuchicheos en los hogares y pensiones
y gritos en las estaciones de policía.
El palacio de Carías apedreado por el pueblo.
Y Managua apuntada por las ametralladoras
desde el palacio de bizcocho de chocolate
y los cascos de acero patrullando las calles.

[Tropical nights in Central America,
with moonlit lagoons and volcanoes
and lights from presidential palaces,
barracks and sad curfew warnings.
"Often while smoking a cigarette
I've decided that a man should die,"
says Ubico smoking a cigarette…
In his pink wedding-cake palace
Ubico has a head cold. Outside, the people
were dispersed with phosphorous bombs.

San Salvador laden with night and espionage,
with whispers in homes and boardinghouses
and screams in police stations.
Carías' palace stoned by the people.
....
....
And Managua the target of machine guns
from the chocolate cookie palace
and steel helmets patrolling the streets.][1]
—Cardenal, "Hora 0"

In the pivotal poetic text "Hora 0" [Zero Hour], Nicaraguan poet Ernesto Cardenal first teases the reader with a recognizable Central America, overly warm, humid, a geography of sweat, and then moves quickly to arrive at governmental corruption and impunity. The first four lines situate the reader in a crossroads between a beautiful, exotic, but potentially dangerous nature (volcanoes) and the even more menacing geography, the region's power structures (executive, military, and legal). The poetic speaker places abusive heads of state (Jorge Ubico Castañeda, Tiburcio Carías Andino, and by allusion, Maximiliano Hernández Martínez and Anastasio Somoza García)[2] atop this corrupt infrastructure under which lies the mostly silent and subjugated "pueblo." The people's suffering is outlined in increasing detail in this stanza: curfew, summary executions, attacks with incendiary weapons, torture, and constant military surveillance. This apparatus, though, is pockmarked by Ubico's cold (*resfriado*) and the fact that the seats of executive power look like tiered cakes. The artificiality and hollowness of the dictators' power is represented visually with both of these images while at the same time its real potency and efficacy is foregrounded by images of well-armed police and military forces.[3] The repeated use of synecdoche to imagine the state and its apparatuses (e.g., the Nicaraguan National Guard's metal helmets) contrasts with the all-encompassing term, *el pueblo*, that refers to civilians. In other words, the contrasting imagery of the oppressor as only one figure of a large repressive machine and of the people as an indistinct "pueblo" intimates the importance of the collectivity in struggles against dictatorial regimes. This strategy serves the poem well as it relates César Augusto Sandino's resistance and rebellion against U.S. economic imperialism and occupation[4] to the 1954 April Conspiracy, a failed attempt to overthrow Anastasio (Tacho) Somoza García. Tacho, the first of the Somoza dynasty to rule Nicaragua, was assassinated two years later in 1956 by the poet Rigoberto López Pérez.[5] In each case, Cardenal's highlighting of the significance of the people and of their heroes (e.g., Sandino and Adolfo Báez Bone) in the rebellion of the few against the distinguishable "one" (e.g., Somoza, U.S. imperialism) turns the struggle into a necessary, feasible goal despite the fact that the region's dictators and *Guardias* exert such overwhelming power.

This collage vision of Central America recognizable both in and out of the isthmus relies on the readers' preconceived, or perhaps lived, experience of a sensual but decadent, poetic but destitute place. Cardenal's Central America in this poetic fragment is not far from the "deadly, diseased, dangerous, disorderly, dissolute and decadent"[6] region that foreigners may stumble upon. At the same time, as Cardenal intones in "Managua 6:30," a Sandinista poem about his life and home: "Y si he de dar un testimonio sobre mi época / Es éste: Fue bárbara y primitiva / pero poética" [If I am to give a testimony of my time / It is this: It was barbaric and primitive / but poetic].[7] Beyond the commonplace Nicaraguan self-conception of being a land of poets, both the opening of "Hora 0" and the closing line of "Managua 6:30" imagine places of excess, whether man-made or innate, situated on the isthmus. In its representation of the Somoza regime and the banana industry's many abuses, "Hora 0" also paints a clear picture of the Central America of the 1930s and 1940s, years of long dictatorships, political repression, economic hardship for the poor majority. While the 1920s saw great growth in the export economy, the Crash of 1929 and subsequent Great Depression were "little short of catastrophic" for economies reliant on commodities like coffee and bananas that were not "basic necessities."[8] And even in Costa Rica, where executive power was not derived from the military, opposition militants "were persecuted with little less zeal than elsewhere in the isthmus."[9] In brief, state violence and repression of the populace "lay at the very heart" of agroexport economies[10] such as the ones portrayed by Cardenal. In my reading, "Hora 0" and Cardenal's post-revolutionary "testimony of [his] time" succinctly represent brutality suffered by victims of economic policies and political oppression. It is the beginning of the road that led to the neoliberal present, post-conflict Central America in which, for critic Ana Patricia Rodríguez, "[t]he image of *garbage* or *waste* surfaces as the metaphor of Central American nations attempting to rebuild themselves from the rubble of armed conflict, while at the same time confronting the disruptive fallout of global capital" (italics in original).[11] The trashed, thrashed region that Rodríguez encounters in recent narrative texts is one glimpsed in oppositional texts of the 1960s and 1970s. These years of a flourishing production of politicized texts often recount the transformation of writers' home countries amid rapid industrialization, authoritarianism, and ever-increasing poverty and social inequality.

The Sandinista revolution's triumph in 1979 and the regime's electoral defeat in 1990 virtually bookend the Salvadoran civil war (1980–1992). In both countries, the revolutionary struggles and the government's concomitant ultraviolent responses (clearly aided by U.S. military and economic intervention) destroyed the very nations contested by the guerrillas and the authoritarian regimes. As is the case with both the Sandinistas and the Salvadoran armed left, writers imagined and invoked new *patrias* in their texts. These revolutionary patrias, infused with oft-idealized images of the future, hotly challenged the representations (propagandized by the right) of a homeland under attack by leftist heretics. In between these competing conceptions of the homeland, for some, Costa Rica stood as a beacon of rationality and well-conceived, well-run, and consensual *patria*. Costa Ricans' home, in other words, may have represented the best-case scenario for places like Nicaragua and El Salvador, where citizens with competing ideologies and interests were dying for their version of the homeland. Contradictorily, of course, Costa Rica played important official and unofficial roles in support of the Contra War and as a destination for exiles and migrants from Nicaragua and El Salvador.[12]

Costa Rican intellectuals question the veracity or adequacy of official images of their homeland as picture perfect: Central American Switzerland, *Arcadia tropical* [Tropical Arcadia], ¡*pura vida!* [life to the core].[13] Their various critiques of the public, and traditional, view of Costa Rica as an idealized Central American home were shared by their Nicaraguan and Salvadoran neighbors living in exile in San José in the 1970s and 1980s. As Gioconda Belli confesses in her autobiography, *El país bajo mi piel* (The Country under My Skin):[14]

> La poesía me abandonó. Apenas un poema ocasional. Sin Nicaragua me secaba. La belleza de Costa Rica no lograba despertarme. Demasiado plácida. Hasta las vacas parecían puestas a propósito en el paisaje bucólico y tranquilo. Echaba de menos los atardeceres furibundos, los árboles enmarañados, las cañadas y los aguaceros. Costa Rica se me hacía un agua mansa, leve como la llovizna interminable de San José.

> [Poetry abandoned me. Barely an occasional poem. Without Nicaragua I was drying up. Costa Rica's beauty didn't manage to awaken me. Too placid. Even the cows looked like they'd been placed there on purpose to create a bucolic and tranquil landscape. I missed furious dusks, tangled trees, gullies and downpours. To me, Costa Rica seemed to be docile water, light like San José's interminable drizzle.]

While in this excerpt Belli romanticizes her own homeland,[15] she also points to the "unnatural" tranquility of her exile experience in the Costa Rican capital. Her description of a poetic "drying up" also relates poetry to tumult and Costa Rica to lack of poetry, a common perception of Costa Rican literary production. Also important is the overall conception of artistic production that underlies Belli's comment. She implies that Nicaragua's turbulent recent history and its nature, including its "furious" evenings, somehow invigorate and inspire literary production, thus exalting a conflict-filled homeland as literary instigator.

These examples demonstrate writers' apparently inevitable imagining of the homeland: as a place to inhabit as a citizen; as a place in which to belong and with which to identify; and, finally, as a place to recreate and reinvent literarily. The aesthetic and sentimental images that arise, though, may or may not coincide with the accepted, official views of the *patria* regardless of how many national monuments, statues of national heroes, or slogans with which the state plasters the nation.[16] Historian Lyman Johnson argues, in his introduction to *Death, Dismemberment and Memory: Body Politics in Latin America*, that across cultures and time periods, societies identify and memorialize national and civic heroes.[17] Through nomenclature, monuments, speeches, stamps, and physical dead bodies, heroes' images are reproduced in order to communicate a particular interpretation of the nation and of its most valued or respected "children." Often these hegemonic representations (through public statuary, for example) are supplemented and/or replaced by popular remembrances of those same or alternative heroes.[18] Johnson's edited essay collection focuses on the political uses of heroes' cadavers and/or body parts. Examples of the signification and resignification of heroes' bodies include the case of Che Guevara's postmortem display by the Bolivian government, the creation of a popular shrine in the village where he died, and his reburial in Cuba. In my reading, the figurative manipulation of the bodies of revered, and hated, heroes to evoke patriotic fervor and nostalgia for a particular national past by both governments and the common people speaks to the emotional, and thus political, power embodied by models of sacrifice and martyrdom.[19] As Johnson argues, cadavers "in Latin America are as likely to speak the language of social protest or to urge resistance to exploiters as to celebrate national greatness."[20] Attempts to represent greatness and the value of sacrifice for the preservation or establishment of patriotic values (whether from a hegemonic or revolutionary perspective)[21] are not limited to popular shrines, street names or national holidays. They are also put into practice *poetically* by paying homage to and disparaging "national" heroes, symbols, and other symbolic representations of the homeland and its possible national identities. The forging of these national identities and images of the homeland are wrought with ideology-specific goals, as in the case of Nicaragua during the Somoza and Sandinista regimes, which David E. Whisnant amply demonstrates. In *Rascally Signs in Sacred Places: The Politics of Culture in Nicaragua*, he points out that beginning with the postconquest, "Nicaragua has been a site for perennial ideological and value conflicts that frequently involved intense argument about what culture is and ought to be, and what if anything the state ought to do about culture."[22] These disputes about culture and official (lack of) support often play out in the literary texts of the region's literati. In these texts, hegemonic versions of the *patria* are poetically displaced by alternative heroes and symbols that legitimate a decentered, revolutionary national imaginary. For instance, in his poetry, Salvadoran Roque Dalton proposes the erasure of his current homeland and the construction of an alternate, inclusive, more "authentic" one. Similarly, in "La tierra es un satélite de la luna" (The Earth is a Satellite of the Moon), Nicaraguan guerrilla poet Leonel Rugama offers a reading of his country wherein the margins are exalted while the center (Somoza and his cronies) is reviled. Rugama, in turn, becomes a figure of heroic dimensions in others' poetry, specifically in Ernesto Cardenal's "Oráculo sobre Managua" (Oracle over Managua), and in the reimagining of Nicaragua as Sandinista. In the cases of all three poets, poetic palimpsest is an effective strategy: hegemonic perspectives and representations of national "greatness" and heroism are supplanted, and sometimes erased, in order to impose "revolutionary" nationhood. Meanwhile younger, post-conflict writers rearticulate differently the unarticulated, fragmented homeland of the 1990s and 2000s.

Roque Dalton (1935–1975), now the most influential contemporary Central American poet, has become a larger than life figure representing Salvadoran literature and its cultural identity as well as the lethality of ideological intransigence. He spent most of his adult life writing poetry, essays, and journalistic articles, and fiction while running from persecution by the Salvadoran government and, at the end of his life, by his own *compañeros*. His aesthetic and political biography is further enhanced by his origins as the illegitimate son of an El Salvador–based U.S. father[23] and working-class Salvadoran mother. With his father's financial assistance, Dalton was educated at a top private Jesuit school in San Salvador and then initiated studies in law at the University of Chile.[24] While in Chile, as he told it, he became politicized. His political education continued upon his return to El Salvador, where he enrolled at the University of El Salvador (UES).[25] At the UES Dalton and other future members of the *generación comprometida* (committed generation) met and began to formulate and publish their views on the responsibilities of artists living under dictatorship.[26] As Hernández-Aguirre notes in his early study of the group, in their "manifesto" they directly espoused their belief in literature's "social function" and in writers' responsibility to work for social betterment.[27] Dalton and his fellow writers' ideological stance, as well as their more expansive view of literature, upended Salvadoran and Central American literary traditions. They injected their literary texts with sociopolitical protest, colloquial language, Salvadoran urban slang, and the "people" [pueblo].[28] Among his peers, Dalton stands out for his militancy and his multifaceted, innovative corpus. For many years, his political life, his travels to the Soviet Union as a youth delegate and to Vietnam for military training, and his extended stays in Mexico, Cuba, and Czechoslovakia[29] overshadowed the importance of his artistic innovation and range as a writer. In the late 1960s and early 1970s he produced some of his most influential and experimental works, including the poetry collection *Taberna y otros lugares* (Tavern and Other Places) (1969), the testimonial narrative *Miguel Mármol: Los sucesos de 1932* (Miguel Mármol: The Events of 1932) (1972), the poem-collage *Las historias prohibidas del Pulgarcito* (Tom Thumb's Forbidden Stories) (1974), and the novel *Pobrecito poeta que era yo* (Poor Poet Was I) (1976). By the time Dalton returned home in December 1973, he had broken with the Communist Party and left Cuba on bad terms.[30] Once in El Salvador he joined the ERP (Ejército Revolucionario del Pueblo [People's Revolutionary Army]), the guerrilla group that condemned and killed him seventeen months later.[31]

Throughout the Salvadoran Civil War and after, Dalton has remained a standard bearer and a burden of both political and aesthetic commitment for young writers. His poems about and to his homeland and compatriots, particularly "Poema de amor" ("Love Poem") (in *Las historias prohibidas del Pulgarcito*), along with his assassination, are examples of these two commitments that loom large in Central American literature. Academic and journalistic appraisals of his literary production have favored the political aspects of his work, but in more recent years scholars such as Rafael Lara Martínez have highlighted Dalton's aesthetic and philosophical complexity.[32]

This complexity of thought and sentiment is abundantly clear in Dalton's poetic meditations on El Salvador and the meaning of home. For instance, in "El alma nacional" ("The National Soul") from *Taberna y otros lugares* (1969), Dalton dissects the national body, revealing its innards and rejecting them as a representation of the nation's "soul." He dissolves the nation's presumed unity, its existence as an "imagined community" of "deep horizontal comradeship,"[33] in the poem's first two lines:

> Patria dispersa: caes
> como una pastilla de veneno en mis horas.
>
> [Dispersed homeland: you fall
> on my hours like a poison pill]

Though apostrophe often signals the initiation of songs of praise or imploration, Dalton's poem is accusatory, as the poetic speaker harangues the nation for its many faults and failures. His homeland fails to nurture its citizens, or "children," and instead poisons them, urinates on them, and generally debases them. The desecration of the homeland, or motherland in this poem's imagery of the *patria*-mother, alludes to the abuse and repeated imprisonment Dalton suffered at the hands of El Salvador's security forces because of his politics,

> ¿Quién eres,
> sino este mico armado y numerado,
> pastor de llaves, que me alumbra la cara?
>
> [Who are you
> but this armed and numbered monkey
> keeper of keys, who lights my face?] (12–14)

The poetic speaker's revenge against the guards and the nation they represent is only rhetorical in this poem. He simply uncovers what lies at the core of the "alma nacional" to his fellow citizens. His public repudiation of the homeland assumes that he has an affective relationship with the *patria* and feels camaraderie with his compatriots. It is this assumption that strengthens the vitriol of Dalton's accusations against his whoring homeland:[34]

> Ya me bastas, mi bella
> madre durmiente que haces heder la noche de las cárceles.
>
> [You're more than enough, my beautiful
> sleeping mother who makes prison nights stink.] (15–16)

The "motherland" lacks a "soul." Rather than uplifting her "hijo[s] bueno[s]" [good or obedient children] (18), she bares, starves, and transforms them into deserters (18–20). Also, unlike Anderson's quasi-religious description of national "communion"[35] among compatriots, Dalton's *patria* is unfit for communion because of its behavior. In religious terms, the homeland must confess its sins to be able to take communion, or less parochially, it needs a do-over or at least a makeover to be a good caretaker to its "children."

While indulging in an unquestioning view of the homeland as mother and of its citizens as male, the poetic speaker rejects traditional conceptions of "appropriate" citizenship. In fact, the I alleges that the nation's smallness (7), literally and metaphorically, is tiresome to all its inhabitants and that it is unworthy of tribute or protection. And, ultimately, in its fragmented condition, it has lost even its name, which should, like its soul, represent its essence,

> ¿Cómo te llamas, si, despedazada,
> eres todo el azar agónico en los charcos?
>
> [What's your name, if, when you're in pieces,
> you are all agonizing chance in puddles?] (10–11)

The homeland's smallness and insignificance, in addition to its parental inadequacy, intensify Dalton's indignation. His poetry portrays a hegemonic but pathetically deficient version of Salvadoran nationhood that the "people" refuse to accept. As Johnson postulates, "The Latin American 'folk' have often rejected the preferred heroes of the elite and embraced or invented their own."[36] The body of the "alma nacional" is fragmented, and its parts do not make the people's home whole. What's more, it does not unite the diverse and divergent visions or experiences of Salvadoran-ness. The poetic speaker, being eaten away by his imprisonment, "me corroen los deberes del acecho" [the duties of vigilance corrode me] (17), endows the poem with an antiestablishment political message that demands a new nation that can represent him and his oppositional politics. Unlike that of younger writers, Dalton's poetry iterates the belief in the possibility of attaining a unified nationhood and in the use of force as a viable strategy to construct that new home.

Along with believing in the "social function" of literature, Dalton and his contemporaries were animated by their belief in the power of the written word—his multiple imprisonments inevitable reminders of his writing's effectiveness.[37] This idealistic belief is made plain in many Daltonian texts, including "El gran despecho" ("Great Indignation"). In this poem, also from *Taberna y otros lugares*, Dalton "disappears" his insufficient homeland. He avenges his exile rhetorically and offers the reader a cynical understanding of El Salvador's geographic minuteness and his expatriation. The poetic speaker tells the reader that earlier he believed El Salvador was simply a tiny place too small to have a North and South (6). He then goes on to confess that he now recognizes its physical nonexistence. In other words, he confesses that he was duped into believing that El Salvador is a recognizable place or geography:

> País mío no existes
> sólo eres una mala silueta mía
> una palabra que le creí al enemigo.
>
> [Country of mine, you don't exist
> you are only a bad outline of me,
> an enemy's word I believed.] (1–3)

The country's body, thus, is reduced from visible fragments ("El alma nacional") to a shoddy silhouette of its "expatriado[s]" [ex-patriots] (14). Further, in this poem the homeland is an insignificant invention (11), useless (8) and dependent on the poetic I for its existence rather than the other way around. Interestingly, at the same time that Dalton denigrates and erases the homeland, he celebrates his own placeless-ness and the *patria*'s dependence on him for its geographical and nationalist self-definition. He loses part of his identity when he becomes an "ex-patriot" but the homeland is also reduced to an "ex-patria" [ex-homeland]. He figuratively transforms the homeland into a cadaver and exiles it, mimicking the *patria*'s trespasses against him. From the edges he declares his power over El Salvador: "Soy pues un diosecillo a tu costa" [So I'm a little god on your coast] (13). This paradoxically marginal godliness illustrates the poetic speaker's decentered position at home. The homeland, in turn, is substance-less, only a silhouette of its citizens. It is this exile condition of ex-patriotism and placeless-ness that outrages Dalton and leads to his erasure of the homeland. Even as he "disappears" El Salvador, his poetic speaker indignantly grasps at the newly nonexistent nation that expels him from its borders.

In these two Dalton poems the homeland's body does not represent its people, and in fact its chosen symbols[38] of national essence fail to create even an inadequate homeland. Dalton challenges the homeland for failing to inspire its citizens to honor it. So that, while the Salvadoran nation possesses typical symbols of nationhood, such as a flag and a coat of arms, that should "flag" its national identity for its citizens,[39] it flounders. In a conventional understanding of nationhood in which citizens share a "deep horizontal comradeship,"[40] the answers to the questions posed by "El alma nacional," "¿Quién soportó tus símbolos?" [Who withstood your symbols?] (5) and "¿A quién aún convences de tributo y vigilancia?" [Who do you still convince to pay you tribute and protect you?] (9), should be the nation's people, citizens, or patriots. But as Dalton responds in one of *Taberna y otros lugares'* prison poems:

> Hoy fue el día de la patria: desperté a medio pudrir, sobre el suelo húmedo e hiriente como la boca de un coyote muerto, entre los gases embriagadores de los himnos.

> [Today was Independence Day: I woke up half rotted, on the floor humid and wounding like the mouth of a dead coyote, among (national) anthems' intoxicating gases.]

On a day formally set aside to honor the homeland, its patriotic hymns sicken[41] the poetic speaker instead of making him proud. His illness contradicts and repudiates the Salvadoran national anthem's chorus and fundamental lesson:

> Saludemos la patria orgullosos
> de hijos suyos podernos llamar.
> Y juremos la vida animosos,
> sin descanso a su bien consagrar.

> [Let's greet the homeland proud
> of being her children
> and let's promise to consecrate our lives to her
> spiritedly and without rest.]

Repeatedly, Dalton's poetic speakers loudly reject conventional, hegemonic representations of nationhood and ideal citizenship. Instead, in these and many other poems, he reimagines the nation from the "coasts" rather than from the center in order to arrive at a more "authentic" place to call home.

Nicaraguan guerrilla poet Leonel Rugama (1949–1970) also joined an armed revolution in search of a more "authentic" homeland. As did Dalton, Rugama received a strong religious education. Before joining the FER (Frente Estudiantil Revolucionario [Revolutionary Student Front]) at the University of León and then the FSLN in 1967, he was a seminarian in Managua.[42] He wrote poetry and political tracts for student, popular, and FSLN publications; but, his poems were not published in book form until after his death.[43] His more immediate notoriety was based on his political commitment and his heroic death for the cause. Unlike Dalton's assassination, which was clouded by chaos and ideological infighting, Rugama's final battle with the National Guard was publicized and celebrated as a victory for a fledgling FSLN. He and two compañeros withstood a heavy weapons attack and the National Guard's repeated entreaties that they surrender.[44] Rugama's well-known retort, "Que se rinda tu madre" [Let your mother surrender], added to his reputation as a heroic guerrilla fighter and poet; and, his bold challenge became a popular revolutionary graffiti.[45] Further, Rugama's defense of the homeland against the Somoza regime and its National Guard was a rallying cry for guerrillas and was poetically memorialized by Ernesto Cardenal, as we will see later in this chapter.

As Dawes remarks, Rugama's revolutionary "credentials" rely on his "excellence" as guerrilla fighter and poet,[46] not unlike Dalton. Rugama also deploys a rhetorical strategy similar to Dalton's in his poetic re-creation of the Nicaraguan homeland. In the well-known poem, "La tierra es un satélite de la luna" ["The Earth is a Satellite of the Moon"],[47] the poetic speaker ironically juxtaposes the scientific sophistication of the 1960s Apollo Space Program to the historic poverty of Acahualinca, an outlying Managuan neighborhood that contains fossils of the footsteps of prehistoric humans.[48] In its first three stanzas, the poetic speaker lists, as if chanting an incantation,[49] the incremental rise in cost of the series of Apollo spacecrafts. In his "incantation," Rugama does not always cite the actual numbers of the different missions and spacecrafts, and he conflates the details from different missions:[50]

> El Apolo 4 costó más que el Apolo 3
> el Apolo 3 costó más que el Apolo 2
> el Apolo 2 costó más que el Apolo 1
> el Apolo 1 costó bastante.
> ....
> El Apolo 9 costó más que todos juntos
> Junto con el Apolo 1 que costó bastante.
>
> [Apollo 4 cost more than Apollo 3
> Apollo 3 cost more than Apollo 2
> Apollo 2 cost more than Apollo 1
> Apollo 1 cost a lot.
> ....
> Apollo 9 cost more than all of them put together
> Together with Apollo 1, which cost a lot.] (5–8, 15–16)

The repetition of the phrase "costó más que" and the numerical progression produce the effect of a litany. This allusion to the liturgy heightens the effects of the irony of enumerating the expenses of a wealthy nation in a poem that prioritizes the needs of the poor. The connotation of religiosity is then made even more explicit in the fourth stanza, where the poetic speaker jumps to Apollo 8 (the first manned spacecraft to orbit the moon and return to earth). Astronauts on Apollo 8 were able to take photographs of earth and transmit via television the first images of the lunar surface.[51] In Rugama's poetic take on the scientific ingenuity of the Apollo Space Program, Apollo 8's high price was less disturbing because of the astronauts' religiosity, "desde la luna leyeron la Biblia" [they read the Bible from the moon] (12). The poem further develops the association between Christianity and the space program more indirectly through the reference to Pope Paul VI. Pope Paul VI is one of the seventy-three world leaders who wrote goodwill messages for the Apollo 11 mission.[52] The messages were etched on a piece of silicon that was left on the moon by the astronauts. The allusion to Pope Paul VI also allows Rugama to comment on the Vatican's official theology and politics. Paul VI ascended to the Papacy during Vatican II (1963–1965), a time when the Church was grappling with heated theological debates in regard to church doctrine and world social inequities. These debates were intensified with the 1968 Medellín Conference and the development of Liberation Theology.[53] The Vatican read the new theology's "option for the poor" and its Marxist interpretation of the Bible as overly radical. Thus by naming Pope Paul VI, Rugama denounces the privileging of space exploration over and above the needs of the poor and reiterates his commitment to social justice.

The second half of the poem replaces the Apollo spacecrafts, monuments of scientific progress, with live monuments of human need. Again using the strategy of poetic repetition and, this time, a gradual increase of hunger from one generation of Acahualincans to the next, the poetic speaker stresses the worsening of the community's situation by repeating that older generations were less hungry than younger ones, that Acahualincans continue to starve. Through four generations of children being hungrier than their immediate predecessors, of children achieving less than their parents, the very poor have remained very poor. Rugama hammers into the reader that ironically in Acahualinca the measure of "progress," or forward movement, is worsening poverty. Meanwhile, for the Apollo program progress is scientific knowledge, technological advancement, and monetary investment.

> Los padres de la gente de Acahualinca tenían menos
> hambre que los hijos de la gente de allí.
> Los padres se murieron de hambre.
>
> [The parents of the people of Acahualinca were less
> hungry than the children of the people from there.
> The parents starved to death.] (23–25)

"La gente de Acahualinca" are a monument of resilience and resistance, unlike the Apollo spacecraft whose utility and durability is limited. Despite their dire living conditions, generations of Acahualincans have striven to be born even if inevitably they will die of hunger:

> Los hijos de la gente de Acahualinca no nacen por hambre,
> y tienen hambre de nacer, para morirse de hambre.
>
> [The children of the people of Acahualinca aren't born of hunger,
> and they're eager to be born, to die of hunger.] (28–29)

Rugama juxtaposes high technology with the Nicaraguan nation and its historic, neglected poor in an attempt to dislodge the poor from the periphery of current issues and place them in the center. It is an attempt to privilege the needs of the majority of the homeland's citizens over the desires and excesses of the more powerful minority. He joins this poetic restructuring of priorities to theology and science by rewriting the biblical Beatitudes (Matthew 5: 3–12) that promise heaven and earth to believers. His beatitude says, "Bienaventurados los pobres porque de ellos será la luna" [Blessed are the poor for the moon shall be theirs] (30). Although the Apollo astronauts may have seen the moon, and eventually Apollo 11 lands on the moon (July 20, 1969), it is the Acahualincans who inherit it. This new beatitude re-emphasizes the poor's virtuousness, their historical importance, and it points to a future in which they will be central rather than marginal to the homeland, as the poem's title reads: "La tierra es un satélite de la luna." The poem's final promise clearly echoes Rugama's political and religious ideologies and constructs a linguistic memorial to the future Acahualincan heroes who will populate a new homeland.

Rugama's poetic uplifting of his homeland's poor and his heroic retort, "¡Que se rinda tu madre!," earn him prominence in Ernesto Cardenal's 1973 long poem, "Oráculo sobre Managua" ["Oracle over Managua"].[54] Cardenal's poem documents Nicaraguan reality after the December 1972 earthquake in Managua.[55] He details Somoza's and his cronies' misappropriation of international aid and Rugama's life and heroism on behalf of Sandinista ideals. As Marc Zimmerman notes, "[I]n post-earthquake Managua Cardenal was eager to see the reincarnation of Rugama's evolution and ultimate revolutionary spirit in the hearts of Nicaragua's young people."[56] In "Oráculo sobre Managua," Rugama's heroic death functions as a strategy to "illustrate and transmit ideals of sacrifice on behalf of a nation, a government, or a party as well as to mobilize resistance to foreign threats or domestic insurgencies."[57] Cardenal's Rugama represents an exemplary armed response to Somoza's tyranny. His life and death in an unjust battle are illustrative of Rugama's unwavering commitment, defiance, and moral and physical fortitude. Johnson's contention that "indeed, Latin American nations typically turn to dead heroes in time of crisis, the very endurance of the hero serving as a model for peoples tested by political or economic threats" underlines the efficacy of Rugama's memorialization as a Sandinista national hero.[58] Cardenal's poem erects a poetic shrine to righteous armed struggle—a righteousness lived through liberatory Christianity and Marxism.

The suitability of Rugama as a heroic figure in "Oráculo sobre Managua" is clearer still when considered in tandem with Cardenal's own biography and poetic production. Cardenal, along with Dalton and Rugama, belongs to a cadre of politically committed poets of 1960s and 1970s Central America. Unlike them, though, Cardenal long advocated for a peaceful revolution, even after openly declaring his support for the FSLN in the dedication to 1973's *Canto nacional* [*National Canto*]. His spiritual experiences in Kentucky with the Trappist monk Thomas Merton, as well as his contemplative peasant community, Solentiname, kept him grounded in a nonviolent revolution. As Cardenal notes in *En Cuba* [*In Cuba*] (1972) and *La santidad de la revolución* [*The Saintliness of the Revolution*] (1976), his visit to Cuba and study of Marxism transformed his view of the compatibility of politics and Christianity.[59] The 1977 destruction of Solentiname by the National Guard forced him to accept "personally the principle of armed struggle."[60] His poetry reflects these spiritual and political transformations. As critics, such as Beverley and Zimmerman and Dawes, have noted, "Oráculo sobre Managua" is a transitional poetic text. The collections that immediately precede it—*El estrecho dudoso* [*The Doubtful Strait*] (1966) and *Homenaje a los indios americanos* [*Homage to the American Indians*] (1969)—amply demonstrate his interest in Latin American history and the lives of the oppressed and his well-known *exteriorismo*. His poetic theory exalts concrete social reality and objects, uses historical evidence and facts, and employs prosaic and figurative language.[61] These characteristics and the "documentary" techniques[62] in evidence in "Hora 0" (1960) are all prevalent in Cardenal's paean to Rugama and the armed revolutionary struggle, a struggle that is part of a "natural" human evolution toward equality and plenitude.[63]

In "Oráculo sobre Managua," then, Rugama's dead body represents the honorableness of martyrdom for political ideals and against injustice and political repression. By quoting a newspaper description of the cadaver's condition, the poetic speaker focuses on the violence Rugama endured,

> Vos Leonel Rugama acribillado y llevado a la morgue
> manchado de tierra y sangre dijo *La Prensa*. (216)

> [You, Leonel Rugama, bullet-ridden and carried off to the morgue
> stained with dirt and blood, said *La Prensa*][64]

Rugama's destroyed body (216, 231), though, signifies the future. A martyr, he will be resurrected in the people, "Pero el pueblo es inmortal" [But the people are immortal] (237).[65] Cardenal echoes the Bible, declaring that death is

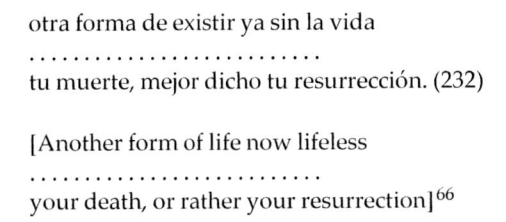

otra forma de existir ya sin la vida
....
tu muerte, mejor dicho tu resurrección. (232)

[Another form of life now lifeless
....
your death, or rather your resurrection][66]

While Rugama's death at the hands of Somoza's National Guard and Managua's destruction in the massive 1972 earthquake seem to be the end of the guerrilla hero and the city, the poetic speaker insists that "para resucitar hay que morir" (237) [to be reborn you must die].[67] Thus, Rugama and his sacrifice function as a vehicle toward a revolutionary future (238), a future in which all Acahualincans cease to exist (223). In "Oráculo sobre Managua" Cardenal displaces Acahualinca, a local living space of abject poverty and an archaeological site, from the center of "La tierra es un satélite de la luna" and replaces it with Leonel Rugama himself, a typical hero who has proven his willingness to sacrifice himself for others. Rugama's persona melds concern for the poor, Christianity, and Marxist ideologies. Through the retelling of the guerrilla poet's development and heroism, Cardenal exalts fearless feats against Somoza and selfless acts of solidarity with the poor. In "Oráculo sobre Managua," he solemnly constructs a burial site for Rugama: Acahualinca. Acahualinca becomes the place that is venerated once the body (Rugama's went to the morgue) is inaccessible. The poetic memorialization of and burial of Rugama illustrates Johnson's highlighting of the political significance of heroes' burial sites. Johnson contends that the "powerful sentiment that martyrs and deceased heroes should be buried in appropriate places, commonly the arenas of their celebrated actions and sacrifices, is often marshaled by governments or political movements."[68] Cardenal intends to mobilize Nicaraguans by poetically burying and resurrecting Rugama's body in Acahualinca, a concrete example of the nation's poverty and vast social inequities. Cardenal erects a monument to an alternative heroism on Nicaragua's socioeconomic margins. His monument rhetorically confronts Somoza's attempts to command loyalty and obedience to his regime.[69] The poet transforms "¡Que se rinda tu madre!" from a threat of violence into a biblical pledge of a new beginning, "He aquí que hago nuevas todas las cosas" [Behold I make all things new] (239, citing Revelation 21:5).

"Oráculo sobre Managua" poeticizes the possibility, and promise for true believers, of "making all things new" through armed struggle. This ideal moved guerrillas, political activists, and fellow travelers. Rugama and Dalton did not live long enough to see the outcome of their revolutions, but they have remained in a privileged position as embodiments of revolutionary fervor and commitment. Now, direct political engagement among literati has ebbed. Even so, Dalton's extensive oeuvre[70] and protest literature's common issues of government repression and social justice resonate in contemporary Central American literature.

This resonance lacks the religious solemnity of Cardenal and machismo-laden threats of guerrilla poets. Idealizations of the *pueblo* and of heroic acts of solidarity have given way to more pragmatic and ironic views of contemporary post-conflict societies. Instead of awed reappraisals of past heroism, the poets and writers who inherited war-torn homelands take more sardonic views of the consequences of Central America's long civil and revolutionary wars. No longer do the heroes and bodies of war victims mobilize social or political actions. Instead, for instance, in the work of Claudia Hernández (1975), a young Salvadoran writer, dead bodies are treated much more practically. Through an acute use of irony, not unlike that of Dalton or Rugama, Hernández critiques the celebration of martyrdom and turns upside-down concepts of citizenship and solidarity that undergird much Central American political poetry.

For several reasons Hernández's narrative dialogues fruitfully with the 1960s and 1970s poetry discussed above. As is much political poetry, it is characterized by brevity, linguistic precision, use of metaphor, and an understatedly ironic narrative voice. While her stories have protagonists and anecdotes that develop in particular settings, most notable are their evocative and allusive qualities. Her stories evoke and allude to Central America's recent history of violence, oppression, and death without dwelling on historical facts, or the "razones detrás de tanto horror" [reasons behind so much horror].[71] Her narrators' apparently detached tone and attitude vis-à-vis the dehumanizing situations and dehumanized homeland they experience distance Hernández from the political commitment of this chapter's revolutionary poets. At the same time, they offer a link to contemporaneous poets. Hernández's poetic short fiction functions as a transition in form, content, and tone between poetry from the 1960s and 1970s—with its heartfelt celebrations of heroes, idealized *patrias*, and violent harangues against oppression—and post-conflict Central American poetry.

Claudia Hernández confronts daily Central American life with "forensic stories dissecting the living and the dead."[72] These "dissections" are performed and presented dryly, with no attempt to tug at readers' heartstrings or awaken social consciousness. In a two-part short story, "Hechos de un buen ciudadano (parte 1)" and "Hechos de un buen ciudadano (parte 2)" ["Deeds of a Good Citizen (Parts 1 and 2)"], the reader encounters national and social fragmentation in the narration of the actions of a "good," perhaps exemplary, citizen who is faced with a seemingly bizarre situation: a recently murdered body in his kitchen.[73] While this situation in itself is strange, more so is the protagonist's unreal but practical solution. He simply places a newspaper advertisement in search of the cadaver's "owner":

Busco dueño de muchacha joven
de carnes rollizas, rodillas saltonas y
cara de llamarse Lívida.
Fue abandonada en mi cocina, muy cerca de
la refrigeradora, herida y casi vacía de sangre.
Información al 271-0122.

[Looking for the owner of a plump young woman
with bulging knees and /
who looks like she's named *Lívida* (Livid)
She was abandoned in my kitchen, very close
to the refrigerator, injured and almost without blood.
For information, call 271-0122.] (17)

The ad specifies the physical state of the body based on the narrator's experiential observations, "He visto muchos asesinados en mi vida" [I've seen a lot of murder victims in my life] (17). But it also reflects his more fanciful thoughts about the dead girl's knees and her possible name. The ad at once objectifies Lívida's body parts and humanizes her by giving her a unique name. The narrator's observations are proven incisive, as one of the several phone calls he receives is from the parents of the cadaver who call to say that they are certain the body is not their daughter's, even though the description fits her exactly. Ultimately, the "good citizen" does not force the parents to admit that their beloved daughter is dead. Instead, the "good citizen" gives the cadaver to a fellow compassionate citizen whose family is frantically seeking a disappeared male family member. Through subterfuge, including weighing down the coffin, the protagonist and the caller with "very fine hands" (18) quell a family's distress and bury the unclaimed body. Lívida's bloodless cadaver substitutes for the disappeared male body. This successful substitution iterates families' need to bury their dead, even if they cannot confirm the body's identity or, as the case may be, even if only fragments of the loved one's body can be buried. Lívida's burial as someone else also critically points, on the one hand, to the insignificance of disappeared citizens as individuals; and, on the other, to the interchangeability of dead bodies when, as during the Salvadoran civil war, dead bodies are abundant. Both of these representations of the dead collide with and satirize the poetic commemorations discussed earlier in this chapter. In Hernández's text, the found dead body requires not homage but rather a discreet solution that allows the narrator and his fellow citizens to feel at home with their treatment of the dead. Her burial also prevents a possible public health crisis in the neighborhood (18, 19). Thus Lívida's murdered body impersonates another citizen in order to maintain her compatriots' health and well-being. Ironically, Lívida's murder and her unpunished murderer transform her into a "good" citizen deserving of accolades and, in the revolutionary idiom of 1960s and 1970s poets, of homage for her "martyrdom."

In the second part of the short story, the reader discovers that the protagonist's dead body disposal service is in great demand. Because of the ad he places, the unlucky custodians of twenty unclaimed cadavers come to him in search of help. Hernández's narrator is characteristically matter-of-fact in the telling of both parts of "Hechos de un ciudadano." And in the second part, when he is offered money for his efforts, he refuses it because were he to accept it, "[L]os estaba declarando a ellos responsables de los gastos que debían ser asumidos por los asesinos o por los familiares de los muertos" [I'd be declaring them responsible for expenses that the murderers or the dead's families should incur] (40). This presumption of malfeasance, the certainty that Lívida was murdered, the revelation that he has seen many murder victims (17), and the description of the new cadavers, female and male, young and old, from the city and beyond (39), all function as a metonymy for the Salvadoran civil war (1980–1992) and its tens of thousands of disappearances and killings. These images and narrative details also foreground Central America's harsh reality: the daily violence that assaults its citizens. Thereby, Hernández's story quietly reflects on the present while conjuring the recent past. Whereas Dalton directly references the *patria* and metaphorizes it as, for example, prison guard and bad mother, Hernández subtly alludes to the homeland by identifying its characters as "citizens." Her narrator-protagonist's matter-of-fact reaction to death and his no nonsense actions are far removed from Daltonian anger- and angst-filled "patriotic" poems. The random, but not entirely surprising, appearance of unidentified cadavers in people's homes leads the protagonist to practical, local solutions.

At the end of the second part of "Hechos de un buen ciudadano," the narrator is left with seven unclaimed cadavers. But he does not rail against criminals or an uncaring *patria*. Instead he finds his own way out of the dilemma: cannibalism. The reader sees that, from the start, he had begun preparing the bodies for consumption. He had salted them to keep them from smelling bad; thus, to prepare them for cooking he must only rinse off the salt cure. He chops up the bodies and shreds the meat, and then cooks it in a tomato sauce made from his homegrown tomatoes. He judges that "[e]l sabor era inmejorable" [the flavor was superb] (41). His lurid, macabre, ironic solution efficiently deals with two serious national problems—hunger and poverty—using surplus local resources—murdered citizens. The dead feed the city's many "pordioseros, indigentes y ancianos" [beggars, indigents, and elderly] (41). The protagonist-chef is content with himself because, in an ironic reference to revolutionary discourse, the meal he prepared allowed him and the dead to "serve their neighbors" (41). And no one is the wiser when he explains that he paid for the delicious stew's ingredients with donations from the cadavers' "owners" (42). His generosity is so appreciated that the city publicly and officially praises him for his good cooking and denominates him a good man and "most meritorious" citizen (41–42). The narrator downplays the applause of his fellow city dwellers, saying that "que sólo había hecho lo que cualquiera—de verdad, cualquiera—habría hecho" [he had done what anyone—really, anyone—would have done] (42).

The *patria*, in Hernández's story, is embodied by the found cadavers and literally cut into pieces and ingested by its poorest citizens (41). The needs of citizens are met by their compatriots' bodies rather than by a caring homeland or oppositional groups or churches, for instance. The homeland's failure to feed its inhabitants forces Hernández's protagonist-narrator to cannibalize other citizens. This cannibalism demonstrates the people's desperation and literalizes rampant crime, including the murders alluded to in the story, as a cannibalization of the citizenry by criminals and by the homeland itself.[74]

Hernández's short fiction is one response to the political ideals and struggles in which socially engaged poets like Dalton, Rugama, and Cardenal participated and, in the case of the first two, for which they died. Her characters represent the civilian populations that "tienen que pagar los platos rotos" [clean up the mess] left by years of armed conflicts and struggles to demonize and memorialize political-military rivals. Hernández's "good citizen" plays the role of "cleaner" impassively but not without sardonically parodying a society that willingly accepts that murders go unpunished and leaves the disposal of the dead to its citizenry. Guerrilla heroism is replaced by that of a citizen who is morally opposed to murder but not to cannibalism, if it is for the good of the poor majority. This moral relativism juts up against the official black and white moralism of the war years' hero-making. Hernández's story thus responds to the literary inheritance bequeathed by her politically committed predecessors and offers up a new ironic vision of solidarity and heroism.

As noted earlier, Dalton died infamously at the hands of his own political movement, the ERP (Ejército Popular del Pueblo [People's Revolutionary Army]), after being found guilty of treason and sentenced to death by a kangaroo court. On May 10, 1975, Dalton and another ERP *compañero* were summarily executed. His death has often been used to exemplify leftist revolutionary intransigency and excess.[75] In 1994, almost twenty years later and after the signing of the Chapultepec Peace Accords, the United Nations (ONUSAL and UN Human Rights division) revealed to Dalton's family where his body had been buried. According to the UN, Dalton was buried "in a grave so shallow that [his] feet stuck out. Animals started the job of unearthing the bodies."[76] The remains were later "tossed . . . into the trash-filled ravine of El Playón,"[77] a well-known dumping site for the victims of state repression. Dalton's remains disappeared, but governmental and cultural institutions have resurrected his image and name. Officially he is considered national cultural patrimony. His name adorns the façade of the Universidad de El Salvador's art gallery, for example. As evidence of his prominence, the governmental publishing house DPI (Dirección de Publicaciones e Impresos) published his complete poetic works.[78] One of his executioners, Joaquín Villalobos, cynically declared in a radio interview, "It would be a very terrible thing, if after that mistake, we didn't make minimal amends, reclaiming Roque as a national treasure and also as one of the people who describes the Salvadoran nature."[79] Dalton, and his nonexistent but Salvadoran cadaver, is thus made into an instrument of unification for a nation he depicted as irreparably torn apart. He imagined replacements for its inauthentic, untruthful symbols and poetically disappeared the homeland he experienced. Likewise, Rugama's poetic resurrection was politically motivated; his heroic sacrifice coalesced new and existent Sandinistas with a contemporary incarnation of the Nicaraguan guerrilla. Similarly in his poetry, Rugama memorialized the forgotten Acahualincans to represent the poor, the potential recipients of the results of his martyrdom. In the poetry of Dalton, Rugama, and Cardenal, the *patria* is redefined to produce other versions of the homeland. As the civil wars and revolutions recede into history, however, and former "heroic" leaders lose their luster and legitimacy as such, there are no ready-made imaginary homelands to poetically capture. But contemporary Central America continually transforms itself even as it is dismembered, strewn about, and consumed from within and without.

Post-conflict Central America's literal and metaphorical self-cannibalization, the chopping up and consuming of its human and physical geographies, forces its inhabitants to constantly piece together their pasts (and presents). As Hernández's story illustrates, Central Americans who remain home on the isthmus must find ways to exist amid corpses and remnants of the places of the homeland. As chapter 2 will show, one way to re-experience and construct imaginary and imagined homes is through pining for a remembered past. Living in the rubble of the post-conflict, neoliberal *patria*, contemporary poets and writers call on nostalgia to belong, and survive, at home.

NOTES

1. Donald D. Walsh, trans., "Zero Hour," *Zero Hour and Other Documentary Poems*, by Ernesto Cardenal, ed. Donald. D. Walsh, trans. Paul W. Borgerson, et al. (New York: New Directions, 1980). Note that in the discussion below, unlike Walsh, I read both "queque" and "bizcocho" as cake.

2. The mentioned dictators ruled Guatemala, Honduras, El Salvador, and Nicaragua, respectively. With the exception of Somoza García, who was in power until the mid-1950s, they ruled in the 1930s and 1940s.

3. Notably during a 2008 summer seminar on Neoliberalism in Nicaragua (CIEE Study Abroad), various invited Nicaraguan speakers proudly mentioned Nicaragua's

safety and its success at keeping state power separate from police and military forces. Speakers also commented on the irony of Costa Rica's pride at not having a national army since 1948 and its insistence on patrolling the San Juan River with firearms. Nicaragua considers the San Juan part of its national territory and opposes Costa Rica's armed patrols. Lastly, it is clear that in El Salvador the separation between civil and military security forces remains hazy to say the least. For a comparative study of post-conflict Guatemala, El Salvador, and Nicaragua see Jack Spence, *War and Peace in Central America: Comparing Transitions Toward Democracy and Social Equality in Guatemala, El Salvador, and Nicaragua*, Electronic Book, (Brookline, MA: Hemisphere Initiatives, November 2004), www.hemisphereinitiatives.org.

4. Carolyn Hall and Héctor Pérez Brignoli, *Historical Atlas of Central America*, cartographer John V. Cotter (Norman: University of Oklahoma Press, 2003), 226, 228; Héctor Pérez-Brignoli, *A Brief History of Central America*, trans. Richard B. Sawrey A. and Susan Stretti de Sawrey (Berkeley: University of California Press, 1989), 112–13. Sandino, the FSLN's namesake, fought a guerrilla war against the U.S. Marines from 1927–1933. The United States. first occupied Nicaragua in 1912, by request of the current Conservative government, to restore peace after it was attacked by a Liberal-Conservative coalition. Through the Byron-Chamorro Treaty of 1916, the United States acquired rights in perpetuity to construct an interoceanic canal, rights to the Corn Islands in the Caribbean, and the right to build a naval base in the Gulf of Fonseca. The United States left Nicaragua in 1925 but returned a year later to quell another civil war. Sandino and his guerrilla army fought past the 1927 signing of peace at Tipitapa by Liberal General José María Moncada. Moncada became president in 1928, but Sandino continued fighting the occupation. In preparation for the U.S. Marines to depart in 1932, the United States trained the Nicaraguan National Guard. Sandino and his forces agreed to put down their arms.
Ralph Lee Woodward, Jr., *Central America: A Nation Divided*, 2nd ed. (New York: Oxford University Press, 1985), 219. However, as Cardenal retells it in this poem, in 1934 after a dinner meeting with the U.S.-backed president, Juan Bautista Sacasa, the National Guard—led by Anastasio (Tacho) Somoza García—assassinated Sandino and his closest lieutenants.

5. Tacho's regime was followed by those of his sons, Luis and Tachito. As in the case of their father, their official presidencies were interrupted with presidencies of loyalists through whom the Somoza family continued to rule. Luis Somoza García's regime lasted until his death in 1967; Tachito's until the Sandinista triumph of 1979 (Woodward, *Central America: A Nation Divided*, 220–23).

6. Stephen Benz, "Through the Tropical Looking Glass: the Motif of Resistance in U.S. Literature on Central America," in *Tropicalizations: Transcultural Representations of Latinidad*, ed. Frances R. Aparicio and Susana Chávez-Silverman (Hanover: University Press of New England, 1997), 59.

7. Ernesto Cardenal, *Antología* (Managua: Nueva Nicaragua-Monimbó, 1983), 127.

8. James Dunkerley, *Power in the Isthmus: A Political History of Modern Central America* (London: Verso, 1988), 59–60, 90.

9. Ibid., 102.

10. Pérez-Brignoli, *A Brief History of Central America*, 107.

11. Ana Patricia Rodríguez, "Wasted Opportunities: Conflictive Peacetime Narratives of Central America," in *The Globalization of U.S.-Latin America Relations: Democracy, Intervention, and Human Rights*, ed. Virginia M. Bouvier (Westport, CT: Praeger, 2002), 230.

12. See Dunkerley's *Power in the Isthmus* for a detailed review of Costa Rica's "national antipathy towards Somoza" and official support of the FSLN (626–29) and of its subsequent support of the Contras (640–45).

13. Chapter 4 discusses in detail Costa Rican self-critiques of their exceptionalism.

14. Gioconda Belli, *El país bajo mi piel* (New York: Vintage Books, 2003), 199.

15. Note this same idealization in Belli's poetry and fiction.

16. It may go without saying that it is not uncommon for the heroic statues that fill public spaces to be fabricated to represent a more adequate or comfortable national identity. Two examples in Central America are Atlacatl and Juan Santamaría. William R. Fowler, Jr. "Ethnohistoric Sources on the Pipil-Nicarao of Central America," *Ethnohistory* 32, no. 1 (Winter 1985): 41. Atlacatl is said to be a rebellious *Pipil* who fended off the Spaniards in El Salvador. He is celebrated in statuary, and during the Civil War an infamous counter-insurgency battalion took his name. But Atlacatl's historical existence is in doubt. Fowler shows that an error in the transcription of a Highland Maya document, by which a place name Panatacat or Atacat was transformed into a proper name, created this folk hero.
Steven Palmer, "Getting to Know the Unknown Soldier: Official Nationalism in Liberal Costa Rica, 1880–1900," *Journal of Latin American Studies* 25 (1993): 70. In the second case, Palmer details the Liberals' creation and use of Juan Santamaría in the 1880s to foment nationalism. Santamaría died heroically in the *Campaña Nacional Centroamericana* (1856–1857) against the U.S. filibuster William Walker. But Santamaría's curly hair, which gave him the nickname "el erizo," did not correspond with attempts to view Costa Ricans as "homogenous and predominantly white." The hero was "brought back into the fold of Costa Rican 'sameness,'" by highlighting his facial similarities with "white" compatriots. Also, see Virginia Q. Tilley, *Seeing Indians: A Study of Race, Nation, and Power in El Salvador* (Albuquerque: University of New Mexico Press, 2005).

17. Lyman Johnson, Introduction to *Death, Dismemberment and Memory: Body Politics in Latin America*, ed. Lyman Johnson (Albuquerque: University of New Mexico Press), 1–26.

18. Johnson, Introduction, 1–2.

19. Ibid., 4.

20. Ibid., 8.

21. One arena in which the Sandinista and subsequent governments imposed their particular view of the Nicaraguan homeland is in educational policy. For an overview of policy changes, see Robert F. Arnove, "Education as Contested Terrain in Nicaragua," *Comparative Education Review* 39, no. 1 (1995): 28–53. Regarding Arnoldo Alemán's erasure of Sandinista murals during his tenure as mayor of Managua (1990–1996), see Dennis Rodgers, "A Symptom Called Managua," *New Left Review* 49 (Jan.–Feb. 2008): 103–20.

22. David E. Whisnant, *Rascally Signs in Sacred Places: The Politics of Culture in Nicaragua* (Chapel Hill: University of North Carolina Press, 1995), 443.

23. Dalton himself popularized the story of his origins as the descendant of the infamous bank-robbing Dalton Brothers. This story has been repeated and held as true by biographers and readers of Dalton's oeuvre. See, for instance, Luis Alvarenga, *El ciervo perseguido: vida y obra de Roque Dalton* (San Salvador: Dirección de Publicaciones e Impresos, 2002); and, Claribel Alegría, *Mágica tribu* (San Salvador: Índole, 2008).
Roger Atwood, "Gringo Iracundo: Roque Dalton and His Father," *Latin American Research Review* 46, no. 1 (2011): 127. In his 2011 article, Roger Atwood debunks this myth of Dalton's family background and demonstrates that in fact his father, Winnall Dalton, Jr., was from a respectable Arizona Mexican-American family. Atwood then develops his theory that Dalton used his father in his work to explore power and identity.

24. Atwood, "Gringo Iracundo: Roque Dalton and His Father," 140–41.

25. Alvarenga, *El ciervo perseguido*; Mario Benedetti, "Una hora con Roque Dalton," in *Los poetas comunicantes* (Montevideo: Biblioteca de Marcha, 1972). In his interview with Uruguayan poet Mario Benedetti, Dalton discusses the importance of his university years in his political education. Alvarenga also highlights these years.

26. Mario Hernández-Aguirre, "La nueva poesía salvadoreña: 'La generación comprometida,'" *Revista Cultura*, no. 20 (April–June 1961): 77–99; John Beverley and Marc Zimmerman, *Literature and Politics in the Central American Revolutions* (Austin: University of Texas Press, 1990); and, Alvarenga, *El ciervo perseguido*. Prior to becoming the Committed Generation, the group called itself the *Círculo literario universitario* (Univer-

sity Literary Circle). In addition to including writers who would revolutionize Salvadoran letters, among them Manlio Argueta, Roberto Armijo, José Roberto Cea, Ítalo López Vallecillos and Álvaro Menéndez Leal, Guatemalan guerrilla poet Otto René Castillo was a founding member of the *Círculo*.

27. Hernández-Aguirre, "La nueva poesía salvadoreña," 87.
28. Ibid., 78
29. Beverley and Zimmerman, *Literature and Politics in the Central American Revolutions*; Alvarenga, *El ciervo perseguido*.
30. Miguel Huezo Mixco, Salvadoran public intellectual, writes in detail of the reasons for Dalton's resignation from his job in Havana's Casa de las Américas and his falling out with prominent Cuban intellectuals in "Roque vuelve a morir," an article commemorating the 35th anniversary of his death. The article was originally published in México's *La Jornada Semanal* No. 816. See http://www.contracultura.com.sv/el-tema/roque-dalton-la-fuerza-literaria-del-compromiso.
31. Alvarenga, *El ciervo perseguido*, 98–104. In addition, see Efren Lemus' critical analysis of internal ERP documents, explaining and defending Dalton's "trial" and condemnation, in "La 'prueba' en el asesinato de Dalton que la justicia salvadoreña se niega a analizar," *El faro*, March 26, 2012. http://elfaro.net/es/201203/noticias/7562/.
32. Lara Martínez's "official" three-volume compilation of Dalton's poetry includes lengthy studies of the production and publication history of poem collections and individual poems. He has also written on Dalton's narrative texts. Roque Dalton, *No pronuncies mi nombre: Poesía completa*, vols. 1–3, comp. Rafael Lara Martínez (San Salvador: DPI, 2005 and 2008). Also, see Yvette Aparicio, "Literary Convention and Revolution in Roque Dalton's *Taberna y otros lugares*," *Revista de estudios hispánicos* XXXII, no. 1–2 (2005): 169–81; Linda Craft, *Novels of Testimony and Resistance from Central America* (Gainesville: University Press of Florida, 1997); Héctor Lindo-Fuentes, Erik Ching, and Rafael Lara Martínez, *Remembering a Massacre in El Salvador: The Insurrection of 1932, Roque Dalton and the Politics of Historical Memory* (Albuquerque: University of New Mexico Press, 2007); and, Ileana Rodríguez, *Women, Guerrillas, and Love: Understanding War in Central America*, trans. Robert Carr (Minneapolis: University of Minnesota Press, 1996); among others.
33. Benedict Anderson, *Imagined Communities: Reflections on the Origins and Spread of Nationalism*, rev. ed. (London: Verso, 1991), 6–7.
34. The conventionality of Dalton's *machista* view of the homeland as an unnurturing, bad *madre patria* is notable but not surprising.
35. Anderson, *Imagined Communities*, 6.
36. Johnson, Introduction, 15.
37. Of course, Dalton went further than some of his compatriots and cast his lot with proponents of armed struggle.
38. Echoes of Dalton's poetic pronouncements can be heard in texts of Salvadoran writers now respected in Latin America. For instance, in his infamous novella *El asco: Thomas Bernhard en San Salvador* (1997) [*Revulsion: Thomas Bernhard in San Salvador*], Horacio Castellanos Moya's protagonist also declares El Salvador's nonexistence and denigrates the country's autochthonous cultural objects and practices (78, 80, 81). *El asco*'s protagonist acridly rejects commonplace symbols of Salvadoran-ness, such as foods (*pupusas*, clams), *Pilsener* beer, and iconic writers (e.g., Salarrúe), for which Dalton yearns in his text. Unlike Dalton, Castellanos Moya rejects fully any possibility of a unified Salvadoran identity. The infamy of this particular narrative is precisely the desecration of closely held symbols of national identity; the author received death threats and was forced to leave El Salvador after its publication.
These two author interviews offer information on Castellanos Moya's literary work and his life in the United States: http://quarterlyconversation.com/the-horacio-castellanos-moya-interview and http://www.pittsburghcitypaper.ws/pittsburgh/uncommonsenselessness/Content?oid=1340617.
39. Michael Billig, *Banal Nationalism* (London: Sage Publications, 1995).
40. Anderson, *Imagined Communities*, 7.

41. Narrative representations of the "illness" caused by the nation can be found in various contemporary Salvadoran writers, including Castellanos Moya and Claudia Hernández. Beatriz Cortez has written of such fictions as "cynical." See her *Estética del cinismo: pasión y el desencanto en la literatura centroamericana de posguerra* (Guatemala City: F & G Editores, 2010).

42. Rugama, Leonel. *La tierra es un satélite de la luna / The Earth Is a Satellite of the Moon*, trans. Sara Miles, et al., (Willamantic, CT: Curbstone Press, 1985).

43. Greg Dawes, *Aesthetics and Revolution: Nicaraguan Poetry, 1979–1990* (Minneapolis: University of Minnesota Press, 1993), 80.

44. Cándida Rugama cited in Rugama, *La tierra es un satélite de la luna / The Earth Is a Satellite of the Moon*, 116–17.

45. Dawes, *Aesthetics and Revolution*, 78, 80, 185.

46. Ibid., 80.

47. Leonel Rugama, "La tierra es un satélite de la luna," in *Poetry Like Bread: Poets of the Political Imagination by Curbstone Press*, ed. Martín Espada, exp. ed. (Willamantic, CT: Curbstone Press, 2000), 218, 220.

48. Currently, there is an open-air museum at the site of the footprints, near the shores of Lake Managua.

49. In *Literature and Politics in the Central American Revolutions*, Beverley and Zimmerman read Rugama's comparison of the U.S. space program and Acahualincans as "a sardonic version of the kind of religious incantation Ernesto Cardenal liked to use" (77). In *Aesthetics and Revolution*, Dawes sees Rugama's use of repetition, like Cardenal's, as an emulation of ordinary speech (82).

50. The manned Apollo missions were: 1, 7–10, 11–17.

51. Information about the Apollo Space Program gathered from the Smithsonian National Space and Air Museum's website: http://www.nasm.si.edu/collections/imagery/apollo/apollo.htm.

52. To access the list of goodwill messages see: http://history.nasa.gov/ap11-35ann/goodwill_messages.html.

53. For an assessment of the importance of the Medellín Conference's interpretation of Vatican II, see the following: Daniel M. Bell, Jr., *Liberation Theology after the End of History: The Refusal to Cease Suffering* (London: Routledge, 2001), 53–55.

54. Cardenal, *Antología* (Managua: Nueva Nicaragua-Monimbó, 1983), 209–39.

55. This 6.2 magnitude shallow earthquake destroyed much of Managua. An estimated 5,000 people died, 20,000 were injured and a quarter of a million were left homeless. See http://earthquake.usgs.gov/earthquakes/world/events/1972_12_23.php. James Dunkerley, *Power in the Isthmus: A Political History of Modern Central America* (London: Verso, 1988), 233–34. Somoza, with the National Guard, plundered emergency supplies. He also appropriated relief funds and gained control of construction contracts.

Héctor Pérez-Brignoli, *A Brief History of Central America*, 150. His regime's scandalous behavior would later play a part in the popular support of the FSLN.

56. Marc Zimmerman, "Introduction: Ernesto Cardenal after the Revolution," *Vuelos de victoria / Flights of Victory* (Willamantic, CT: Curbstone Press, 1988), xv.

In his memoirs, Cardenal notes that he was midway through writing this poem about Rugama when the 1972 earthquake struck Managua. He then rewrote the poem to integrate the destruction of Managua. Cardenal published a preview of these anecdotes in 2000 in the Managuan daily *El nuevo diario* (16 September) under the title, "Reevaluación de Leonel Rugama." http://archivo.elnuevodiario.com.ni/2000/septiembre/16-septiembre-2000/cultural/cultural8.html.

57. Johnson, Introduction, 5.

58. Ibid., 18–19.

59. In *En Cuba* (Buenos Aires: Ediciones C. Lohlé, 1972) and *La santidad de la revolución* (Salamanca: Ediciones Sígueme, 1976), Cardenal expounds on his theology and conversion to Christianity and to Marxism.

60. Beverley and Zimmerman, *Literature and Politics in the Central American Revolutions*, 83.

61. *Exteriorismo* owes much to Ezra Pound's poetics and the American poet's contention that anything which can be said in prose can be poetry. On the influence of Pound on Cardenal's poetics, see Tamara Williams, "Reading Ernesto Cardenal Reading Ezra Pound: Radical Inclusiveness, Epic Reconstitution, and Textual Praxis," *Chasqui: Revista de literatura latinoamericana* 21, no. 2 (November 1992): 43–52.

62. Robert Pring-Mill, "The Redemption of Reality Through Documentary Poetry," introduction to *Zero Hour and Other Documentary Poems*, by Ernesto Cardenal, ed. Donald D. Walsh, trans. Paul W. Borgeson, Jr., Jonathan Cohen, Robert Pring-Mill, and Donald D. Walsh (New York: New Directions, 1980), ix–xxi.

63. In *Aesthetics and Revolution*, Dawes rightly asserts that the most significant new feature of "Oráculo sobre Managua" is its use of scientific research, which will be particularly notable in later works that reveal Cardenal's "greater understanding of historical materialism and of scientific socialism" (78).

64. Donald D. Walsh, trans., *Zero Hour and Other Documentary Poems*, 48

65. Ibid., 67. Also, see James Iffland's *Ensayos sobre la poesía revolucionaria* (San Jose: EDUCA, 1994) on revolutionary self-sacrifice in Central American poetry as viewed through the lens of historical materialism.

66. Ibid., 62.

67. Ibid., 67.

68. Johnson, Introduction, 21.

69. Years earlier, in "Somoza desveliza la estatua de Somoza en el estadio Somoza" ["Somoza Unveils the Statue of Somoza in Somoza Stadium"] (*Epigramas*, 1961) [Epigrams], Cardenal imagines Somoza's cynical justification for commissioning a statue of himself: "No es que yo crea que el pueblo me erigió esta estatua / porque yo sé mejor que vosotros que la ordené yo mismo. / Ni tampoco que pretenda pasar con ella a la posteridad / porque yo sé que el pueblo la derribará un día. / Ni que haya querido erigirme a mí mismo en vida / el monumento que muerto no me erigiréis vosotros; sino que erigí esa estatua porque sé que la odiáis" [It's not that I believe the people erected that statue for me / because I know better than you that I ordered it myself. / Nor do I intend through it to live on in posterity / because I know the people will topple it one day. / Nor is it that I erected for myself in life / the monument you'd erect upon my death; rather I erected that statue because I know you hate it.] (16). This epigram exemplifies the political utility of monuments and the desire for veneration, even if the "hurrays" are a forced civic duty.

70. There are numerous examples of young writers' directly referencing Roque Dalton's works and life. For instance, Eunice Shade, a writer discussed in chapter 5, imagines Dalton's return to Santiago, Chile after death and his encounters with a mythified former lover. This multipart short story's title, "No pronuncies mi nombre" ["Don't say my name"], is a frequent allusion to Dalton's early, prophetic poem, "Altas horas de la noche" ["Small Hours of the Night"] from *El turno del ofendido* (1962).

71. Nadine Haas, "Claudia Hernández y lo surreal de la violencia," *Revista Luna Park* 31 (n.d.) http://www.revistalunapark.com/index.php?option=com_content&view=article&id=71:felipe-granados-la-foto-en-la-que-me-dabas-la-espalda&catid=69:31-literatura-salvadorena&Itemid=331.

72. Ana Patricia Rodríguez, *Dividing the Isthmus: Transnational Histories, Literatures, and Cultures* (Austin: University of Texas Press, 2009), 226.

73. Claudia Hernández, *De fronteras* [*Of Frontiers*] (Guatemala City: Piedra Santa, 2007). The first edition of this short story collection, titled *Mediodía de frontera* [*Frontier Midday*], was published in 2002 in San Salvador by CONCULTURA's Dirección de Publicaciones e Impresos. Also, see Haas's working paper on violence in Central America, *De fronteras*, and Guatemalan Javier Payeras' work. Nadine Haas, "Representaciones de la violencia en la literatura centroamericana," German Institute of Global

and Area Studies (GIGA) Working Papers, Institute of Latin American Studies, GIGA, Hamburg, Germany, October 2010.

74. The poor's consumption of fellow citizens' bodies is also a degradation of the human body as yet another object to consume. In an ironic turn, Hernández's story represents Jesús Martín-Barbero's contention in *De los medios a las mediaciones: Comunicación y hegemonía* that the poor's consumption can express "sus justas aspiraciones a una vida más digna" [their just aspirations to a more dignified life] (294). Cited in Carlos A. Jáuregui, *Canibalia: Canibalismo, calibanismo, antropofagia cultural y consumo en América* (Madrid: Iberoamericana-Vervuert, 2008), 570.

Carlos Monsiváis, "De la sociedad tradicional a la sociedad postradicional," in *Imaginarios de nación: Pensar en medio de la tormenta*, Cuadernos de nación (Bogota: Ministerio de Cultura, 2001). Hernández's citizens also contradict and support Monsiváis' contentions about nationalism. Using Martín-Barbero's assertion, we can see that Hernández's characters demonstrate a sense of solidarity, which he sees as absent, while at the same time they literalize the concept of nationalism as consumption.

75. On this point, see, for example, Dunkerley, *Power in the Isthmus*; Beverley and Zimmerman, *Literature and Politics in the Central American Revolutions*; I. Rodríguez, *Women, Guerrillas, and Love*; and, Cynthia McClintock, *Revolutionary Movements in Latin America: El Salvador's FMLN & Peru's Shining Path* (Washington, D.C.: United States Institute of Peace Press, 1998).

76. Cited in Barbara Harlow, *After Lives: Legacies of Revolutionary Writing* (London: Verso, 1996), 79.

77. Ibid.

78. For a tongue-in-cheek reaction to Dalton's literary canonization in El Salvador and the publication of the final volume of his complete works, see: "Roque Dalton comienza a aburrir (Cinco tesis sobre la imagen pública del poeta salvadoreño)," (December 1, 2008) at www.elfaro.net. The article's author, Miguel Huezo Mixco, was the director of the DPI for several years after the civil war. He, too, participated in the armed left.

79. Cited in Harlow, *After Lives*, 83.

More recently in 2010, Dalton's family demanded that Salvadoran President Mauricio Funes dismiss and prosecute Jorge Meléndez, his administration's director of *protección civil*, for Dalton's assassination. Jorge Meléndez has admitted his role in Dalton's sentencing to death although he denies pulling the trigger. Like Villalobos, Meléndez has presented Dalton's death as an "error." Funes, in the name of national reconciliation, refused to dismiss Meléndez; in fact in June 2011, Meléndez became *secretario de vulnerabilidad*. See www.elfaro.net for more details. The *Los Angeles Times* also published a "special report" on this controversy: Alex Renderos, "El Salvador, in Celebrating Roque Dalton, Confronted by Bitter Past," May 25, 2010, *Los Angeles Times*.

TWO

(Re)membering Central America

¿Dónde igual que tú están los otros
los desaparecidos de las madres
los hijos que esperamos,
los malditos traidores rompehuesos
los santos hijos de putas,
los mejores del mundo,
aquéllos que tanto amamos?

[Where, like you, are the others
the mothers' disappeared
the children we expect,
the damned bone-breaking traitors
prostitutes' saintly children,
the best in the world,
those we love so much?]
—González, "Los otros: III"

In post-conflict Central America the acts of travelling across (*recorrer*) and crossing (*cruzar*) are important metaphors to describe the effects of and inhabitants' reaction to the isthmus's fragmentation. Both those who stay home and those who immigrate north are themselves fragmented and traverse imaginary homelands in pieces. The armed conflicts and their social, economic, and cultural consequences, as well as massive immigration, are key elements of post-conflict identities. Contemporary inhabitants of Central America and Central American immigrants share a nostalgia for an (imaginary) wholeness at home and of home. The former travel daily through remnants of the homeland, while immigrants search for a sense of belonging in diasporic communities where they partake of nostalgia products (synecdoches of home) promising to temporarily transport them home.[1] In short, Central Americans' dismembered identities and bodies, as in chapter 1's examples, reflect the homeland's fragmentation.

> Después de 12 años de guerra, mucha gente perdió familia y las familias se descompusieron. Es que uno [se] sient[e] [sic] en pedazos. Los inmigrantes aquí somos los pedazos de esos fragmentos. Quizás sólo es un sueño de recomponerse y volver.[2]
>
> [After 12 years of war, a lot of people lost family members and families disintegrated. It's just that one feels in pieces. Immigrants here are the pieces of those fragments. Perhaps it's only a dream to be refashioned and return.]

This interview subject, a Salvadoran woman living in Washington, D.C., as a legal permanent resident, attests to the metaphorical and literal dismemberment of Central American subjects at home (*fragmentos*) and in the North (*pedazos de esos fragmentos*). Her word choice makes it abundantly clear that the sense of not being whole and not belonging is a constituent element of contemporary subjectivities regardless of residence in or away from the homeland. Lack of wholeness, this feeling of fragmented existence, or a sense of being broken into pieces and emotionally disintegrated, is crucial to remembering the past and maintaining homesickness. And, in the isthmus, this fragmentation also complicates definitions of *nosotros* (Nicaraguans, Salvadorans, etc.) and *los otros* (the others). Now, unlike during the Cold War era when ideologies demarcated good and evil, us and them, notions of Central American-ness, "home," and "homeland" are harder to apprehend. Even in-country national identity becomes fuzzier as more and more Central Americans are legal citizens of their countries of birth and also (un)documented immigrants; and, isthmian-born Central Americans and foreign-born *guanacos*, *nicas*, and *ticos*[3] coexist sometimes uneasily both in and away from the isthmus.

Feelings of national belonging (regardless of geographic location) and of solidarity between those who stay and those who leave are of great political and economic importance. This importance is clearly seen, for instance, in Salvadoran candidates' campaigning in U.S. Salvadoran enclaves[4] and in the fact that remittances to El Salvador are the country's second largest source of GDP.[5] In addition, the significance of citizens' identification with each other, their sense of community, is not only obvious in official pronouncements made by politicians or government entities, but it is also propagated by the Central American media. For instance, major national dailies in El Salvador and Nicaragua maintain regular sections on immigrant compatriots ("los que se han ido" [those who have left]). In fact, one of San Salvador's major dailies, *La Prensa Gráfica*, metaphorically draws *los hermanos lejanos* (distant siblings)[6] closer by dubbing their section "Departamento 15."[7] In this way it figuratively expands and deterritorializes El Salvador's geography. Whereas the neoliberal policies Central American governments have implemented in the last two decades reach out to the rest of the world, mostly through free trade and privatization and its exportation of cheap labor via illegal immigration, nationalist discourse and its appeals to patriotic feeling continue to be part of the official rhetoric. For instance, the August 2010 kidnapping and killing of seventy-two immigrants (including twelve Salvadorans, fourteen Hondurans, and four Guatemalans) by the Zetas drug cartel, condemned across Latin America, constituted an opportunity for the Salvadoran government to defend its citizens' human rights as they immigrate illegally.[8] This discourse also trades on immigrants' sense of responsibility for their extended families and, more generally, their desire to stay connected to their cultural, social, and familial roots. One can see the power of family ties in the amounts of remittances sent from abroad to countries like El Salvador, Nicaragua, and Costa Rica.[9] When recent research on globalization and immigration focuses on the cultural aspects of immigration, the focus is often on immigrants' sentiments and the nostalgia industry they sustain as consumers. The immigrant-tourist nostalgia market includes the trinkets sold in arts and crafts markets (trinkets that no self-respecting in-country citizen would buy) and their updated, cleaned up, or "modernized" versions sold in urban shopping malls. The ties to the homeland and home are also obvious in the sale of food products packaged for visiting native immigrants and their families.[10] In a manner similar to national monuments, these consumer goods, an accessible point of entry into the neoliberal, free trade economies of contemporary Central America, evoke citizenship for buyers and/or interlocutors and are embodied by the family. Thus, the homeland ties that Nicaraguans, Salvadorans, and Costa Ricans feel pull at them in and out of the isthmus.[11] Family members, the family home, childhood friends, and familiar haunts represent home for Central Americans.

Regardless of their physical location, these Central American subjects, living in and away from rapidly changing, highly fragmented but still recognizable homelands, often yearn for a nostalgia-infused version of home; their nostalgia "depends on where the speaker stands in the landscape of the present."[12] As Kathleen Stewart convincingly argues, nostalgia always depends on context, "[H]ere are texts that are contingent and they are *about* contingency."[13] She uses the loss of home to yuppie tourism on Long Island and to economic collapse in Virginia coal country to demonstrate how local inhabitants reconstitute their (local) places, filling "ruins" and "emptied spots" with meaning. This loss of home to economic imperatives, whether to "development" or "collapse," parallels Central Americans' situations. For Central American nostalgics, their displacement in the world and the scars left by armed conflicts and the neoliberal economic regimes that have followed lie at the core of their lives' and their texts' contingencies. Nostalgia helps to give meaning to their post-conflict homes, *here* in Central America and *there* in the North. Just as immigrants fill their shelves with knickknacks from home, those who have remained home also seem "haunted inescapably by the images [of the homeland] they dwell in."[14]

The prevalence of nostalgia, as well as displacement, is also the subject of Svetlana Boym's *The Future of Nostalgia*.[15] Her book meditates on and explores the nature of nostalgia with examples from post-Communist cities and Russian émigrés that offer interesting similitudes to post-conflict Central America. Boym affirms, "Outbreaks of nostalgia often follow revolutions."[16] In Boym's estimation, nostalgia, named and identified in the seventeenth century as a disease causing the ill to hallucinate, hear voices, and lose touch with the present,[17] is an ailment of the present, as surprising as it may seem:

> Somehow progress didn't cure nostalgia but exacerbated it. Similarly globalization encouraged stronger local attachments. In counterpoint to our fascination with cyberspace and the virtual global village, there is a no less global epidemic of nostalgia, an affective yearning for a community with a collective memory, a longing for continuity in a fragmented world. Nostalgia inevitably reappears as a defense mechanism in a time of accelerated rhythms of life and historical upheavals.[18]

Post-conflict Central Americans reel from socioeconomic and cultural changes. They may long for a mythical or imaginary past, for the "unrealized dreams of the past and vision of the future that became obsolete,"[19] but they must also look forward to what is possible in the future as it is informed by the past and present. Globalization, including the passage of CAFTA-DR and massive immigration within and out of the region, opens up the isthmus to greater mobility, flexibility, and (virtual) connectivity. At the same time, the isthmus remains fragmented, with accumulated piles of itself strewn about for its inhabitants to reassemble into a whole.[20] Central American locals and immigrants share the desire to reconstitute the homeland, to make it and the past "whole." Easy global communication and connections, however, are not the cure for nostalgic longing and imaginings. Rather, they are a palliative to ease the pain of detachment from the *patria* and its memory, as Boym asserts: "To unearth the fragments of nostalgia one needs a dual archaeology of memory and of place, and a dual history of illusions and actual practices."[21]

Claribel Alegría's poetry is illustrative of the imaginary reconstitution of the homeland from afar.[22] Alegría (El Salvador-Nicaragua, 1924) was exiled from El Salvador for many years because of her political beliefs. She was a fellow traveler, not a militant, of the Central American left and produced much socially committed political literature in the 1970s and 1980s. Like her contemporaries Roque Dalton and Ernesto Cardenal, during the Cold War Alegría depicted Nicaragua's and El Salvador's armed conflicts as struggles between idealist guerrillas and deadly military regimes.[23] Alegría began publishing poetry books in the late 1940s and published her first novel in the mid-1960s. Her first book, *Anillo de silencio* (1948), was heavily influenced by her mentor and teacher, the Spanish poet of "poesía desnuda" [naked poetry] Juan Ramón Jiménez,[24] and touches on traditional lyric poetry themes, such as nature and love, in free verse. This initiation into poetry production is noteworthy as it highlights the breadth of Alegría's career-long aesthetic and ideological transformations. Her first forays into socially conscious poetry began in the 1960s with critiques of bourgeois women's daily lives.[25] Her critiques of women from her own class joined with her concern for the poor and the political situations of her two native countries, El Salvador and Nicaragua, in the novel *Cenizas de Izalco* [*Ashes of Izalco*] (1966). Considered one of the isthmus's first experimental novels, it retells the story of the 1932 *matanza* (massacre) and its effects on a woman of the Salvadoran high bourgeoisie. Cowritten with her late husband Darwin (Bud) J. Flakoll, the novel directly addresses Alegría's political awakening. Her status as a fellow traveler was cemented during the Nicaraguan Revolution and Salvadoran Civil War when she committed herself to producing protest, or "emergency," poetry and prose to testify to the injustices suffered by Central Americans. In 1978, *Sobrevivo* [*I Survive*], along with Gioconda Belli's *Línea de fuego* [Line of fire], won the Casa de las Américas Prize in Poetry and further established Alegría's reputation as a leftist writer.[26] Through the 1980s, Alegría's protest poetry and fiction gained her notoriety in and away from the isthmus.[27] Unfortunately, her less politicized work has received scant critical attention. In the post-conflict era, her poetry has focused on mythology, aging, and longing.[28]

In more recent years, the longing of Alegría's poetry has had to do with the death of Flakoll and with the passage of time. But before this stage of her life, her poetic I expressed the exile's longing for home and homeland. Her militant contemporaries, primarily Dalton, also express longing for an imagined homeland, as noted in chapter 1, but do so with the bravado of hardened cynics. Alegría's longing, in contrast, openly reveals emotional vulnerability and a visceral, unfulfilled need to come home.

Her homesick poem, "La ceiba" ["The ceiba tree"], from her utterly "Salvadoran" *Luisa en el país de la realidad* [*Luisa in Realityland*] (1997),[29] pays homage to the ceiba tree of her childhood.[30] She yearns for this ceiba tree that may now only exist in her memory. She begins with a question that immediately calls on memory:

> ¿Cómo era aquella ceiba
> aquella frente al parque
> con que tengo cita?
>
> [What was that ceiba tree like

that one in front of the park
with which I have a date?] (1–3)

The ceiba is the poetic speaker's "sentry" (8). It represents her longing for the many different homes she has inhabited. In the park of her memory, the ceiba is a fundamental pillar for the entire town. It is the ceiba "que sostenía el cielo" [that held up the sky] (7) and under which the street vendors "reposaban" [rested] (12–13). And, most importantly, in the poem's last lines we learn that this tree is the poetic speaker's *kaaba* (48), the object she ritually circles in her imagined pilgrimages home (42-44). The kaaba is the black stone cube in Mecca that is the most sacred, most holy of pilgrimage sites for Muslims. Muslims face the kaaba during daily prayers and circle it during pilgrimage seasons. The poetic speaker's comparison of the kaaba to the ceiba tree, a representation of the Mesoamerican "world tree,"[31] effectively illustrates the significance of personal monuments to deep-set spiritual feelings of belonging to a home. It also iterates monuments' fundamental place in the memory of the homesick. In this and other poems, Alegría's attention to Central American geography[32] and to its role as a marker of nationality and cultural identity tightly situates her work in the region, despite her physical distance and "innumerable" absences (18–21). Her ceiba, like her malinche tree and her "tamalitos" [little tamales] made with "manteca de indios de Panchimalco" [Panchimalco Indian lard],[33] embodies the Salvadoran home she misses. Her ceiba *santaneca* (from Santa Ana) with its thick branches and a trunk too wide to encircle in an embrace (10, 35–38) also reminds her of the "fuerzas hostiles" [hostile forces] (43) that keep her out of El Salvador. This prohibition clearly alludes to the country's history of repression and social injustice. Alegría's homage is bittersweet. She yearns for the homeland in spite of her many years away and in spite of its trespasses against her. She is a homesick yet socially conscious expatriate. Contrary to Dalton, however, she does not threaten the *patria* with erasure. Her poems celebrate the Central American homeland even if only to then demand serious changes. In Alegría, the *patria*'s presence is palpable, "tourable," alive.

Alegría links the poets of chapter 1 and chapter 2. She is socially committed but not willing to take up arms, and she remains "patriotic." Her poetic speakers imagine they share a comradeship with others like them.[34] Her poetry mourns the loss of the homeland and of national "monuments," and advocates for compatriots. For instance, in "Mi ciudad" ["My City"] from *Luisa en el país de la realidad*, the poetic I misses and runs from her painful home:

y yo quería huir de mi ciudad.
. . . .
y me dolió su ausencia
y cundió la nostalgia entre mis sueños.

[and I wanted to flee the city
. . ..
and its absence pained me
and nostalgia spread in my dreams.] (10, 21–22)

The young poets I discuss below also poetically traverse home in search of a remembered belonging and also imagine becoming whole. Unlike Alegría, though, advocacy or direct social critique does not accompany them on their walks through the homes of their memories. And, more significantly, their *paseos* confirm that important markers of their pasts have disappeared from home. They are not left to wonder if their "ceiba" still holds their place on the homeland's landscape. This realization urges on nostalgics to fill emptiness with new meanings.[35]

Marta Leonor González and Susana Reyes, Nicaraguan and Salvadoran poets discussed here, feel the numbing pain and nostalgia the city evokes in Alegría. For Reyes, who lived the Salvadoran Civil War, wounds are embedded on the streets of the city and on the skin of its inhabitants. Memories, scars, and nostalgia keep the poetic speakers in these texts from severing the ties that bind them to their places, places that they may no longer physically occupy or which may no longer exist.

Marta Leonor González's poetic speakers are akin to Alegría's, who "cling to [their] souvenirs."[36] Material objects, similar to the ceiba tree, open doors to buried homesickness and nostalgia, and the family is a place to find home in the past as well as in the present. González (Nicaragua, 1972), founding member of the *400 Elefantes* journal and small press[37] and current editor of *La Prensa*'s literary section, explores different types of homelands and homes in her second poetry collection, *La casa de fuego* [*The House of Fire*].[38] Home is the family ("La casa de fuego"), the metaphorical ship-house inhabited by the poet ("El barco del poeta" ["The Poet's Boat"]), the margins of society ("Los otros" ["The Others"]) and the social world inhabited by abused women ("Cuando ellas beben" ["When They (females) Drink"]).[39] In the first two sections of *La casa de fuego*, the poems' tone is quiet, more intimate. Allusions are abstract, less specific than in the book's latter sections in which the poetic speaker names places (e.g., the Nicaraguan Atlantic Coast), social sectors (e.g., the homeless), sociohistorical realities or events (e.g., the Ciudad Juárez femicides), and in which the tone becomes denunciatory, angry, and disillusioned. The second half of this collection echoes the tone and themes of González's 1999 poems, *Huérfana embravecida* [*Enraged Orphan Girl*]. The rage and feelings of alienation characteristic of her first book are present in the second, but their expression is more nuanced and encompasses a broader spectrum of topics and places. *La casa de fuego* speaks to the "mysterious" hold that home has on individuals, regardless of their social and/or ideological positioning.

In *La casa de fuego*'s third poem, "Paseo en la casa de los padres" ["Stroll Through My Parents' House"], the poetic speaker leads the reader on an impressionistic, sensorial walk through her childhood, the home she inhabited, and the people who inhabit(ed) her. Her *paseo* is through both a physical and an imaginary place. Similar to Alegría's imaginary encircling of the yearned-for ceiba, González's walk attempts to regain the "paradise" (23) she occupied as a child.[40] She ends the poem with the word "paraíso," although the stanzas that precede that conclusion illustrate a more complex and tense experience than homesickness for a paradisiacal beginning suggests. In the first three stanzas of this five-stanza poem, the reader accompanies the poetic speaker on a visual, auditory, and tactile tour of the past all under the veil of a dream.

> En la casa de la infancia
> hay un sueño escondido
> y no lo encuentro
> busco los días iluminados que me ciegan
> como cuchillo que se clava
> huella de la humanidad.
>
> Sigo las voces por los corredores
> y me descubro eterna
> mientras me consuelan en silencio
> como un gesto alto.
>
> Como si se tratara de cenizas
> que me calientan
> el hueco de la mano infantil
> y me cantan con golpes de puerta.
>
> [In the childhood home
> there's a hidden dream
> and I can't find it
> I look for the illuminated days that blind me
> like a knife that drives itself in
> a trace of humanity.
>
> I follow the voices through the hallways
> and I discover myself eternal
> while they console me in silence
> like a high gesture.
>
> As if it were ashes
> that warm
> the hollow in my childhood hand
> and sing to me with knocks on the door.] (1–14)

The poem's title conjures a concrete, tangible house. As the poem begins, however, it quickly establishes a dreamlike atmosphere and places the poetic I in an illusory "casa de infancia" (1). She enters a phantasmagoric house that promises to contain forgotten or lost dreams and the light (in both literal and figurative terms) of the past. The light and the voices she encounters wound her. It is this pain, caused by violence (5), that marks her humanity and membership in the family that witnessed her childhood and which is now only "ashes" (11–12). These first stanzas convey the poetic speaker's sense of loss and desire for the place, the people, and the sensations that made her feel home when she was a child. But once she returns home, the reality of her past blinds her (4), injures her (9–10), makes her acknowledge its emptiness (13), and feel again the violence of the past (14).

The knocks on the door, calling her away from the house of memories she has entered, invoke more concrete images of her parents, caretakers of family history and home:

> Son los rostros de esta casa
> que me hablan,
> y mis padres son guardianes
> de lo perdido
> olvidado por otros.
>
> Hay sombras de fantasmas
> en esta casa
> de habitada vida feliz
> donde encontré el paraíso.
>
> [It is the faces of this house
> that speak to me,
> and my parents are the guardians
> of that which has been lost
> forgotten by others.
>
> There are phantom shadows
> in this house
> of a happy inhabited life
> where I found paradise.] (15–23)

The poem's last stanzas transform the poetic speaker's childhood experiences and her rambling search for "lo perdido" (18) into the remembrance of a happy life in paradise. González's haunting family home parallels Alegría's ceiba tree, the place and object that she recreates and then encircles in an attempt to return home and feel belonging. This desire for belonging leads González's poetic speakers to travel through their childhoods and family homes and ultimately to build new places in which to dwell, places such as that from another poem, "Quinta travesía," the fifth "crossing" in "Gulf King el barco del poeta" ["Gulf King the Poet's Boat"]: "juntamos conchas, / espuma, arenas, huesos de ballena / para hacer nuestra casa" [we collect shells, / foam, sands, whale bones / to make our house] (15–17).

González's new house made of shells and sea surf reuses the homeland landscape to imagine and build a new home at home. The poetic speaker responds to the loss of her childhood *paraíso* and to the past's dragging her down by constructing a fanciful seashell abode. However, in the poetry of other contemporary poets who have also remained in Central America, fantastical homes are harder to come by. Susana Reyes (El Salvador, 1971), for example, vainly traverses her scarred hometown in search of a livable place. Reyes, who earns a living teaching young Salvadorans who have inherited an unlivable homeland, is a leader of the cultural foundation Alkimia. Alkimia sponsors weekly poetry readings, Miércoles de poesía [Poetry Wednesdays], and other cultural events, and it has also ventured into publishing. Reyes's participation in Alkimia is one way in which she endeavors to build connections in her disintegrating city. The other is through her poetry. Her 2004 collection, *Historia de los espejos* [*Story of the Mirrors*],[41] offers the reader a poetic glimpse of post-war, neoliberal, "democratic," or in Robinson's terms, "polyarchic,"[42] El Salvador. It is a vision that does not hide the nation's many scars. Instead her poetic speakers tread on the city's scars, battling the surrounding hopelessness. They acknowledge that their home is not a shadow of what it was in the past. Adrift, they attach themselves to images, objects (often in the urban geography) that align with their memories of a collective, violent past. Their remembrances are tinged with "reflective" nostalgia. Boym characterizes this longing as a meditation on the past, on the ruins that remain[43]

> concerned with historical and individual time, with irrevocability for the past and human finitude. *Re-flection* suggests new flexibility, not the reestablishment of stasis. The focus here [vs. "restorative nostalgia"] is not on recovery of what is perceived to be an absolute truth but on the meditation on history and the passage of time.[44]

Reflective nostalgics do not share restorative nostalgics' goal of reviving or reconstructing a national mythical past. Neither is their return to the past like the politicized and functional rereading of national and regional history by poets such as Roque Dalton, Leonel Rugama, or Ernesto Cardenal. Susana Reyes and her contemporaries do not rail against the destruction of home and its monuments or in favor of the reconstruction of a former (official) version of the homeland. Instead, Reyes's poems travel through the Salvadoran landscape and give the reader an intimate, personal, and recognizable look at the consequences of recent historical events. At the same time, Reyes's poetic texts make plain that "longing and critical thinking are not opposed to one another, as affective memories do not absolve one from compassion, judgment or critical reflection."[45] In short, her poems neither see the world around them through the rose-colored glasses of unreflective nostalgia nor return to her literary predecessors' politicized interpretations of the homeland's past and present.

One of Reyes's ironically titled "Postales urbanas" ["Urban Postcards"] bemoans the loss of public spaces in an increasingly poor and dangerous San Salvador. City dwellers and observant visitors will quickly discern that many Salvadorans, from a broad social spectrum and of many different ages, window shop at malls rather than take their families to city parks and plazas for traditional weekly family outings.[46] Reyes's "Los parques" ["The Parks"] meditates on the significance of this loss of community. A two-part poem, "Los parques" is a "postal urbana" of a place that has lost its significance. It has become empty space. In this poem the poetic speaker searches for an absent interlocutor (*vos*) to reminisce with her about "aquel parque" [that park] (8) of their youth as she now stands in "este parque" [this park] (13–14). As the poetic speaker remembers the vos and the happiness they shared, she also resignifies "this" park by memorializing the significance of "that" park of her past.

Part I of "Los parques" begins with the poetic speaker basking in both the sun and her memories of the interlocutor whose presence she joyously invokes. The *vos* represents a light, airy, free adolescence:

> Tu luz, la luz de la tarde
> felizmente me rodea y sonríe
> al ver que te recuerdo como una adolescente.
>
> [Your light, the afternoon light
> happily surrounds me and smiles
> as I remember you as an adolescent.] (5–7)

The light and lightness of happy memories momentarily embrace the poetic speaker until she recalls "that" park full of yellow cortés trees (8, 16). Reyes's park, like Alegría's ceiba, is a reminder of both a happy past and a deteriorated present. The park and the *vos* also evoke who the poetic speaker used to be, "y yo soy apenas una sombra" [And I am but a shadow] (9) but is no longer. She is a shadow, like her childhood friend, a voice on the phone (12) and also a nostalgic "promise," "una promesa que se reafirma en el verano / y este parque" [a promise that is confirmed in the summer / and this park] (13–14). Significantly, Reyes's poetic speaker finds promise in the past rather than in the present. In her *paseo* through "este parque" she is transported to "aquel parque," and thus sees through the eyes of her adolescence and feels her friend's presence all around her: "Te aspiro" [I inhale you] (3). This inhalation allows her to temporally rebel against the homeland's "progress," its present. In short, her nostalgic meditation temporarily frees her from the passage of time and from the present's grasp.

The poem's second half explains the allure of the past and the poetic speaker's rejection of, or disdain for, the present. Images of the present park superimpose themselves over "aquel parque amarillo / que invitaba al sueño" [that yellow park / that made you want to sleep] (16–17). The streets where the poetic I and the *vos* ran freely and the park adorned with its civic equestrian monument are now clogged with the detritus of post-conflict urban development. "Aquel parque" has been overrun by the signs of war and marginal urban living: blood, street vendors' baskets and boxes of goods, vagrants, yelling, and violence. It is not a "tourable" or photogenic place. It is not a postcard-ready image:

> en aquellas calles por las que corrimos
> sin pudor y sin espanto.
> ¿Te acordás?
> antes también hubo ahí sangre,
> pieles y ropas.
> Zapatos y gritos
> quedaron haciendo eco en las paredes,
> ahora hay grandes claxons [sic] gritando sus verdades,
> no se parece más que por la memoria
> no es el mismo, aunque aquel caballo
> siga a galope eterno en el mismo pedestal,
> ahora hay alambres como hebras de piscuchas de viejos octubres,
> como hilos de algodón de dulce de las ferias,
> hay manos, cuchillos y olores perpetuos,
> hay llantos y ruido
> hay prisa, hay ecos.
>
> [down those streets where we ran
> without shame and without fright
> Remember?
> before there was also blood,
> skin, and clothes.
> Shoes and screams
> remained echoing from the walls,
> now there are car horns declaring their truths,
> it doesn't resemble it except in memories
> it's not the same one, although that horse
> continues to gallop eternally on the same pedestal,
> now there are wires like kite tails from old Octobers,
> like the threads of cotton candy at the fairs,
> there are hands, knives, and perpetual smells,
> there is sobbing and noise
> there's a rush, there are echoes.] (21–39)

The pasts of the poetic voice, park, and streets reverberate in the transformed city. They are the sound equivalent of the physical pain the city and its inhabitants endure(d). The constant claxons are echoed in the poem by the repeated visual image of loose filament: wires that remind the poetic speaker of kite tails and cotton candy but that also lead her back to reality (37–39). Reyes renders the homeland's past and present traumas sensorially: we can hear, see, touch, smell, and taste what the homeland was and what it has become. Reyes's poetic "urban postcards" stand on end the official images and rhetoric of urban renewal and development.[47] Their nonconfrontational, unadorned language upsets the well-planned national image of "progress" and "development" that San Salvador's new highways, many shopping malls,[48] and many transnational businesses are supposed to propagate.[49] They parody the postcard genre that celebrates places, peoples, monuments. Her postcards refuse to "sell" places in order to entice recipients to visit or to feel envious of the sender. Instead, she addresses her postcard poems to former compatriots who know or knew places that have been disappeared by war and peace's "progress."

Unlike immigrants and exiles, whose memories can sustain them while they are away from home, Reyes's poetic speaker is an eyewitness to the supplantation of the landmarks of her youth by developed tracts of land that transform the geography of the urbanscape and the past:

> Cuando vuelvas, ya no preguntes
> por aquella casa.
> Ya no pidas que te dejen frente a su puerta,
> ....
> Cuando vuelvas, pregunta por un parqueo,
> por un centro comercial
> por un moderno edificio.
>
> [When you come back, don't ask about
> that house anymore.
> Don't ask to be dropped in front of its door
> ....
> When you come back, ask about a parking lot
> about a shopping center
> about a modern building.]
> ("Las cosas sencillas: IV" ["The Simple
> Things: IV"], 14–16, 23–25)

Changes to its physical landscape, the effects of modernization, and consumption scar San Salvador. The poetic speaker warns her visiting compatriot, the "hermano lejano" [distant sibling], of the disappearance of the places that populated their youth and the symbols of progress that have replaced them. The past existence is confirmed only by dusty photographs that make the poetic speaker weep, "la desempolvo y lloro un poco" [I undust it and cry a little] ("Las cosas sencillas: V" 31). The poetic speaker's tears memorialize both the loss of the personal monuments of her past as well as the filling of the city's landscape with meaningless places (e.g., parking lots).

The city's new buildings and parking structures, though, cannot erase the scars or soothe the pain and memory of the Salvadoran Civil War. As Reyes affirms in the thirteenth, and penultimate, poem of "Sobreviviente del silencio" ["Survivor of Silence"], the scarred city is not very different from its pained citizens. Its body is also in pain: "dolor de ciudad / herida en su calles" [city's pain / wounded in its streets] (2–3). The wounds that scar the city's streets are also tattooed on its inhabitants' bodies. Another poem by Reyes imagines those tattoos as a literal and figurative branding. The city's poorest inhabitants, vagrants baptized "dragones de cartón" [cardboard dragons], amble about their homeland embodying, indeed etched with, its sorry condition:

> Otros llevan noticias
> con la primera plana en sus caritas
> con la tristeza y la alegría
> que son una y la misma cosa
> de sonrisas agrietadas
> y llantos de llovizna.
>
> [Others carry the news on them
> with the front page on their little faces
> with the sadness and happiness
> that are one and the same thing
> of cracked smiles
> and drizzled weeping.]
> ("Dragones de cartón: IV" ["Cardboard
> Dragons: IV"], 34–39)

The "little faces" of the city's lamentable beggars report on and reflect "cracked," "teary" current events. By referring to the homeless men in the diminutive and with a synecdoche, "caritas," Reyes infantilizes, humanizes, and shows tenderness toward them. These homeless are a metaphor for the city of San Salvador, home to over a million people. The capital city and its wayward citizens fill newspapers with stories revealing and reveling in the "cracks" of post-conflict national life. Stories of violence and hardship are daily fodder for the media and provoke tears and readers' incredulity.[50] But for Reyes's poetic speaker, the beggars who stand in the city's congested intersections also inspire fear. They are

> dragones de bulevares
> frente a caballeros
> en resplandecientes armaduras rodantes.
>
> [dragons of the boulevards

facing knights
in resplendent rolling armor.] (27–29)

This image of beggars, inhabitants of the socioeconomic margins, is simultaneously fanciful and menacing. They are the danger faced by car-armored knights; the obstacle that drivers and pedestrians must maneuver in order to get home. These begging dragons are also reminders of post-conflict San Salvador's uneven modernization and unrelenting poverty.[51]

This poem subtly recognizes the desire for change in daily life, for a new place "donde pasar el invierno" [in which to spend the winter] (41), and protection from the rain (42–43), within the Salvadoran polity. This desire for a new beginning within the limits of the status quo also concedes the homeland's viability. This concession represents a change in perspective in contemporary Central American literature. As the poets in chapter 1 illustrate, writers have often searched for more radical social transformations regarding the isthmus's structural problems. The negotiated end to the Salvadoran Civil War in January 1992's Chapultepec Accords inspired hope for a better future at home without having to resort to further violence. As Roberto Turcios, former director of *Tendencias* (1991–2000), an important post-war cultural-political journal, writes,

> San Salvador era una ciudad esperanzada el 16 de enero de 1992. En las dos plazas centrales de la ciudad se celebraba el fin de la guerra. . . . En medio de las celebraciones transitaban con la incredulidad a cuestas los personajes silenciosos de una aventura nueva, quienes estaban en la invención de las más diversas empresas culturales de todo tipo.[52]

> [San Salvador was a hopeful city on January 16, 1992. The end of the war was celebrated in the city's two central plazas. . . . Amid the celebration, silent figures walked around incredulous; they were actors in a new adventure, in the middle of planning the most diverse cultural projects.]

But opportunities to effect the transformative changes imagined by Salvadorans did not readily emerge. The post-conflict "new world" did not turn out to be fundamentally different from the "old world." Salvadoran poet María Cristina Orantes (Mexico, 1955) writes of the frustrations of the post-war present and the longing for the ideals that motivated many to make war. In a classical hendecasyllabic sonnet, "El nuevo mundo" ["The New World"], she writes,

> Todo está permitido en esta tierra:
> volver a conquistar lo conquistado,
> poner la bota como buen soldado
> sobre el sobreviviente de la guerra.
>
> Jugar a ser Dios que al hombre aterra,

apremiar y oprimir al desgraciado,
arrancarle hasta el nombre y al desarmado
ponerlo bajo el filo de la sierra.

Ésta es la ley que rige el nuevo mundo,
en el que hay que obligar al moribundo
a estrellarse en la roca del olvido

donde entregue esperanzas, sangre, canto,
polvo, memoria, fe, sueños y llanto
aferrados al último latido.[53]

[Everything is permitted in this land:
re-conquer what was conquered,
put the boot down, like a good soldier,
atop the war survivor.

Playing a God that terrifies man
pressures and oppresses the wretch,
takes away his name and puts the unarmed
under the saw.

This is the law that governs the new world,
in which the moribund must be forced
to crash against the rock of forgetfulness

where he will surrender hopes, blood, song,
dust, memory, faith, dreams, and tears
seizing the last heartbeat.]

Orantes, the daughter of two artists and intellectuals, Salvadoran Elisa Huezo Paredes and Guatemalan Alfonso Orantes, is a cultural promoter, member of Alkimia (as is Susana Reyes) and current director of SECULTURA's[54] Sala Nacional de Exposiciones. She has published widely in poetry anthologies, local newspapers, and literary journals as well as in book form.[55] One notable aspect of her poetic practice is the use of poetic meter and classical forms. This practice speaks to her literary education as well as to her ability to apply traditional forms to contemporary themes.[56] In this poem from her 2005 poetry collection, Orantes gives the reader a panoramic view of what has not changed since the end of the Civil War. Her poetic speaker recognizes the maintenance of the prewar and war status quo, the homeland's stubborn addiction to military violence, repressive governments, and social injustice. Her dying, nameless compatriots (7, 10) gasp for air and grasp at the remnants of hope and memory they still hold (12–14). Orantes's sonnet illustrates the difficulty of both remembering the war and its suffering and remaining faithful to dreams and "song" (12). As Reyes does, Orantes's poetic speaker stands in the present, on "esta tierra" [this land], looks at the awful consequences of the war, and longs for the dreams of the past and a "promise" for the future.

This poem takes a long view of the national situation and its future by affirming survivors' strength. At the same time, it asserts that hope is not easy to maintain, as Orantes's word choice implies (14). The dying struggle to survive in a world where forgetfulness is an easier, socially sanctioned strategy. Those who wish to reflect on the past must fight the post-conflict homeland's efforts to force citizens to share space, to forget past experiences as victims and victimizers (1–4). In recent Salvadoran and Nicaraguan histories, the reality of "El nuevo mundo" is the lived reality of post-conflict societies where forgiveness, reconciliation, and solidarity are difficult to achieve. The scars of the past—constant reminders of conflict—assail the homeland and its inhabitants and cannot be camouflaged behind the isthmus's globalizing efforts. Or as Rosanna Reguillo posits about Latin America as "space object," in these poems we cannot "evade the scars and tattoos now making up the skin that unavoidably covers and forms the surface of a Latin America of multiplicity and profundity."[57]

The image of a scarred or tattooed surface with profound depths metaphorizes the experience of poetic speakers who travel around and through their homelands and homes in search of (lost) meanings and identities. In her tripartite poem, "Los otros" ["The Others"], Marta Leonor González explores the alienation in both her local home, as in "Paseo en la casa de los padres," and in the *patria grande* of Central America.[58] The poem's three sections thread together the homes for which the poetic speakers search and yearn. They long for personal intimacy with family members as well as for connections with "the others," or coinhabitants of the homeland.

González begins her trip toward intimacy with others at home. "Los otros: I" narrates the poetic speaker's desperate search for her mother, a link to her past that she has lost. "Recorrer" [to travel across / tour / scan or investigate] appears in the first line; "Fábulas recorren tu nombre / deletreado" [Rumors travel over your name / spelled out] (1–2) describes the experience of looking for home and belonging at home. The motherless and homeless poetic speaker espies her origins in the home laid out in front of her by the letters of her mother's name and whispered "pistas" [clues] of her whereabouts (4–5). The daughter must decipher clues and riddles to reach her mother and to understand herself,

> Escasos cuatro años para adivinar acertijos
> para preguntar dónde está mi madre,
> cuántos colores me cubren el rostro.
>
> [A short four years to decrypt riddles

to ask where is my mother
how many colors cover my face.] (6-8)

Of course, this desire for family—and self-knowledge—insinuates the significance of the homeland's history for its inhabitants and their identities. The poetic speaker tries to remember her mother and home, but memory does not serve her well. Rather, she stumbles around mistaking strangers for her mother:

> Borrado todo el deseo,
> volví a pensar que eras
> sin ser, te vi frágil
> embravecida y ajena a mí.
> Nada era cierto.
> Nuevamente mi memoria
> traicionó mi deseo y el amor se fue.
>
> [With the desire erased,
> I thought again that you were
> without being, I saw you as fragile
> enraged and alien to me.
> Nothing was certain.
> My memory again
> betrayed my desire and love left.] (15–21)

Once her desire dissipates, the poetic speaker realizes that her visions of her mother's name, her face, her fragility, anger, and foreignness are hallucinations. González's poetic I, as does Reyes's, yearns to find her place in a changing landscape and reaches into the past to attempt to situate herself in the present. But unlike Reyes's, González's memory is untrustworthy.

The second poem of this series transfers the point of view from the daughter to the mother. Whereas the daughter's search is surrounded by silences (including not knowing the whys and hows of the mother's disappearance), echoes, and unrecognizable voices, the mother's is surrounded by noise. The mother looks for her daughter amid urban commotion (*tumulto*) (2), listens for her screams (3), looks for her on the street (8), in bus windows (12), and among the market vendors (13). The mother also searches blindly, without clues about how to distinguish her daughter from those around her:

> ¿Con qué esfinge de la calle te confundo
> y finjo hablarte,
> de qué color te vistes mejor que el negro?
>
> [With what street sphinx do I confuse you
> and pretend to speak to you,
> what color do you wear better than black?] (8–10)

Both poetic speakers and interlocutors fail to communicate because they do not recognize each other as family. Like the daughter who hears her mother's name in the wind, the mother only glimpses her daughter's name in dreams:

> Otra vez, el sueño me golpea
> y es la brisa de septiembre
> que me trae tu nombre
> escrito en los rótulos de los parques.
>
> [Again, sleep hits me
> and it's the September breeze
> that brings me your name
> written on park signs.] (14–17)

The park signs with "tu nombre" (16) call to mind waving flags and other emblems representing membership in a specific, differentiated homeland. But the signs emblazoned with the daughter's name do not identify or embody her. By the end of the second part of "Los otros," mother and daughter remain lost, history-less, and without a lasting sense of identity or belonging in a family or at home.

The third and final section of "Los otros" expands the scope of the poem to include the social context. The reader learns that the poetic speaker's "pura realidad" [total reality] (9) lies on the edges of dreams, memory, and death:

> vos en el borde,
> yo en el sueño.
> Ambas en la muerte que nos une.
>
> [you on the edge,
> me in the dream.
> Both in the death that unites us.] (8–10)

This placement on "el borde" (8) discloses the poem's conception of home. Home and its inhabitants are disconnected (except maybe in death), and individual and collective memories are elusive. The wandering mother and daughter represent the mis- and un-recognition underlying present society:

> ¿Dónde igual que tú están los otros
> los desaparecidos de las madres
> los hijos que esperamos,
> los malditos traidores rompehuesos
> los santos hijos de las putas,
> los mejores del mundo,
> aquéllos que tanto amamos? (11–17)[59]

The disconnection and lack of knowledge in the poetic speakers' private lives play out socially. Loved ones and compatriots live parallel but not interconnected existences. The poetic speaker's desire for intimacy is obvious in the closing stanza's language and sentiment. The poem also recalls Roque Dalton's beloved and oft-quoted "Poema de amor" ["Love Poem"].[60] Dalton's poem, read as an alternative Salvadoran national anthem,[61] reimagines Salvadoran-ness. He exalts those fellow citizens who would be easily discarded from hegemonic conceptions of the homeland (e.g., poor people, criminals, prostitutes, etc.).[62] González employs a similar strategy to draw together and make visible the inhabitants of the social margins. But "Los otros" does not identify the "others," nor does it equate their otherness with Nicaraguan-ness. Nationality seems unimportant. Instead, as the poem asks after the disappeared, those who have gone away, violent traitors, and prostitutes' children (11–15), it amasses them together with few marked characteristics beyond their place on the margins (8) of their globalizing home. The last two lines, "los mejores del mundo / aquéllos que tanto amamos" (16–17), confess the poetic speaker's affection. In similar fashion to Dalton, who ends his poem with overt sentimentality, "my compatriots / my brothers" (34–35), González closes her poem with a declaration of love for those others with whom she shares the homeland.

Longing for a sense of belonging with and to "others" colors González's love declamation. In her listing of loved ones she emphasizes those with tight interrelations: mothers of the disappeared and lost children, and traitors, for instance. The relationships she mentions, including those of prostitutes' children, suggests broken-ness among intimates. The image of "damned," "bone-breaking" traitors (14) is particularly ripe with allusions to desire for interpersonal connections and acceptance of (dis)trust and (dis)loyalty. By professing her love even for those who have betrayed her, the poetic speaker makes an emphatic statement about the importance of bygone sentimental bonds and disparate memories of those bonds. After all, those we love so much (17) lie "en el borde" (8) of our dreams (9).

Sentiment and dreams (as experiences we "live" as we sleep and as ideals and aspirations) are significant in conceptions of nostalgia and nostalgic reflection. A recently published short story by Salvadoran Jacinta Escudos (1961), "¿En qué libro guardé tus cabellos, Elsa Kuriaki?" ["In Which Book Did I Keep Your Hair, Elsa Kuriaki?"] poetically explores the effects of love and nostalgia on the protagonist's psyche and body.[63] In summary, after a typical night of heavy drinking the protagonist awakens suddenly and cannot figure out where he is or even who he is. When he realizes Elsa, a woman for whom he has been secretly yearning, is lying in bed next to him, he cannot remember how she got there or if they had sexual relations. She leaves before morning, and thus begins his emotional spiral. This last point, whether or not they had sex, is the question that eventually leads the protagonist to Elsa's house, to his loss of consciousness at her door, and a hospital stay to treat amnesia. The title holds the short story's core question. The story, even more than a study of unfulfilled love and desire, is a meditation on nostalgic longing for another and for the belief in happiness. The strands of hair Elsa leaves on the protagonist's bed, and which he places in a book of aphorisms by E. M. Cioran,[64] are the only "souvenirs" he has to help him remember the paradoxically memorable but un-rememberable night he is sure he spent with Elsa. The strands of hair sustain his tenuous hold on reality and hope (22).

Jacinta Escudos, a fiction writer well-known for her texts' innovation, cynicism, and black humor,[65] details in poem form the protagonist's fall into amnesia. His arrival at Elsa's door fragments into one and two word phrases that combine his dream and daily life: "Llegúe a la puerta, / tropezándome en el asfalto / ardiente /. . . / mar / yo" [I arrived at her door / tripping on the asphalt / burning / . . . / sea / me] (22–23). These beginning and ending lines show the protagonist's fragile state of mind and prepare us for his subsequent loss of consciousness. His next conscious statement is "soy un hombre en un hospital" [I'm a man in a hospital] (23) and shortly thereafter, "eso es lo que soy" [that is what I am] (24). The fragmentation of his subjectivity and erasure of his memory, caused by extreme fear or happiness according to the doctor, free him from his alcoholic blackouts but not from the feelings Elsa causes him when she looks at him, "me punzan los testículos" [my testicles burst] (24), or from his desperate search for the bits of her he lost. The answer to the short story's title, "¿En qué libro guardé tus cabellos, Elsa Kuriaki?" becomes an "imperiosa necesidad" [imperious need] that haunts the protagonist (25) and leaves him in limbo. He has no access to the memories that would prompt nostalgia and a retelling of his night with Elsa.

The lost strands of hair represent the protagonist's longing for Elsa and for happiness, and a way out of his neuroses and cynicism (22). He saves the hair as a keepsake as well as proof of his sanity if not of his bad memory. Even in his amnesiac state he knows the "souvenir" is a significant trace of his past and of himself. It represents the intimate experience of a "solitario" (22), or social orphan, with another. Morever, it proves the authenticity of the protagonist's love for Elsa. As Susan Stewart posits, objects (souvenirs) authenticate unique experiences: "We need and desire souvenirs of events that are reportable [rather than repeatable], events whose materiality has escaped us, events that thereby exist only through the invention of narrative."[66] When Escudos's protagonist loses his memory to emotion-provoked amnesia, he forgets everything, even his pre-amnesia desire for "amnesia absoluta en los tejidos de su sexo" [absolute amnesia in the fabric of her sex] (20). What he does not forget is his possession of Elsa's wayward strands of hair. His souvenir is a metonymy of the experience[67] he longs to remember and reflect upon. At the end of the story, the protagonist longs for nostalgia itself, although he does not remember the cause of his nostalgia.

The strands of hair that mark the (erased) geography of the protagonist's memory resemble the personal monuments and the scars of the poems discussed in this chapter. They are material objects that serve to recall the past, to trigger nostalgic reflection, and thus to bring near what is temporally and spatially distant. They also bring order to disordered, fragmented, and lost memories, as in Escudos and González, and meaning to significant places, as in Reyes and Alegría. Material reminders of the past, as Susan Stewart says of souvenirs, "transform and collapse distance into proximity to, or approximation with, the self."[68] Their distant closeness allows poetic speakers and narrators to travel through time and space to re-experience and re-evaluate their place(s) in the past and, in this book, at home and among their fellow inhabitants.

This chapter's poetic speakers and narrator travel across their homes and homelands nostalgic for the fragments of the past they still recall. Their texts are dotted with scars, keepsakes, hints, and clues of their personal as well as their homes' and homelands' pasts. They locate themselves in the present of sometimes unmentioned homelands and look forward by looking back.[69] Their backward glances make visible home's empty spaces, the loss of meaning,[70] and thus the loss of their sense of belonging in the places where they stand. In attempts to repopulate the emptiness around them and alleviate the latent pain; keepsakes gain significance as anchors to each other and to the local home. As in the case of compatriots who have immigrated, Central Americans at home in Central America also grasp onto objects with metonymic significance to meditate on the past and present *here* in the homeland and on them over *there*. They recognize the contours and, at times, yearn for their slowly disappearing home(s) and for their compatriots. This nostalgia reveals a sentimental attachment to the homeland as well as the recognition of loss, without tears, of that irreversibly changed homeland.

In the chapter that follows, fragments of the homeland are etched on the faces of the poorest and on the scarred landscape of blighted capital cities decaying beside bourgeois enclaves. They inspire disgust and rejection. Rather than nostalgic meditation about loss, the emptiness and decay of ruins means, literally, shit. Yet, writers' attachment to home and homeland, however frayed, remains intact. In other words, writers' acknowledgement of home and homeland's significance changes in tenor but not in substance. Nicaraguan Juan Sobalvarro, discussed in chapter 3, exemplifies this difference as he writes about the insignificance of abstract notions and sentiments, and the importance of material experience. In "No hay poesía" ["There Is No Poetry"],[71] Sobalvarro denies poetry's impalpability ["lo impalpable"] and its unutterability ["indecible"] (8, 9), both of which lie at the core of nostalgic remembrances. He argues for the greater importance of daily life and its tedious chores, as he complains "*planchame este pantalón por dios que soy mortal*" [iron these pants for me, for god's sake I'm mortal] (17; italics in the original). Mortality and life's gory details supersede and surpass literature's ability to enrich lived experience or to dream of future possibilities. Sobalvarro ends his poem asserting,

> Sin poesía, se vive sin poesía,
> sólo con vida,
> con este cautiverio de uno mismo
> y el mundo barato.
>
> [Without poetry, one can live without poetry,
> only with life,
> in captivity with oneself
> and the cheap world.] (18–21)

Chapter 3, then, contemplates visions of home from the ground. Homesickness is evident but lies deep beneath the weight of "el mundo barato" with its cheap thrills and constant letdowns. While chapter 2's poetic speakers can be imagined as compassionate, still hopeful observers of post-conflict Central America, chapter 3's are like the poetic speaker in "No hay poesía," a man moved by his filthy dwelling and life, but immobile.

NOTES

1. See Sarah Gammage's and Diana Santillán's articles "Viajeros y viajeras en El Salvador: enlazando mundos, estrechando vínculos" and "Renegociar las identidades nacionales: los vínculos transnacionales, los discursos de las diasporas y las comunidades pan étnicas" in *La transnacionalización de la sociedad centroamericana: Visiones a partir de la migración* (San Salvador: FLACSO Programa El Salvador, 2005), 61–100, 101–38.
2. Cited in Gammage, "Viajeros y viajeras en El Salvador," 73.
3. These are the nicknames that Salvadorans, Nicaraguans, and Costa Ricans call themselves. Other Central American nicknames are *chapines* (Guatemalans) and *catrachos* (Hondurans). As with other nicknames that serve as identity markers, Central Americans use their and each others' nicknames as both points of pride and to offend and ridicule.
4. See Beth Baker-Cristales on the double disenfranchisement of Salvadorans living in the United States in *La transnacionalización de la sociedad centroamericana* (139–56). As non-U.S. citizens, they can vote neither in their host country nor in El Salvador.
5. Based on Central Reserve Bank (El Salvador). *Americas Quarterly* (July 13, 2009) also reports that remittances make up 17% of El Salvador's GDP. http://www.americasquarterly.org/remittances-el-salvador (accessed July 22, 2011).
6. See chapter 5 of Baker-Cristales's *Salvadoran Migration to Southern California: Redefining El Hermano Lejano* (Gainesville: University of Florida Press, 2004) for a discussion on the renaming of San Salvador's 1990s monument to the "distant sibling," "El Monumento al hermano lejano." For an interdisciplinary reading of the construction of a Salvadoran transnational homeland, see "'Departamento 15': Salvadoran Transnational Migration in Narration" in Ana Patricia Rodríguez's *Dividing the Isthmus: Transnational Histories, Literatures, and Cultures* (Austin: University of Texas Press,

2009). Also, see Nora Hamilton and Norma Stoltz Chinchilla, *Seeking Community in a Global City: Guatemalans and Salvadorans in Los Angeles* (Philadelphia: Temple University Press, 2001).

7. El Salvador is divided into fourteen provinces (*departamentos*).

8. See contrapunto.com, a Salvadoran internet newspaper, for one of the many reports on the deaths: http://www.archivocp.contrapunto.com.sv/violencia/identifican-a-12-salvadorenos-de-los-72-migrantes-asesinados-en-mexico.

9. According to statistics compiled by the World Bank, for 2010 it is estimated that remittances, in U.S. millions, would be as follows: Costa Rica, $622; El Salvador, $3,648; Nicaragua, $803. In *Migration and Remittances Factbook 2011* at http://econ.worldbank.org/WBSITE/EXTERNAL/EXTDEC/EXTDECPROSPECTS/0,,contentMDK:21352016~pagePK:64165401~piPK:64165026~theSitePK:476883,00.html (accessed January 18, 2012).

10. For instance, Comalapa International, the San Salvador airport, has its own Pollo Campero where the longed-for fried chicken is packaged especially for air travel. Salvadorans' craving for Pollo Campero chicken is even more notable considering that the chicken chain now operates restaurants in the United States. Also on sale at the airport, bags of Central American dry red beans emblazoned with the Salvadoran flag are another example of the allure and consumption of nostalgia products by immigrants.

11. Examples of studies on the nostalgia food market in the United States include: S. Patricia Batres-Márquez et al., "Salvadoran Consumption of Ethnic Foods in the United States," Working Paper 01-WP 289 (Center for Agricultural and Rural Development, Iowa State University, October 2001); and, Mirian Cruz, Carlos López Cerdán and Claudia Schatan, "Pequeñas empresas, productos étnicos y de nostalgia: los casos de El Salvador y México," Serie estudios y perspectivas, no. 17 (Mexico City: Sede de la CEPAL en México, Unidad de Desarrollo, United Nations, 2004).

12. Kathleen Stewart, "Nostalgia—A Polemic," in *Rereading Cultural Anthropology*, ed. George E. Marcus (Durham, NC: Duke University Press, 1992), 252.

13. Ibid., 253.

14. Ibid., 260.

15. Svetlana Boym, *The Future of Nostalgia* (New York: Basic Books, 2001).

16. Ibid., xvi.

17. Ibid., 3.

18. Ibid., xiv.

19. Ibid., xvi.

20. K. Stewart, "Nostalgia—A Polemic," 261.

21. Boym, *The Future of Nostalgia*, xviii.

22. In his book of testimonies and literary criticism, Trigo explores the creation of *ciberpatrias* by Uruguayans who have immigrated to the United States. He asserts that online his compatriots can sever themselves from official, "ideological" versions of Uruguay and create and sustain a "more real experience" of a "community of phantoms" whose existence relies on memory and language. Abril Trigo, *Memorias migrantes: Testimonios y ensayos sobre la diaspora uruguaya* (Rosario, Argentina: B. Viterbo Editora / Montevideo: Ediciones Trilce, 2003), 18.

23. Rafael Lara Martínez, "Postestimonio y disolución de la guerrilla en El Salvador," in *La tormenta entre las manos: Ensayos sobre literatura salvadoreña* (San Salvador: Dirección de Publicaciones e Impresos, 2000). This essay harshly criticizes Alegría. He judges her incapable of recognizing the Salvadoran guerrillas' missteps in her highly laudatory, *No me agarran viva* [*They Won't Take Me Alive*] (1987), a *testimonio* about Eugenia, a guerrilla fighter.

24. "Juan Ramón Jiménez (Mantecón)," *Contemporary Authors Online* (Detroit: Gale, 2003), *Literature Resource Center*.

25. On the development of a feminist consciousness in Alegría's early poetry, see, Yvette Aparicio, "Reading Social Consciousness in Claribel Alegría's Early Poetry," *Cincinnati Romance Review* 18 (1999): 1–6; and *Negotiating Politics and Aesthetics: The*

Poetry of Claribel Alegría, Ernesto Cardenal and Roque Dalton (PhD diss., University of California, Irvine, 2000).

26. One essay collection, *Claribel Alegría and Central American Literature: Critical Essays* (Athens: Ohio University Center for International Studies, 1994), edited by S. Boschetto-Sandoval and Marcia Phillips McGowan, is dedicated to Alegría's oeuvre. Notably, only a few essays focus on her poetry. Most scholars focus on her fiction and testimonial texts. For example, see Arturo Arias, *Taking Their Word: Literature and the Signs of Central America* (Minneapolis: University of Minnesota Press, 2007); Laura Barbas-Rhodens, *Writing Women in Central America: Gender and the Fictionalization of History* (Athens: Ohio University Press, 2003); Linda Craft, *Novels of Testimony and Resistance from Central America* (Gainesville: University Press of Florida, 1997); and, Ileana Rodríguez, *Women, Guerrillas, and Love: Understanding War in Central America*, trans. Robert Carr (Minneapolis: University of Minnesota Press, 1996).

27. In various interviews Alegría speaks of her inability to return home in 1982 for her mother's burial because of threats to her life. She has also described the burning of her books by the National Guard when they took over the Universidad de El Salvador. See Marcia McGowan Phillips, "Closing the Circle: An Interview with Claribel Alegría," in *Claribel Alegría and Central American Literature*, 228–45.

28. These include *Umbrales* [*Thresholds*] (San Salvador: Dirección de Publicaciones e Impresos, 1997), *Saudade* [*Longing*] (San Salvador: Dirección de Publicaciones e Impresos, 2000), and *Soltando amarras/Casting Off* (Willamantic, CT: Curbstone Press, 2002). Various anthologies of her poetry have also been compiled. The most comprehensive is that of the Salvadoran DPI, *Esto soy: Antología poética* (San Salvador: Dirección de Publicaciones e Impresos, 2004).

29. *Luisa en el país de la realidad* (San Salvador: UCA Editores, 1997). In the book's prologue, Alegría affirms: "A los cincuenta años de haber publicado mi primer libro de poemas, *Anillo de silencio* [1948], vuelvo con un libro muy salvadoreño, tan salvadoreño como *Cenizas de Izalco* y con el agravante de ser santaneco, como diría Roque" [Fifty years after publishing my first poetry book, *Ring of Silence*, I return with a very Salvadoran book, as Salvadoran as *Ashes of Izalco*, and with the aggravating circumstance of being from Santa Ana, like Roque (Dalton) would say] (11). Alegría's enthusiastic claim to Salvadoran-ness is more notable considering that she is Salvadoran-Nicaraguan. She was born in Nicaragua to a *nica* father and a Salvadoran mother and was reared in El Salvador's second largest city, Santa Ana. Despite the book's Salvadoran identity, some events take place in and/or refer to Nicaragua and other places.

30. In this collage of poems and short prose vignettes, Luisa travels down the rabbit hole of Central America. During her trip, she is awed by the everyday reality of great wealth and poverty as well as by revolutionary political action. The implied idea that Central American reality does not need embellishment to inspire wonder recalls Gabriel García Márquez's Nobel lecture, "La Soledad de América Latina," http://www.nobelprize.org/nobel_prizes/literature/laureates/1982/marquez-lecture-sp.html.

31. See Ana Patricia Rodríguez, *Dividing the Isthmus: Transnational Histories, Literatures, and Cultures* (Austin: University of Texas Press, 2009) on the importance of returning to the home "center" in Guatemalan Maya post-traumatic narratives.

32. *Luisa en el país de la realidad* also contains poems to the malinche tree and to important rivers and volcanoes.

33. "Tamalitos de cambray," *Estoy soy*. Panchimalco, a town outside San Salvador, is one of few areas recognized as "Indian" in El Salvador. In her book on El Salvador's largely unacknowledged indigeneity, *Seeing Indians: A Study of Race, Nation, and Power in El Salvador* (Albuquerque: University of New Mexico Press, 2005), Virginia Q. Tilley includes Panchimalco as a "famous" Indian area (74).

34. Benedict Anderson, *Imagined Communities: Reflections on the Origins and Spread of Nationalism*, rev. ed. (London: Verso, 1991).

35. K. Stewart, "Nostalgia—A Polemic."

36. McGowan, "Closing the Circle: An Interview with Claribel Alegría," 230.

37. http://400elefantes.wordpress.com.

38. Marta Leonor González, *La casa de fuego* (Managua: 400 Elefantes, 2008).

39. In a short piece about González's new book in *La Prensa*, "Versos de fuego" ["Verses of Fire"] (June 20, 2008), Cindy Regidor states that the focus of "Los otros" is "violencia de género" [violence against women] (accessed on August 27, 2008). In my reading, these poems do denounce violence against women (e.g., in "Ciudad Juárez: los muros hablan" ["Ciudad Juárez: the Walls Speak"]), in addition to other types of violence, such as that of the government against its citizens (e.g., in "Día entre Cuscatlán y Managua" ["A Day Between Cuscatlan and Managua"]).

40. At the same time, the poem makes clear that this "paradise" is not an ideal place—in other words it is not really a paradise. This gesture is comparable to Alegría's recasting of Lewis Carroll's "Wonderland" as "Realityland," a conflict-filled home.

41. Susana Reyes, *Historia de los espejos* (San Salvador: Dirección de Publicaciones e Impresos, 2008). This poetry collection is divided into six sections tellingly titled: "Cuenta regresiva" ["Countdown"], "Recuento de daños" ["Damage Counts"], "Sobreviviente del silencio" ["Survivor of Silence"], "Postales urbanas" ["Urban Postcards"], "Historia de los espejos" ["Story of the Mirrors"], and "La felicidad de las piedras" ["The Happiness of Stones"]. In addition, Reyes coauthored a poetry book with the collective "Poesía y más" ["Poetry and More"] titled *El libro de los conjuros* [*The Book of Spells*] (2001). Most recently, she published *Los solitarios amamos las ciudades* [*We Solitary Ones Love Cities*] (2009).

42. Robinson characterizes polyarchy as the political counterpart of the neoliberal economic system, a "low-intensity democracy." In it, a select group of elites rule through elections in which this group makes up the electoral slate. William I. Robinson, *Transnational Conflicts: Central America, Social Change, and Globalization* (London: Verso, 2003), 53, 54.

43. Boym, *The Future of Nostalgia*, 41.

44. Ibid., 49.

45. Ibid., 50.

46. García Canclini notes that the preference for shopping centers and metro stations as places to congregate in Latin America "suggests that younger generations are drawn to what Marc Augé has called 'non-places.' The proliferation of these 'installations necessary for the rapid circulation of people and commodities,' which affects the use of space and the citizenry's habits, reveals a displacement in urban agglomerations, a decrease (but not a disappearance) of the distinctive in favor of the deterritorialized and dehistoricized." Néstor García Canclini, *Consumers and Citizens: Globalization and Multicultural Conflicts*, trans. George Yúdice (Minneapolis: University of Minnesota Press, 2001), 73.

47. See the websites for El Salvador's Ministry of the Economy and Ministry of Tourism: http://www.minec.gob.sv/ and http://www.elsalvador.travel/en/. Both promulgate El Salvador as a safe, secure, appropriate place for foreigners to invest funds and spend leisure time.

48. Examples include the luxury shopping malls that have sprung up in the city's outskirts populated by the bourgeoisie: La Gran Vía (The Grand Way), Multiplaza, and Las Cascadas (The Cascades), all in Antiguo Cuscatlán. According to Reyes, La Gran Vía is an "obscene" representation of consumer culture and of the vast chasm that separates the poor majority from the wealthy minority in El Salvador (personal communication, July 2008).

49. For a discussion of branding and consumer culture in San Salvador, see Luis Armando González, "Implicaciones culturales de la globalización," *Revista de estudios centroamericanos (ECA)* 62, no. 703–04 (May-June 2007): 377–96.

50. A recent *Los Angeles Times* article, "El Salvador Grapples with Rising Bloodshed" (May 13, 2009) reported that according to government figures the homicide rate in El Salvador is ten times that of the United States. The Salvadoran major dailies *La Prensa Gráfica* and *El Diario de Hoy* reconfirm perceptions of being under siege on a

daily basis in El Salvador. Both papers seem to carry stories of murders and other miseries every day. There is also a growing body of scholarship on violence in Central America. See, for instance, Mario Lungo and Roxana Martel, "Ciudadanía social y violencia en las ciudades centroamericanas," in *Estudios culturales centroamericanos en el nuevo milenio*, ed. Marc Zimmerman and Gabriela Baeza Ventura (Houston: LACASA Publications, 2007), 265–82.

51. For a less whimsical portrayal of homelessness, see chapter 3.

52. Roberto Turcios, "Made in Posguerra," in *Visiones del sector cultural en Centroamérica*, coord. Jesús Oyamburu (San Jose: Embajada de España, 2000), 225.

53. María Cristina Orantes, *Paso leve que el polvo avanza* (San Salvador: Alkimia Libros, 2005).

54. SECULTURA (President's Secretariat of Culture) replaced CONCULTURA (National Council of Culture and Art) in 2009. See http://cultura.presidencia.gob.sv/institucion/marco-institucional/decreto.html.

55. In addition to collaborating with Reyes and other members of "Poesía y más" in *El libro de los conjuros* (2001), she recently published *El grito hacia adentro* [*The Scream Inside*] (San Salvador: Dirección de Publicaciones e Impresos, 2012).

56. Other contemporary Salvadoran poets who also write metered verse include Carmen González Huguet (1958) and David Escobar Galindo (1943).

57. Rosanna Reguillo, "Latin America: A Story in Three Movements," *Radical History Review* 89 (Spring 2004): 36, 37.

58. Rubén Darío, *Poesías completas*, 9th ed., ed. Alfonso Méndez Plancarte (Madrid: Aguilar, 1961). Darío, in "Retorno," from *Poema del otoño y otros poemas* (1910), posits that "Si pequeña es la Patria, uno grande la sueña" [If the Homeland is small, one dreams it large].

59. This stanza is the chapter's epigraph. See translation at the beginning of the chapter.

60. Roque Dalton, *Las historias prohibidas del Pulgarcito*, 11th ed. (Mexico City: Siglo XXI Editores, 1997).

61. Dalton's poem was musicalized and popularized by Yolocamba I Ta, a political folkloric musical group formed in the mid-1970s in San Salvador. For more information, see their website: http://yolocambaita.com/historia.htm.

62. Dalton's poem resonates with Salvadorans, in part, because he not only names them directly (both as "salvadoreños" and as *guanacos*) but also indirectly through lexicon and the repetition of accepted views of Salvadoran-ness (e.g., industriousness, shrewdness, ingenuity). A national survey conducted by CONCULTURA revealed that that over half of those polled saw "industriousness" as a characteristic trait of Salvadorans. Maria Tenorio and Miguel Huezo Mixco, *Resultados consolidados del diálogo nacional por la cultura* (San Salvador: CONCULTURA, 2007), 33–35.

63. Jacinta Escudos, *Crónicas sentimentales* (Guatemala City: F & G Editores, 2010).

64. The Romanian philosopher is known for his nihilism. In relation to Escudos's story, his paradoxical belief in human beings' insignificance in the "material universe" and in the sentiment that "one is located at the conscious center of existence" is notable. Robert Wicks, *Modern French Philosophy: From Existentialism to Postmodernism* (Oxford: One World Publications, 2003), 79–80.

65. In addition to *Crónicas sentimentales*, Escudos's publications include the novels *El desencanto* [*Disenchantment*] (San Salvador: Dirección de Publicaciones e Impresos, 2001) and *A-B-sudario* [*A-B-C Shroud*] (Guatemala City: Alfaguara, 2003), and the short story collections *Cuentos sucios* [*Dirty Stories*] (San Salvador: Dirección de Publicaciones e Impresos, 1997) and *El diablo sabe mi nombre* [*The Devil Knows My Name*] (San Jose: Uruk Editores, 2008). Her work has received the critical attention of scholars of Central American narrative. For instance, see the many articles at http://istmo.denison.edu, the e-journal of Central American literature and culture; and, see Beatriz Cortez, *Estética del cinismo: pasión y desencanto en la literatura centroamericana de posguerra* (Guatemala City: F & G Editores, 2010).

66. Susan Stewart, *On Longing: Narratives of the Miniature, the Gigantic, the Souvenir, the Collection* (Durham, NC: Duke University Press, 1993), 133.
67. Ibid., 136.
68. Ibid., xii.
69. Boym, *The Future of Nostalgia*.
70. K. Stewart, "Nostalgia—A Polemic."
71. Juan Sobalvarro, *Unánime* [*Unanimous*] (Managua: Nuevo Signo Fondo Editorial INC, 1999)

THREE
The Stench of Belonging

> De cerca el lago es color café y cuando creí
> ver un pez, me dije: 'nues', porque simplemente
> era una bolsa plástica
> inhalaba su tufo con patriotismo, tratando de
> hacer cuentas de la cantidad de mierda que lo
> nutre.
>
> [Up close the Lake is brown and when I thought
> I saw a fish, I told myself: "s'not,"
> because it was simply a plastic bag
> I inhaled its stench with patriotism, trying to
> count the shit
> that feeds it.]
> —Sobalvarro, from "Del desempleado H#896440"

When read alongside celebratory songs of Nicaragua, Juan Sobalvarro's view of Lake Managua (or Xolotlán[1]) illustrates the tension between visions of home in Central America. One such celebratory song—Tino López Guerra's[2] praise-filled 1946 *corrido* celebrating Managua's centennial—describes a "marvelous" pre-earthquake[3] Managua and "crystalline" Lake. Sobalvarro's view, as noted in the epigraph to this chapter, is more up-to-date. Once, before 1927 when it became a depository for raw sewage and then, in 1972, for construction waste, the Lake was a prime fishing and hunting area.[4] Today it remains Managua's central reference point. Street directions and official addresses are often given in relation to distance to and from the Lake. And despite its dangerously polluted state, poor communities subsist on its contaminated shores using it as a resource.[5] Guerrilla poet Leonel Rugama's "La tierra es un satélite de la luna" ["The Earth is a Satellite of the Moon"], discussed in chapter 1, offers a vivid depiction of the neighborhood's historic poverty. Rugama's ironic comparison of Acahualinca's incremental poverty and the United States' expanding space program efficiently criticizes global economic priorities. His concern and commitment for the poor, and his heroic death, made him an ideal figure for Ernesto Cardenal's elegiac and utopian "Oráculo sobre Managua" ["Oracle over Managua"] (1973). But Juan Sobalvarro, born in the late 1960s and beginning his writing career in the late 1990s, almost a decade after the Sandinistas' electoral loss to Chamorro, writes against texts like Cardenal's and Rugama's. Sobalvarro, who came of age during the Sandinista revolution and regime, wrote a series of articles[6] critical of Cardenal's *exteriorismo* and its imposition on younger poets, gaining notoriety in Managuan literary circles for himself and the then-fledgling cultural journal and small press, 400 Elefantes.[7] He also recently published a *testimonio* narrating his military experience as, initially, a Sandinista. *Perra vida: memoria de un recluta del Servicio Militar* [*Doggone Life: Memories of a Military Service Recruit*] (2005), relates Sobalvarro's life during the Contra War. Drafted into the Sandinista Army with the passage of the Servicio Militar Patriótico (SMP [Patriotic Military Service]) Law (1983), he encountered many physical, emotional, and philosophical difficulties that led him, like many others, to desert. Eventually, though, he was forced to return to the army to complete his tour of duty. Both of these bio-bibliographical details help to explain Sobalvarro's oppositional position vis-à-vis what was still the dominant Nicaraguan literary culture of the late 1990s: exteriorism,[8] politicized poetry, and, more directly, the singing of Sandinista heroes and victories.

In his most recent poetry publication, *Agenda del desempleado* [*The Unemployed's Datebook*] (2007),[9] Juan Sobalvarro offers readers the musings of a poetic speaker who, unemployed, either ambles around Managua a broke *flâneur* or sits at home, hungry and observant. The back cover tells the reader that Sobalvarro received a datebook when he was unemployed and decided to put it to an alternative use, given that he did not have appointments to keep. The resulting "escritura libre" [free writing], unlike his previous literary works, does not fit preset genre limitations. It wavers between poetry and prose, between prosaic and poetic language, and between cynicism and hope. The back cover declares this latest book by Sobalvarro to be "anarchic" and out of the ordinary in its aesthetic sensibilities ["fuera de agenda"], unconcerned with "literary precepts" or "canons." It further describes the book as a combination of poetry, prose, "reflexión" [meditation], and "algo que se interna entre fronteras" [something seeped in between borders]. This in-between place represents risk: "no hay arte sin riesgo" [there is no art without risk]. Reviews of *Agenda del desempleado* also use a variety of descriptors to discuss Sobalvarro's literary risk-taking, including "secuencias prosódicas" [prosaic sequences] (Toledo Keysler), "automatic writing" (Peña), and "poema, prosema, relato, crítica, comentario, cuento y leyenda urbana" [poem, "prosem," tale, criticism, commentary, short story, and urban legend"] (Duarte).[10] But, in fact, 400 Elefantes' editorial narrative about Sobalvarro's writing echoes Michel Delville's characterization of contemporary American prose poetry. In his 1998 study, Delville concludes that prose poetry, a hybrid between poetic and narrative genres, is a "site of [critical] struggle" with the "competing camps of contemporary literature and aesthetic criteria underlying the current literary canon."[11] He, as other critics have, sees this genre as radical and "self-critical" and integral to the debates on aesthetic convention and innovation.[12] In the Latin American context, prose poetry's hybridity expands linguistic possibilities to deal with the "tensions [that] exist between traditional culture and modernization, where dirt roads eventually lead to glassy corporate headquarters."[13] Its open, rebellious form potentializes poets' aesthetic representations of conflict.[14] In these ways, *Agenda del desempleado* challenges prose and poetry by making prose poetic and poetry prosaic. The narrative logic and development of poetic speakers join forces with personal sentiment to create texts that I read as prose poetry.

The emphasis on urban life, tone, and lexicon from Sobalvarro's earlier works (poetry, short stories, and testimonio)[15] is visible in *Agenda del desempleado*'s prose poems. However, they appear with a more cynical worldview. Comparing "No hay poesía," Sobalvarro's poem that ends chapter 2, and *Agenda del desempleado*'s eponymous first poem gives us a glimpse of a change in the tenor of his cynicism and sarcasm. This difference between the two poems is not evolutionary in terms of his poetry's development. *Agenda del desempleado*'s opening poem was originally published in 1999. It is the second poem in *Unánime*, the same collection in which "No hay poesía" is published.[16] These texts bring to light the noxious effects of boredom and its significance in Sobalvarro's work. Both bored poetic speakers search for something "poetic" to say. In "No hay poesía," the poetic I limits poetry's inspirational qualities. He makes random observations about sunsets simply "porque le viene la gana" [because he feels like it], or as an act of self-pleasure (6–7, 12–13). He also denies poetry's power to communicate profound truths—"lo impalpable" (8) or "lo indecible" (9)—or to secure daily needs—food or ironed pants (10, 17). Of course this denial of poetic language is expressed as a poem, a poem that closes by stating the obvious: to live one needs life, not poetry, even if one exists in a "cheap" world. While the world of "No hay poesía" is markedly negative, the poetic speaker finds comfort in poetic expression despite its supposed insignificance to daily life. In "Agenda del desempleado," republished with its content unchanged, the poetic speaker has completely lost hope and interest in his present and future life: "Estoy acostado, pensando en lo fatal que es la vida" [I'm lying down, thinking about how dreadful life is] (5). While the poetic speaker does not directly invoke poetry, the phrase "lo fatal" immediately recalls the poem of that name by *modernista* poet Rubén Darío (1867–1916), Nicaraguans' "inevitable compatriot" as he was dubbed by Nicaragua's *van-*

guardia (1920s–1930s).[17] In Darío's famous poem, the poetic speaker laments human beings' consciousness of death and their helplessness in daily life, and expresses envy for unfeeling nature (rocks, trees). Through polysyndeton, or the overuse of conjunctions, the three-stanza poem masterfully expresses the poetic speaker's increasing fear and panic at his life's uncertainty and mortality: "y no saber adónde vamos, / ni de dónde venimos!" [and to not know where we're going / or where we came from]. Darío's poem, published in the 1905 collection *Cantos de vida y esperanza* [*Songs of Life and Hope*], beats quietly beneath Sobalvarro's "Agenda del desempleado."[18]

Sobalvarro's setup of the poetic speaker lying in bed contemplating his life is followed by the conclusion that this topic is "decepcionante y aburrido" [disillusioning and boring] (5). His boredom and life's dreadfulness lead him to consider committing suicide. In his pitiful condition, suicide has stopped being a risk ["riesgo"] to his life and become a real opportunity for him to exercise personal agency ["un poder"] in a world in which he has been made helpless by doubt, similar to Darío's poetic speaker. Unlike Darío's terrified poetic I, however, Sobalvarro's poetic speaker falls asleep to thoughts of mortality and dreams of suicide and homicide. In his dream a gun is aimed at his temple by his own hand, and he runs through the street "nebuloso y aburrido" [hazy and bored], feeling like he is being watched. The poetic speaker runs without knowing where he is going and ends up in a dead-end alleyway, a metaphor for eventual death. He comes upon a group of men talking about themselves. His boredom and haziness dissipate, and he realizes that the gun in his hand is now pointing away from him and at his future victims:

> Llego a un callejón
> sin salida, una tribuna sobre la que unos hombres hablan de sí mismos, me obstruye el paso,
> repentinamente mi arma ha cambiado de sentido
> y experimento placer, apunto hacia la tribuna y
> disparo. Soy feliz. Ha nacido un criminal.
>
> [I arrive at a dead-end
> alleyway, a grandstand where some men
> talk about themselves, it blocks my way,
> suddenly my weapon has changed directions
> and I experience pleasure, I point at the grandstand and
> I fire. I'm happy. A criminal has been born.] (5)

Rather than crying out his doubts and anxieties, Sobalvarro's bored poetic speaker calmly raises his pistol and destroys the talking heads. The killings verify that a magic-less world cannot be made magical ("No hay poesía") and life's vicissitudes (e.g., unemployment) cannot be allayed by poetry. In "Agenda del desempleado," as well as the rest of the collection, the poetic speaker surveys his urban surroundings and reiterates the substitution of "magic," the "impalpable," and inspiration with disillusion, decay, and poverty. The opening poem's final lines coalesce some of the collection's important themes: the lack of options (life is a dead-end street), the uselessness of talk (particularly politicians'), the viability of violence as a solution, and self-serving pleasure. In this short text the world-weary poetic speaker announces his boredom twice and only gets beyond it after firing his gun. Ironically, shooting the self-centered men in his dreams is akin to shooting himself, for he too is indulging in mental masturbation. As *Agenda del desempleado*'s back cover forewarns, Sobalvarro's writing "linda con la masturbación porque su principal aspiración es la autosatisfacción" [borders on masturbation because its main goal is self-satisfaction]. At the same time, this virtual masturbatory release of sorts does not take place in his "dreadful" life, but instead as he sleeps. Thus his escape from the antithetical "paz desquiciante" [maddening peace] that thoughts of "lo fatal" [dreadfulness] provoke is utterly temporary. Because his ability to kill is imagined, the power that comes from committing homicide is weakened. And, in actuality, the helplessness he feels as a "desempleado" [unemployed person] is integral to his imaginary criminality and may foretell a descent into violence in his everyday life. As Sobalvarro alerts us in "No hay poesía" and further develops in "Agenda del desempleado," (poetic) words are useless when confronted by a tawdry world ["el mundo barato"] and dead-end streets ["callejón sin salida"].[19]

Sobalvarro's poetic speaker inhabits a thoroughly "unpoetic" but paradoxically inspiring world. It is polluted, dirty, "modernized," and sometimes loved. I began this chapter with lines of poetry that are a synecdoche of Sobalvarro's Managua and of the unemployed's reality. "Del desempleado H#896440," the collection's second poem, broadens the first's concerns with the most intimate thoughts of the poetic speaker and integrates his perspective of his social context. It introduces the reader to Managua and its citizens, including the poverty-stricken children who play in the city lake. As in previously discussed texts, here the reader goes on a *paseo* with the poetic speaker. In this case we stroll through a downtrodden Central American capital city. The well-worn path through Managua's everyday tires even the day itself:

> Caminaba el día como quien "hace
> camino al andar", así llanamente, un pie alter-
> nando con el otro, pisando la carne polvosa de la
> tarde a orillas del Lago Xolotlán...
>
> [The day walked as someone who makes
> his way as he goes, straightforward, one foot alter-
> nating with the other, stepping on the dusty flesh of the
> afternoon on the edges of Lake Xolotlán...] (6)

The day, personified, tramps along at the edges of the city's central landmark. Time passes, and the poem focuses on the poetic I's agency and perception of home. Unlike the corrido writer cited at the beginning of this chapter, the twenty-first century poetic speaker has inherited an unpleasant, stench-filled homeland. The Lake, as any Managuan or visitor to Lake Managua can attest, is malodorous. Its deficiencies inspire the poetic speaker, tired of brilliant visions ["cansad(o) de espectacularidades"], to designate it concisely as the "monumental cloaca capitalina" [capital city's monumental sewer] (6). As the text continues, he justifies his epithet for the Lake. His re-creation of Lake Managua becomes increasingly detailed and distasteful, its tone more and more acerbic.

Besides offering the reader a thoroughly realistic vision of the Lake-sewer, the poem is a metaphor for Nicaraguan life and society.[20] Specifically, the poetic speaker reveals in the second stanza that the gray of the sky is so similar to the lake's gray water that the horizon is a "fusión del gris etéreo y fecal" [fusion of gray ethereal and fecal]. In other words, the horizon—the future—is excrement: "Es decir, en la distancia cielo y tierra parecían la / misma mierda" [That's to say, from a distance the sky and the earth looked like / the same shit] (6). Once Sobalvarro establishes his text's and Managua's landscape, he slowly adds more elements to the picture, enlarging the scope of his (eventual) critique of the abuse the Lake has sustained and of investors' and politicians' self-interested, pathetic attempts to make it into a tourist attraction, "alguien detectó que un lago licuado en heces es divisa" [someone realized that a lake of liquefied feces is capital] (6). Mostly visible in cosmetic changes, such as the addition of park benches, faded lanterns, and an improvised pier, these attempts do not decontaminate the Lake and its environs. Neither do they create a (foreign) tourist zone with its attendant luxury hotels and hordes of scantily dressed tourists. The area's un-touristic traits are attested to by the speaker's presence, "y yo no estaría allí" [and I wouldn't be there] (7). The plastic bags the poetic speaker temporarily confuses with fish flourish in the Lake. Their ubiquity has become fodder for jokes: plastic bags are Nicaragua's national flower.[21] If the area were successfully renovated to attract tourists able to afford five-star accommodations, the poetic I and the poor *nica* children he sees playing in the Lake would not be able to enjoy "la dicha de ser nicaragüense, de la mera tierra de lagos y volcanes" [the good fortune of being Nicaraguan, of being from the real land of lakes and volcanoes] (7). The realization that, ironically, its pollution is what makes Lake Managua a *local* living space and hangout produces surprising sentiments in Sobalvarro's poetic speaker—that is nostalgia and patriotism, "quería estar triste por el lago" [I wanted to feel sad for the lake] (7). The image of Managua that emerges from this prose poem is one of a vitiated home. The poetic speaker's sense of patriotic pride, inspired by a contaminated Lake, is equally degraded. Notably, though, Lake Xolotlán's stench does not awaken in him an active or activist patriotism. What I call "activist" patriotism here is akin to Maurizio Viroli's "patriotism of liberty," by which citizens demonstrate their "love of country" by mobilizing when their compatriots and/or their country's laws are abused or violated.[22] In contrast, the poetic speaker's attachment to the homeland and his willingness to breathe in its stench does not go beyond the acknowledgment of patriotic sentiments. He identifies himself as someone who values the *patria*, scat-filled Lake and all, but he does not propose a plan of action to decontaminate the Lake nor does he ultimately critique the actors who have played a part in the Lake's present condition.[23] This poem's walk along Lake Managua flips on its head the concept of ecotourism, progressives' earth-friendly tours through "pristine" nature, by finding benefit in the presumably unresolvable environmental disaster that has befallen Lake Xolotlán. Sobalvarro's presentation of highly polluted Lake Managua as a place for *local* enjoyment of nature can also be read as an ironic twist on what have been termed "toxic tours," tours of environmentally compromised neighborhoods led by community members to raise awareness and, hopefully, to promote social justice.[24] By the end of this short text, the poetic speaker rejoices, even if sarcastically, at the Lake's accessibility to ordinary Nicaraguans.[25] And while his reaction demonstrates a sense of belonging to his poor, decaying homeland, it also communicates resignation and acceptance of its present condition.

Sobalvarro's disillusionment differs from the nostalgia-laden poems discussed in the previous chapter. In Sobalvarro's poetry, nostalgia for home, love of home, drips with sarcasm and irony. For example, the poetic speaker of "Del desempleado H#896440" confesses he is saddened and nostalgic for Nicaragua, his home; however, he does so in a backhanded manner. The tone and imagery of those texts that could be called "nostalgic" or "patriotic" also express bitterness and relish in revealing the underside of Nicaraguan life, in exposing its deficiencies without looking forward to possibilities or looking back at better times. "No hay" [There isn't any] begins with the presentation of a common problem in Central America: lack of (sufficient) potable water, "No hay agua en el barrio" [There isn't any water in the neighborhood]. Besides drinking water, the inhabitants of the urban *barrio* have neither paved streets nor land deeds: "Estas tierras no son de nadie, la gente aparejó sus tablas y se dispuso a vivir" [These lands don't belong to anyone, the people put planks together and got on with living] (31). What the *barrio* does have are rabid stray dogs, an old woman babbling in the street, and implicit desperation. It is "[c]omo asilo de pretéritos" [like a shelter for preterits] (31), the human version of Sobalvarro's Lago de Xolotlán, a "Sumidero de especies humanas mal facturadas" [a wastepipe of poorly made human species] or a "costra encarnada al corazón tieso de Managua" [an ingrown scab on Managua's hard heart] (31).

The poetic speaker juxtaposes this neighborhood, this scab, with a Managua that becomes iridescent with its new "acrílicos and smoking y el nylon embute vítreos muslos de reciente promoción" [plastics and dinner jackets and nylons crammed with new glass thighs] (31). Managua's artificiality, its unnaturalness (including the use of English) stand out. It is a city masking the existence of the poor *barrios* that dot its landscape. The shiny city wears disguises and cosmetics to feign economic development:

> La Managua que se maquilla
> de fantasías y quincalla. Donde los pendejos se
> ceban de progreso en bolsas plásticas.
>
> [The Managua that makes herself up
> with fantasy and trinkets. Where idiots
> delight in plastic bags.] (31)

The glimmering Managua that Sobalvarro alludes to is the one that can be viewed from atop Tiscapa Lagoon,[26] with its multinational buildings and fancy restaurants.[27] In "No hay," believing that plastic bags prove modernization is idiotic and ignores the quotidian reality of most inhabitants. Those plastic bags seen floating in the Lake-sewer in "Del desempleado H#896440," perhaps emblazoned with the names of transnational supermarkets, highlight the fragility and incompleteness of modernization processes in Central America. Nicaraguan elites who benefit from the city's plasticization do not contemplate the "No hay" reality of the majority of their compatriots.[28] Managuans who experience "no hay," or "nues" [s'not] ("Del desempleado H#896440) are banned from the city "que se maquilla" [that makes herself up]. They are those who must follow the edict: "Algo se hace o como sentenció el poeta: uno hace lo que puede" [Something is done or as the poet declared: you do what you can] (31).

The places that inhabit Sobalvarro's prose poems are those in which "you do what you can" to survive. The poor and indigent "infest" Managua's modernity. In her research on indigence in San José, which also applies to other Central American capital cities, social scientist María del Carmen Araya Jiménez pinpoints the root cause of increasing urban poverty: the "actual modelo de desarrollo urbano" [current urban development model] and its associated "consumo masificado" [mass consumption].[29] Araya Jiménez surveys the mass media's treatment of "los excluidos," or the poor, in comparison to press representations of middle class and elite citizens and municipal leaders. She focuses on three socially marginal groups that, according to press reports, mar San José's aesthetics and disturb the urban experience of "legitimate" citizens.[30] *Cuidacarros* (literally car guards), informal vendors, unlicensed taxi drivers (often called *piratas*, or pirates), and indigents. All three groups play roles in diminishing middle class urban dwellers' enjoyment of and spending in the city. As William I. Robinson argues, globalization has brought about "worldwide polarization" in which "broad swathes of humanity have experienced absolute downward mobility."[31] In this scenario, Central American elites, such as those who hire a *cuidacarros* while they shop, are "global consumers" like their transnational peers; meanwhile, most Central Americans "do not consume."[32] Sobalvarro poetically illustrates Araya Jiménez's and Robinson's estimation of contemporary Central America: the poor are left behind, slowly made invisible by shiny modernization processes that manufacture "iridescent" buildings that (momentarily) display national "advancement" while hiding the "pústula hedionda" [foul-smelling pustule] ("El olor de la lástima"; 51), or the tremendous poverty that plagues much of Central America.

Araya Jiménez contends further that indigents, the face of poverty on the street, can become normalized if they fulfill the roles of "picturesque" or "folkloric" urban figures—homeless street performers, for instance—for locals and visiting foreigners. Nonthreatening indigents provide an opportunity for alms giving and quaint photos or postcard images for foreign tourists, and they can (temporarily) awaken social altruism in national citizens.[33] Threatening poor people, "monsters," or those who otherwise fail the "folklore" test hinder development and beautification projects.[34] As Araya Jiménez attempts to do in her study, Sobalvarro and Marta Leonor González humanize these urban "monsters." Gone is Susana Reyes's fanciful image of urban beggars as "dragones de cartón" [cardboard dragons] from chapter 2. They are replaced by toothless, "fetid" vagabonds, diseased and abused bodies of sex workers, and "rotting" bodies.[35]

"El olor de la lástima" ["The Smell of Pity"] effectively exemplifies the dreadful realities of life on Central American streets and the use of repulsion by the repulsive to survive. "El olor de la lástima," as does Sobalvarro's poem about Lake Xolotlán, challenges readers with its explicit descriptions of its subject: necrosis. The poetic I asserts that beggars display their necrotic limbs to arouse sympathy and to "justify" their begging (51), and thus earn a living. The title and first sentence set the tone and tenor of the entire poem: "Lo peor de la lástima son sus moscas, el enjambre de bichos que danza en torno a la pústula hedionda de lo que perece" [The worst thing about pity are its flies, the swarm of bugs that dances around the foul-smelling pustule of what is dying] (51). The images of swarming flies and pus-filled wounds surely awaken disgust in readers and perhaps indignation at Sobalvarro's central premise: that human beings are fascinated with decay and dying. Disgust expresses human aversion toward an object with the power "to contaminate, infect, or pollute by proximity, contact, or ingestion";[36] in short, it is "a rejection of a possible contaminant."[37] It reminds us our bodies can also decay and we can also be unclean. Our indignation,[38] on the other hand, represents our feeling that Sobalvarro, by asserting that we revel in rot, has offended our humanity and likened us to scavenging animals. Sobalvarro argues further that we are incapable of pity or compassion and that our demonstrations of pity are really signs of necrophilia: "Por eso la lástima no es ni piedad, ni caridad sino necrofilia" [That's why pity isn't mercy or charity, it's necrophilia] (51). The poetic speaker implicitly defines the disorder as a (nonsexual) fixation on necrosis.[39] This obsession goes hand in hand, in Sobalvarro's poetic world, with human beings' urgent need to survive. In a skewed way, the relationship between the necrotic indigent and the necrophiliac passers-by is one of supply and demand. The indigent supplies passers-by with decay, satisfying their demand to feel pity, and in turn they (may) give him alms. The resolute beggar employs not just ingenuity but any and all available resources, including his "disgusting" body, to endure life. The poetic speaker finds great determination and agency in the beggar's mendicancy, "un residuo, un acto mínimo y casi parasitario" [a residue, a minimal action, and almost parasitical] (51), and he maintains that, although begging seems to express passivity, in reality it requires action and sacrifice (51). In fact, not only does the poetic speaker see[40] the beggar as someone with agency and persistence, he also draws him nearer to himself by remarking on their likenesses, thus unothering an other.

By resisting the urge to turn away in disgust from the rotting leg, the poetic speaker gives himself time to contemplate the mendicant's display of his dying limb. His epiphany about necrophilia stops him in his tracks, "me estacionó" [it parked me] (51). He wonders, is the beggar provoking him or simply justifying his mendicancy? Power dynamics and the expected exchange between himself and the other, or socially excluded, are disturbed. As Sara Ahmed theorizes disgust in *The Cultural Politics of Emotion*,

> disgust at 'that which is below' functions to maintain the power relations between above and below, *through which 'aboveness' and 'belowness' become properties of particular bodies, objects and spaces*.[41] (italics in original)

The disgusted person confirms his/her superiority by exhibiting intolerance in the presence of "asquerosidad" or "lo asqueroso" [that which is disgusting]. By not turning away from a "disgusting" body, Sobalvarro's poetic speaker challenges social and cultural barriers and distinctions that separate him from the beggar. By acknowledging the similarities between the beggar, himself, and his readers, Sobalvarro also questions the validity and sturdiness of his (our) own "aboveness." If he (and the reader) were to inhabit the beggar's place, as his current unemployment suggests is a very real possibility, then "aboveness" like "belowness" would no longer be *"properties of particular bodies."*[42] The "below" contaminates, and thus the beggar's disgustingness is both contagious and dangerous, or "polluting."[43] Sobalvarro's poetic speaker directly confronts the reader with human vulnerability and decay by asking,

> Qué distancia me separa de
> ese hombre semipodrido en el semáforo cuando
> asisto al trabajo con el pie lesionado con la excu-
> sa de no tener tiempo para ir al médico.
>
> [What separates me
> from the semi-putrid man at the traffic light when
> I go to work with an injured foot with the excu-
> se that I don't have time to see a doctor.] (51)

Using the mendicant's strategy, the poetic speaker garners sympathy through displays of his (temporarily) damaged body. Though his injury does not directly earn him money, the act of dragging himself to work injured is comparable to the beggar's hygienic inaction. Inattention to his leg and tolerance of pain and decay preserve the beggar's ability to successfully solicit handouts. For the poetic speaker, the ill worker's willingness to sacrifice his health for a salary parallels the sacrifice the beggar makes for the sake of survival.

As noted above, Sobalvarro's implicit argument is that sustaining the pain caused by disease allows the mendicant to survive on Managua's streets. This argument echoes seemingly incongruous patriotic feelings at seeing Nicaraguan children playing in the city's polluted Lake. The children's willingness to play in the "ill" Lake and the beggar's high level of tolerance for the pain and stench of physical decay are great achievements of sorts that do not make the poor and indigent substantially different from mainstream Managuans. The poetic speaker again crudely challenges the reader to scrutinize the similarities shared between all who inhabit the homeland:

> Entonces la diferen-
> cia sólo está en el número de moscas que uno con
> la carne podrida es capaz de atraer. La diferencia
> fundamental es la capacidad que tengamos para
> tolerar el tufo.
>
> [So the difference lies in the number of flies one with
> rotting flesh is able to attract. The fundamental
> difference lies in the capacity we have
> to tolerate the stench.] (52)

In the poetic speaker's view, everyone has rotting flesh literally or figuratively. The difference between visible "others" (marginalized individuals like the beggar) and everybody else (the office worker from the following paragraph, for example) lies in the way they utilize the decay they embody. The "tufo" [stench] that the gangrened, foul-smelling beggar emits and proudly bears repels passers-by and readers, making them fear contagion from both his foulness and low social status.[44] It gives power to the disgust he elicits, and it endangers passers-by because odors "cross barriers" as they travel through the air.[45] Sobalvarro's poetic speaker sees himself and his readers in the beggar. For him, the beggar's wherewithal to use the only things he has—rot and the pain it causes—to survive demands a morbid acceptance of the state of the world as well as the acknowledgment of our human compulsion to endure.

In another poem Sobalvarro explores this compulsion—"siempre surge la comezón de sobrevivir" [the itch to survive always arises]— among office workers, mainstream counterparts of the beggar from "El olor de la lástima." "Quietud sin paz" ["Stillness Without Peace"] is annotated with an epigraph from "El Derecho a la Pereza" ["The Right to Be Lazy"] that speaks against capitalist society's "extraña pasión" [strange passion] for work, an "aberración mental" [mental aberration] (56). The poem's text explores the mental anguish of an office worker who, in order to live, feigns faith in the "system," "sólo caben las opciones preestablecidas: / adentro o afuera" [only the pre-established options are possible: / inside or outside] (57). The poetic speaker reveals the inner life of a worker who has been subsumed into the job, "[N]o puedo empu- / ñar ni una queja si hasta yo me he expiado" [I can't bran- /dish even one complaint for I have atoned] (57), but who remains aware of the system's power and his own weakness. This understanding—of his smallness and his need to be "inside" for fear of ending up "outside"—certainly does not prevent him from recognizing, and perhaps allows him to recognize, the "itch" to search for the "fissures" that crack reality: "y darle vuelta al traste de la realidad para hallarle sus fisuras" [and flip over reality's backside to find its fissures] (56). It summarizes the poetic speaker's struggle to survive and keep alive his sense of self while distancing himself from his mind-numbing employment. The cracks that scar reality are the spaces inhabited by "los otros," like the beggars who populate busy intersections in Managua, San Salvador, and San José; like the beggars who, as Sobalvarro insists, are not fundamentally different from the poetic speaker or the reader. As "El olor de la lástima" unflinchingly concludes, the difference between those on the lowest social rungs and those above is ephemeral and not innate. Our distinction relies on the number of flies our rot attracts and, in that sense, in our ability to "profit" from bodily decay (whether literal or figurative).

The human ability to "live with the stench" is taken to its extremes by Claudia Hernández in "Lluvia de trópico" ["Rain of the Tropics"], a short story from *De fronteras* (2007).[46] In descriptive but terse language and in a blank voice, Hernández creates visual, sensory images of an environmental disaster that befalls a "tropical" city. Her antithetical ode to waste and its stench provoke disgust by compelling the reader to imagine (and smell) the situation. As in Sobalvarro's prose poems, in Hernández's short stories narrators seem to almost relish pointing out and dwelling on everyday degradation and resigning themselves to an existence in social conditions that readers interpret as untenable. Critics have noted that Hernández's fictions narrate "extreme realities."[47] Her characters take their strangely transformed realities in stride, as we saw in "Hechos de un buen ciudadano parte 1" and "parte 2" in chapter 1. Hernández intensifies the critique of human tolerance for stench and "lo asqueroso" [the disgusting], upping the ante on Sobalvarro's perturbing image of a polluted Lake Managua, a "lago licuado en heces" [lake of liquefied feces] that is somehow inviting to poor Nicaraguan children.[48] In "Lluvia de trópico," Hernández tells the story of urbanites who learn to live, and love, the smell of excrement. The short story begins, and the reader is (as are the protagonist and his family) immediately and rudely faced with the arrival of a new type of "tropical rain": "Nos despertó el olor a caca" [The smell of shit woke us up] (67). Believing he had a particularly vivid dream and ended up having an accident in his sleep, the first person narrator's reaction is to run to the bathroom. Once he discovers that he is not the source of the stench, however, he and the rest of his family conclude that their annoying neighbor, who owns several loud dogs and with whom they often quarrel, must have spread dog excrement on their house, "Esa mujer es capaz de cualquier cosa con tal de molestarnos" [That woman is capable of doing anything to annoy us] (67). The neighbor's corresponding reaction is to think that the overwhelming stench must be her neighbors' retribution for her dogs' excessive barking. Both conclusions reveal social insecurity and distrust. A sign of the family's social isolation includes the narrator's surprise at the many phone calls he receives inquiring about the origin of the stench. Also, we learn that the family can be reached only because it is listed in the phone book (68). Interestingly, in the search for the origin of the stench, it does not occur to anyone to open the door and look outside. These narrative details exemplify the emptying of Central American streets of "legitimate citizens,"[49] who have shuttered themselves in homes protected by iron bars. Gaby Küppers, in her presentation of Hernández as an Anne Seghers award winner, accurately senses the sadness felt by those in post-conflict Salvadoran society, "una sociedad destrozada, de familias fragmentadas, de metas extraviadas y de la carencia de una base social comunitaria intervenida por la moral y la conciencia" [a destroyed society of fragmented families, lost goals and without a moral, conscientious communal social base].[50] Lungo and Martel's article, "Ciudadanía social y violencia en las ciudades centroamericanas," analyzes these phenomena in post-conflict Central America. Their study shows that, due to everyday urban violence, citizens have retreated from public spaces to private ones. The consequences of this retreat are profound:

La desconfianza en "el otro", la amenaza que éste representa, han venido a deteriorar las relaciones en las comunidades tradicionales. Esto es más evidente en las relaciones en las comunidades de barrio. La proximidad del vecino, los espacios de socialización con éste se cierran a partir de la desconfianza que prima en las relaciones interpersonales, imponiendo patrones de conducta que obstaculizan la integración comunitaria y reducen los niveles de tolerancia a lo diferente.[51]

[The distrust of the "other," the threat that he/she represents, has deteriorated traditional communities' relations. This is most evident in relationships in neighborhoods. The proximity of the neighbor, the social spaces with him/her are closed off because of the mistrust that prevails in interpersonal relations; models of conduct are imposed that hinder community integration and reduce the levels of tolerance of difference.]

This disconnect among neighbors takes form as a general lack of solidarity and as tolerance, or acceptance, of increasingly worsening social conditions. The texts I discuss in this chapter portray these social phenomena through the use of detached poetic speakers and narrators who exist in and critique the rotting, waste-filled homeland yet express no desire to leave.

Hernández takes this imperturbable attitude to the extreme in the narration of her characters' reactions to the "tropical rain" and its (temporarily) intolerable odor. When they finally venture out of their homes to go to work, the city's inhabitants are appropriately disgusted by what they find: streets caked with dog waste, "Era como una nevada café: una nevada de trópico. Y apestaba" [It was like a brown snowfall: a tropical snowfall. And it stank] (69), and an odor "tan denso que casi podíamos tocarlo con las manos" [so dense that we could almost touch it with our hands] (68). The permeating stench alarms them. As pragmatists, however, they leave the cleanup for later lest they be late for work. Their work ethic reminds us of Sobalvarro's contention that workers are subsumed by the "system," and that in a manner of speaking, we all stink in the end. Also lending credence to Sobalvarro, Hernández's characters attempt to find a way to tolerate the stench using handkerchiefs or face masks. They protect themselves from the invading odor, or "foul other," by covering up; the fact that they arrive at their jobs demonstrates their temporary victory against the odor's disruption of their daily routines.[52] Their ability to adapt to an environmental disaster is in full display when, after the sun has baked the excrement into a brown crust, they become accustomed to the stench and are able to have dinner as usual (70). This lightning-fast "olfactory reversal,"[53] a process in which subjects assimilate formerly foreign and/or offensive odors, transforms the citizens' initial (expected) repugnance into desire for "tropical rain." While readers may barely keep from gagging as they read Hernández's story, her characters long for the noxious smell: "nos producía una sensación de comodidad muy cercana a lo agradable" [it produced in us a sensation of comfort very similar to pleasantness] (70). Interestingly, their heightened level of "comfort" steers them toward each other and away from the authority figures. The government puts forth a number of measures to deal with the "enfermedad ambiental" [environmental sickness] (70), but the citizens resist, finding ways to release the dried excrement's smell. For instance, women purposely wear high heels to poke holes in the excremental crust. In a perverse way, the all-encompassing repellent air brings the people together against clean-up efforts.[54] The foul odor literally "breaks down barriers" between the walled-in, alienated citizens and turns out to be "a powerful force for integration."[55] Classen comments, in reference to the integrative power of scent in religious ceremonies, that a "shared smell can give the partakers a strong 'we' feeling."[56] Such is the feeling of belonging that the odor of excrement actualizes in Hernández's "tropical" city. It functions as a force that brings together a disparate society. The people become so dependent on the stench that they become ill without it, and it leads them to develop a black market for dog waste to circulate the smell indoors (71). Incomprehensibly for the reader, rather than joining forces to eliminate their city's toxic air, they struggle to maintain it because they "enjoy" it.

As we compare Sobalvarro's prose poems and this story, we perceive that the characters' adaptation and survival strategies are reflections of each other. Implementing these strategies in the face of horrific, inhumane situations attests to citizens' determination to survive without abandoning their homelands. Similar to the children who joy in Lake Managua and the beggar who treats his decay as a saleable object, the characters of "Lluvia de trópico" enlist coping mechanisms when the rain first falls but then come to glory in their own degradation. In some ways, this story parodies Central American resistance literature much touted during the region's various internal armed conflicts. Protest literature—poetry as well as testimonial narrative—presents the reader with images and stories of social injustice calculated to elicit indignation and perhaps action on behalf of the texts' victims. In Hernández, the reader witnesses the populace's efforts to procure that which the government has denied them by not "allowing" it to rain dog waste again (71). In the short story's world, citizens' newly acquired (disgusting) need replaces recognizable basic human needs (e.g., potable water, sufficient food) demanded in protest texts. And, ironically, the government's attempts to protect public health are interpreted by the narrator and his fellow citizens as misdeeds and abuse: "Nos obliga a velar por nosotros mismos" [They force us to watch over ourselves] (71). If the reader replaces the image of excrement (as a vital necessity) with food or water, the story would follow the pattern of the war years' dominant literary model. It would demonstrate the people's struggle to have their needs met by an ineffective, unresponsive government more interested in maintaining control over its citizenry than in providing quality of life. The inhabitants' success at fulfilling their "need" privately by getting dog waste from neighbors, away from the government's eyes, is again an upside-down representation of resistance and survival strategies found in protest literature of various genres. The city's inhabitants find ways to have "olor suficiente" [sufficient smell], which they rejected at first, as an oppositional act against the authorities (71). The oppositional nature of the relationship between the populace and the government is further highlighted by the narrator's last revelation (and point of pride): he and his family get their excrement for free from their neighbor in exchange for not reporting her dogs' "unbearable" (71) racket. This ending strongly, absurdly indicates to the reader that the narrator's family is *almost* used to the neighbor's barking dogs, an aural nuisance; therefore, not denouncing her to the authorities in exchange for her dogs' waste is a pretty good deal. The world that Hernández imagines is one in which everyone can get used to everything, even the unimaginably noxious and disgusting, and in which everything is saleable, even dog's excrement. The goal is to survive in a ravaged homeland.

Perhaps more forcefully than Sobalvarro, Hernández draws all citizens into the same category. In this city that reminds the reader of Central America, with its houses of "muros gruesos y rejas" [thick walls and iron bars], no one is safe from "tropical rain" or from its foul smell (68, 69). The waste blankets the entire city, leaving nothing uncovered. This "environmental" event, then, equalizes all citizens while still leaving the government in its position of authority. While the citizens resist government policies and find adequate ways to survive, their idea of survival (maintaining the effects of an environmental calamity) is, at least to the reader, less than desirable. Hernández's presentation of "lluvia de trópico" as not only welcomed but also worthy of risking government punishment reveals a deep disillusionment with current Central American society and daily life; what is more, it reveals a profoundly cynical view[57] of fellow citizens, their aspirations, and their willingness to suffer indignities.

In her story, Hernández accuses her compatriots of asking for the dire straits in which they find themselves. Her characters' literal need for excrement is also a metaphorical compulsion to be treated like excrement and to resist opportunities for betterment when they present themselves (as when the government attempts to clear the streets of the "tropical rain"). The fact that characters at the beginning of the narrative are distrustful of each other, assuming their neighbors are out to get them, but by the end effectively collaborate with each other in a (twisted) sense of solidarity, results in a text that challenges its readers to consider their daily lives, the constancy of resistance, and the results of conformity.

In a vein similar to Sobalvarro's and Hernández's graphic meditations on human kinship, but with less savagery and grotesque images, "Invierno no" ["Not Winter"] by Marta Leonor González is a poetic illustration of the daily lives of decaying citizens. González meditates on the physical manifestations of the passage of time in a deteriorating home and on human beings' shared mortality. While Hernández's short story tells of the effects of environmental disaster on urban dwellers from a distance, González's early poem conjures a vision of home using close-up images of the decaying life and body of a destitute Managuan. In this poem from González's first poetry collection, *Huérfana embravecida* [*Enraged Orphan Girl*],[58] a foul-smelling, ill *vagabundo* becomes a metaphor for urban life and citizenship. The inhabitants of this poem's city lack historical memory and consciousness; nevertheless, they still suffer from the passage of time. In the first stanza of the poem, the day is made human, a toothless human without index fingers: "Este día no tiene dientes, / le han cortado sus dedos índices / para no tocar la historia" [This day has no teeth / they've cut off its index fingers / so it can't touch history] (1–3).[59] As the imagery of the vagabond develops, González transforms the day into a decrepit beggar who ambles around Nicaragua's capital city,

> Lagrimoso impaciente vagabundo por Managua,
> con melena hedionda y dril arrugado
> lleva consigo bandadas de pájaros sordomudos
> y los mediodías le han curtido la piel.
>
> [Teary impatient vagabond around Managua
> with stinking mane and wrinkled canvas
> he carries flocks of deaf-mute birds
> and noons have hardened his skin.] (4–7)

The day-turned-teary-vagabond wears time like a skin, wrinkled and stinking as it ages. The birds he carries are as "deficient" as he is, for they cannot sing or hear singing. Further, this "fetid" vagrant is both diseased and a disease-producing element of urban life. An "other," he exists as an infectious "cancer" (8) on Managua's streets among "indomitable" (10) trash. This image of the urban homeless man living among waste is not unlike the inhabitants of Hernández's tropical city or of Sobalvarro's Lake Xolotlán or Managuan intersections.

Both González's vagabond and the vagabond's city survive despite their unmitigated disintegration. In the Managua that she poetically photographs, the vagrant's body molds and becomes infested with bugs and ticks (14), infected with ulcers (20), pus, and blood (21). It is a snapshot of time itself (the day, the month, the season), a lifetime spent on the city streets. Simultaneously, the brambly, craggy (17) world that the poetic speaker describes is that of the interlocutor, an urban dweller also trapped in Managua,

> Arañado por los segundos de una
> tarde en alambrados

el invierno
tiene tu rostro
y gente en los buses llegando tarde a sus trabajos.

[Scratched by the seconds of a
fenced-in afternoon
winter
has your face
and people, late to work, on the bus.] (22–26)

In spite of time's putrefaction, the city and its inhabitants continue doing and living as they always have, yet those left by the wayside, like the homeless and other poor, are left without resources or recourse to better their conditions. In contrast, Sobalvarro's mendicant and Hernández's compatriots do find ways to access resources and, if not better their conditions, at least resist death, even if the means are dehumanized and degraded.

In "Invierno no," the poetic speaker's naturalist description of time passing as a process of decomposition reviews life cycles unflinchingly, realistically, and even objectively. González's use of a homeless man's body as a surface on which to inscribe this fact of life can reveal a morbid interest on her part if we do not reread the poem's title, "Invierno no." The word "invierno" appears three times in the text: in the title and in the middle and last stanzas. Throughout the text, the poetic speaker uses winter in Managua to frame the vagrant's (and time's) journey. As a framing tool, winter helps the reader fill in the details of daily urban life and comprehend the title's refusal, "not winter." The weight of the "not" becomes more perceptible when we consider the meaning of winter in the city and for the poor: illness, discomfort, storms, damage.[60] The poem's *no*, while not exclaimed, sounds nonetheless like a muted protest. The poem does not hint at the idea of resistance conveyed by the joy that poor Nicaraguan children feel as they play in their polluted Lake, or the illusory homicidal happiness of the unemployed, or, finally, the relief that "tropical rain" brings. Instead, the poetic speaker's interjection cries out quietly for compassion or, perhaps, solidarity. Notably this "no" is not tangled up in the politics of recent Nicaraguan revolutionary or protest literature. González, as do many of her contemporaries, refuses to align with (post-) Sandinista political positions. Simultaneously, with "Invierno no," she expresses her acceptance of the malodorous status quo and the ill *patria* without imagining or dreaming of ways to remake Nicaragua or, more broadly, the Central American homeland.

In their renditions of post-conflict homelands, young writers exercise their critical skills. They foreground the cracks of Central America's globalizing economies and cultures and wearily present the "real" conditions of their homes and fellow citizens but not without compassion. This compassionate sentiment that founds detailed depictions of the disgusting, though, does not rise to the level of indignation in textual tone, attitude, or action. The portrayal of disgusting objects and conditions does not disgust the poetic speakers or narrators. They simply assimilate the images and adapt to conditions as they exist. The reader, on the other hand, may retch or feel like retching at the smells evoked by Sobalvarro, Hernández, and González. It is also the reader who may feel indignant both for being subjected to descriptions of the disgusting as well as for the disgusting subjects themselves. Indignation "impels us to do justice, to do the work of setting the balance right."[61] This possible (probable) sentiment, however, lies beyond the realm of the narrators' and poetic speakers' passive evocation or provocation of disgust. They manage to vividly evoke their decaying homelands from an antithetically intimate distance. Disgust, which "operates in a kind of miasmic gloom,"[62] oozes from their homelands, but the narrators and poetic speakers manage to mostly remain aloof. Cynical acceptance of the present foregoes indignation. Instead, Sobalvarro, González, and Hernández witness and ironically photograph their disintegrating, rotting, excrement-filled homes. Then, they leave it at that. Sobalvarro expresses this impassivity in a graphic example from "Protesta pacífica" ["Peaceful protest"] (*Agenda del desempleado*): "Concluye que ya es demasiado, que vamos a ser drásticos, ahora sí. Y se tira un pedo" [He concludes that now it is too much, that we're going to be drastic, now for sure. And he farts] (18).

Sobalvarro's gaseous, unemployed poetic speaker recognizes the socioeconomic and political issues that underlie and explain the whys of his filthy existence. He also understands that he belongs in the place he inhabits: "se siente nombra- / do en un espacio cafezusco que entona hedores veteranos" [he hears himself na- / med in the brownish space that intones veteran stenches] (18). He listens to the heavily polluted Lake Managua acknowledge his belonging. This reciprocal recognition keeps the poetic speaker in the decayed and decaying homeland, "¿para dónde me voy a / mover?" [where am I going / to move?] (18). Feet grounded at home on figurative and literal excrement, Sobalvarro's, as well as Hernández's and González's, texts claim their place in the homeland but hold their nose while doing it.

In contrast, the poets and writers in the next chapter situate themselves at an even farther remove from home. In their texts the homeland stinks, but they are too far away to smell it. In chapter 4, Central Americans survey and travel across and through the homeland as if they were tourists. Viewing home from a distant and distanced stance, they imagine themselves as visitors in an "exotic" locale. But their knowledge of home gives them away as they comment on the homeland's slow decay and their own lost memories of what was. These meditations on loss and change also reveal the artificiality of texts' studied remoteness. In short, despite purporting a touristic sensibility, chapter 4's poetic speakers and protagonists desire interpersonal links with compatriots and a place at home.

NOTES

1. Jaime Íncer, "El Lago de Managua (Historia, geografía y geología)," *Revista de la Academia de Geografía e Historia de Nicaragua*, Segunda época, LXV (2007): 233; Jorge Eduardo Arellano, "Presentación: Managua en el tiempo," *Revista de la Academia de Geografía e Historia de Nicaragua*, Segunda época, LXV (2007): 8; Roberto Sánchez Ramírez, *Breve historia de la navegación en el Lago Xolotlán* (Managua: PAVSA, 2008), 11; and, Fernando Silva, "Xolotlán," *El nuevo diario*, November 16, 2002. The meaning of Lake Managua's indigenous name, Xolotlán, is a topic of debate. Jaime Íncer traces the name to indigenous mythology, stating that the name alludes to Xolotl, the twin brother of the Mesoamerican deity Quetzalcoátl. Arellano adds that besides being a deity, Xolotl was the name of a Nahua leader. According to Sánchez Ramírez, however, the most widely accepted view is that Xolotlán alludes to "xolotli," a water salamander eaten by Nicaraguan indigenous people. Finally, in a series of articles published in the Managuan daily *El nuevo diario*, the Nicaraguan writer Fernando Silva disputed the meanings of place names and their indigenous origins. In "Xolotlán" (November 16, 2002), he argues that this word is derived from "xonoctla," a place in Mexico named after an indigenous leader. Silva asserts that the lake's proper name is "Lago de Managua."
2. For the *corrido*'s lyrics, see Sánchez Ramírez, *Breve historia de la navegación*, 55–56. According to T.M. Scruggs, Tino López Guerra, a prominent Nicaraguan composer, wrote "several well-known *corridos*. These were non-political *corridos* written in praise of the various cities of the country ("Granada de Nicaragua," "Corrido Chinandega," etc.), which were performed by Nicaraguan mariachis in a manner indistinguishable from their northern-Mexican counterparts." T. M. Scruggs, "Socially Conscious Music Forming the Social Conscience: Nicaraguan *Música Testimonial* and the Creation of a Revolutionary Movement," in *From Tejano to Tango: Latin American Popular Music*, ed. Walter Aaron Clark (New York: Routledge, 2002), 45.
3. A massive 6.2 earthquake destroyed much of Managua on December 23, 1972. The Nicaraguan government's misappropriation (theft) of international disaster aid is often cited as a turning point in the growth of organized popular opposition to Somoza, his National Guard, and his cronies.
4. Sánchez Ramírez, *Breve historia de la navegación*, 11, 27.
5. According to Íncer, estimates say that the Lake is contaminated by approximately 100 million gallons of wastewater; in addition, its pollutants include solid waste and trash (236).
6. For a discussion of Sobalvarro's early poetry and his critiques, see Yvette Aparicio, "Poesía nicaragüense escrita después de Darío, de Cardenal, de la Revolución," in *Literatura y otras artes en América Latina: Actos del XXXIV Congreso del Instituto Internacional de Literatura Iberoamericana*, ed. Daniel Balderston et al. (Iowa City: University of Iowa, 2004), 151–57.
7. See http://400elefantes.wordpress.com.
8. See chapter 1 for a definition of Cardenal's *exteriorismo*. This poetic theory formed the basis for the controversial popular poetry workshops Cardenal ran as Minister of Culture. For more information on the debates surrounding the Ministry of Culture and aesthetics, see Greg Dawes, *Aesthetics and Revolution: Nicaraguan Poetry, 1979–1990* (Minneapolis: University of Minnesota Press, 1993).
9. Juan Sobalvarro, *Agenda del desempleado* (Managua: 400 Elefantes, 2007).
10. Sobalvarro has posted all these reviews on his blog: http://juansobalvarro.blogspot.com/p/agenda-del-desempleado.html. Duarte's posting is a version of his introduction given at a presentation of Sobalvarro's book in Managua.

11. Michel Delville, *The American Prose Poem: Poetic Form and the Boundaries of Genre* (Gainesville: University of Florida Press, 1998), 249.
12. Ibid., 249–50.
13. Susan Briante, Introduction to "Hybrid Cultures: The Prose Poem in Spanish," *Sentence: A Journal of Prose Poetics* 2 (2004): 48.
14. Jesse Fernández, *El Poema en prosa en Hispanoamérica: Del modernismo a la vanguardia (Estudio crítico y antología)* (Madrid: Ediciones Hiperión, 1994), 31, 73.
15. In addition to publications mentioned in this chapter and published in literary journals, Sobalvarro's creative work includes two short story collections, *¿Para qué tanto cuento?* [*Why So Much Talk?*] (Managua: 400 Elefantes, 2000), and the recently published *El dueño de la pelota* [*The Ball's Owner*] (Managua: 400 Elefantes, 2012).
16. Juan Sobalvarro, *Unánime* (Managua: Nuevo Signo Fondo Editorial Inc., 1999).
17. For more information on the Nicaraguan *vanguardia*, see Leonel Delgado Aburto's *Márgenes recorridos: Apuntes sobre procesos culturales y literatura nicaragüense del siglo XX* (Managua: Instituto de Historia de Nicaragua y Centroamérica, Universidad Centroamericana, 2002).
18. Rubén Darío, *Poesías completas*, 9th ed., ed. Alfonso Méndez Plancarte (Madrid: Aguilar, 1961).
19. Under- and unemployment, alongside feelings of destitution, as Sobalvarro leads us to believe, are alarmingly high in Nicaragua and neighboring countries. In nonindustrialized countries across the globe, underemployment looms around 30%. In 2011 unemployment ranged from an estimated 6.5% in Costa Rica to an estimated 7.3% in Nicaragua to an estimated 7.6% in El Salvador. Keeping in mind these figures and local living conditions, the congruousness of the poetic speaker's depression and desperation as well as his sarcasm and cynicism is evident. Figures are from https://www.cia.gov/library/publications/the-world-factbook/fields/2129.html?countryName=&countryCode=&regionCode=Á (most recently accessed June 11, 2012).
20. In consideration of similar issues of a degraded Central American landscape, Ana Patricia Rodríguez explores waste as "signifier of development and progress" focusing on narratives by Carmen Naranjo, Fernando Contreras Castro and Gioconda Belli. *Dividing the Isthmus: Transnational Histories, Literatures, and Cultures* (Austin: University of Texas Press, 2009), 221.
21. Florence Babb, *The Tourism Encounter: Fashioning Latin American Nations and Histories* (Stanford, CA: Stanford University Press, 2011), 141. Babb mentions this joke, retold in a 2004 newspaper interview with the then-president of INTUR (Instituto Nicaragüense de Turismo), Lucía Salazar. See Gabriel Sánchez Campbell, "Turismo lanza grito de guerra contra la basura," *La Prensa*, August 5, 2004.
22. Maurizio Viroli, *For Love of Country: An Essay on Nationalism and Patriotism* (Oxford: Oxford University Press, 1995), 185.
23. For an example of "ecological" Central American poetry, see Nicaraguan Esthela Calderón, *Soplo de corriente vital (Poemas etnobotánicos)* (Managua: Ediciones 400 Elefantes, 2008).
24. Phaedra Pezzullo, *Toxic Tourism: Rhetoric of Pollution, Travel, and Environmental Justice* (Tuscaloosa: The University of Alabama Press, 2007).
25. Sánchez Ramírez, *Breve historia de la navegación*, 26.
Recently the remodeled Xolotlán pier and surrounding area have become a low-cost entertainment destination for Nicaraguans. The restoration began in 2007.
26. For decades Somoza's presidential palace sat on this hilltop. The palace was heavily damaged by the 1972 earthquake. Now this area forms part of the Tiscapa Historical National Park, and its dominant monument is a silhouette sculpture of Sandino by Ernesto Cardenal that can be seen throughout the city.
27. "A Symptom Called Managua" posits that after the Sandinista defeat, then Mayor and future President Arnoldo Alemán oversaw "development aimed to 'beautify' the metropolis in order to make it more attractive to private investors: a huge illuminated fountain in front of the Metrocentro mall that spouted multicolored water;

showpiece public works such as the construction of a new cathedral in the city center or the restoration of the lakeside Malecón." Dennis Rodgers, "A Symptom Called Managua," *New Left Review* 49 (Jan.–Feb. 2008): 110–11.

28. See William I. Robinson, *Transnational Conflicts: Central America, Social Change, and Globalization* (London: Verso, 2003) on *maldevelopment*: further "progress" for the few and marginalization for the many.

29. María del Carmen Araya Jiménez, "El lado oscuro de San José: Miedos de comunicación y construcción de pánicos morales," in *El lado oscuro: Ensayos sobre la violencia*, ed. Anacristina Rossi and Nora Garita (San Jose: Uruk Editores, S.A., 2007), 96.

30. Ibid., 64.

31. Robinson, *Transnational Conflicts*, 313.

32. Ibid., 314.

33. Araya Jiménez, "El lado oscuro de San José," 103, 107. As an example of the attempt to awaken charity, Araya Jiménez also cites an advertisement campaign in which Bancrédito urged Costa Ricans to share their wealth with the less fortunate. The newspaper ads displayed photographs of "los excluidos" alongside bank slogans.

34. Ibid.,107.

35. These are images from González's "Invierno no" and "Visaje de jinetera" in *Huérfana embravecida* (1999) and Sobalvarro's "El olor de la lástima" from *Agenda del desempleado*, respectively.

36. William Ian Miller, *The Anatomy of Disgust* (Cambridge, MA: Harvard University Press, 1997), 2.

37. Martha Nussbaum, "Secret Sewers of Vice: Disgust, Bodies, and the Law," in *The Passions of the Law*, ed. Susan A. Bandes (New York: New York University Press, 1999), 26.

38. For Miller, indignation has to do with questions of "owing and paying back" and revenge (*The Anatomy of Disgust*, 36). Nussbaum characterizes indignation as a reaction to being wronged or harmed ("Secret Sewers of Vice," 26).

39. Dany Nobus, "Over My Dead Body: On the Histories and Cultures of Necrophilia," in *Inappropriate Relationships: The Unconventional, the Disapproved, and the Forbidden*, ed. Robin Goodwin and Duncan Cramer (Mahwah, NJ: Lawrence Erlbaum Associates, Publishers, 2002), 171–89. Nobus explains that definitions of necrophilia have been wrought with misconceptions and variations. The most common views are of cadaver desecration and of the sexual desire for the dead. But necrosadists and "lust" murderers have often been categorized as necrophiliacs as well.

40. Unlike most city dwellers for whom mendicants are invisible, as Araya Jiménez argues ("El lado oscuro de San José," 99), Sobalvarro's poetic I acknowledges the mendicant's existence and empathizes with him.

41. Sara Ahmed, *The Cultural Politics of Emotion* (New York: Routledge, 2004), 89.

42. Ibid., 89.

43. Miller, *The Anatomy of Disgust*, 9.

44. Miller, *The Anatomy of Disgust*.

45. Constance Classen, "The Odor of the Other: Olfactory Symbolism and Cultural Categories," *Ethos* 20, no. 2 (June 1992), 160.

46. Claudia Hernández, *De fronteras* (Guatemala City: Editorial Piedra Santa, 2007).

47. Ana Patricia Rodríguez, *Dividing the Isthmus*, 227.

48. The children's apparent unawareness of the Lake's contamination can also be read as an example of their age and developmental stage (Miller, *The Anatomy of Disgust*).

49. Araya Jiménez, "El lado oscuro de San José," 64.

50. Gaby Küppers, "Provisiones creativas de energía para un futuro que, con esfuerzo, debe establecerse fuera del caos reinante," trans. Marisol Batres, in *De fronteras*, by Claudia Hernández (Guatemala City: Editorial Piedra Santa, 2007), 117. The Anna Seghers award is awarded annually to young writers, one German and one Latin American. Hernández won the award in 2004.

51. Mario Lungo and Roxana Martel, "Ciudadanía social y violencia en las ciudades centroamericanas," in *Estudios culturales centroamericanos en el nuevo milenio*, ed. Marc Zimmerman and Gabriela Baeza Ventura (Houston: LACASA Publications, 2007), 277.
52. Classen, "The Odor of the Other," 160.
53. Ibid., 152, 153. Classen's examples include travelers from one culture who become accustomed to another culture's, or the supernatural world's, odors (152–54).
54. For a discussion of the evolution of theories about and behaviors surrounding olfaction, particularly in reference to public hygiene and excrement, see Alan Corbin's *The Foul and the Fragrant: Odor and the French Social Imagination* (Cambridge, MA: Harvard University Press, 1986).
55. Classen, "The Odor of the Other," 160.
56. Ibid.
57. Beatriz Cortez, *Estética del cinismo: Pasión y desencanto en la literatura centroamericana de posguerra* (Guatemala City: F & G Editores, 2010). Cortez has characterized post-war Central American literature as an "aesthetic of cynicism" in which violence, chaos, and disillusionment reign over daily life and in which subjectivities are (re-)constituted through intimate exploration of the self as opposed to in relation to revolutionary projects.
58. Marta Leonor González, *Huérfana embravecida* (Managua: Ediciones de Bolsillo 400 Elefantes, 1999).
59. In another prose poem from the same collection, "Retrato de hombre callejo" ["Portrait of a Street Man"], González keenly depicts physical deterioration. The protagonist is a semihuman, semianimal, hunchbacked, bearded street person, and poet with "una nariz con secrecio / -nes, abrupta, indecisa al estornudo, al contacto con la / respiración entrecortada de una bronquitis" [a nose secreting, / abrupt, hesistant to sneeze, touching / bronchitis' irregular breathing] (27).
60. A comparison with Costa Rican Luis Chaves's poetic rendition of winter in the tropics highlights the urgency of González's lament for her poem's vagabond. Chaves, in "Niccolo," a poem in which the poetic subject passively watches his life go by as if watching television, presents a wholly different and more "modern" view of winter. In his poem, winter, or the rainy season, is one in which to join global, international trends: "Invierno en el trópico, estación fértil / para talleres de feng shui o el karaoke" [Winter in the tropics / fertile season / for workshops on feng shui or karaoke] (1–2). Luis Chaves, *Historias Polaroid* (San Jose: Ediciones Perro Azul, 2000). Chapter 5 considers in detail Chaves's globalized poetic renditions.
61. Miller, *The Anatomy of Disgust*, 36.
62. Ibid.

FOUR
Touring the Homeland

Lotes baldíos esconden sus misterios
tras latas de zinc.
A través de un agujero rodeado por la herrumbre
hay uno que descubre lo que fue una casa
y—entre la maleza crecida—
eso que parece siempre
resistir el olvido y la intemperie:
medias paredes de ladrillo,
baldosas artesonadas, el inodoro blanco.

[Vacant lots hide their mysteries
behind corrugated metal.
Through a rusted hole
someone discovers what was once a house
and—among overgrown weeds—
that which always seems to
resist oblivion and bad weather
half brick walls,
coffered tiles, the white toilet.]
—Chaves, "Heredades"

En el fondo sólo una cosa querías
y nada tiene que ver con esta ciudad
vista de noche desde las laderas,
ni con el lugar que dejaste hace un par de horas
donde en el espejo detrás de la barra
los desconocidos de ambos lados
parecían tu familia.

[Deep down you only wanted one thing
and it didn't have anything to do with this city

seen at night from the hillsides,
nor with the place you left a couple of hours ago
where in the mirror behind the bar
the strangers on both sides
seemed like your family.]
—Chaves, "Salir de 'El Caracas'"

The headline of a February 13, 2009, *BusinessWeek* article on outsourcing reads: "Costa Rica: Cultural Similarities Make It an Outsourcing Favorite."[1] The article praises Costa Rica as a potential source of "highly skilled workers, a location not more than two hours' time from [the] in-house developers" and as "a safe and pleasant locale." As evidence of the country's attractiveness to investors, the article relates the experience of a U.S. software development firm looking for offshore programmers. According to the president and chief executive officer of the U.S. firm, he considered outsourcing to India or Ukraine but was deterred by time differences and the "sometimes hard to understand accents."[2] In contrast, besides fulfilling the company's basic requirements, Costa Rica extends an additional perk to visiting U.S. software partners: its weather and beaches.[3] It goes without saying that Costa Rica also offers international business partners a stable political and economic environment and a more highly developed infrastructure[4] than its neighbors on the isthmus and in much of the rest of Latin America. As now former President Óscar Arias Sánchez[5] put it at the Costa Rica Services Summit 2009 (June 3–4, 2009), a meeting of domestic and international businesspeople involved in the service sector (including information technology and communication, the audiovisual industry, medical tourism, architecture, and construction):

> La conexión de Costa Rica con el mundo, es la que le permite hoy disfrutar de una posición de privilegio en material de integración comercial. El país que está dibujado en nuestro Escudo Nacional ha tenido algunos cambios notables, que han sido transcendentales para alcanzar un nivel mayor de desarrollo, particularmente en el sector de comercio internacional. Nuestros barcos mercantes ya no abandonan nuestras costas cargados únicamente de fanegas de café o de cajas de banano; ni parten hacia una decena de países que unos días nos quieren comprar y otros días no."[6]

[Costa Rica's connection to the world is what allows it to enjoy a privileged position in commercial integration. The country that is drawn on our national coat of arms has had some notable changes that have been very significant to reach a higher level of development, particularly in the international commerce sector. Our merchant ships leave our shores weighed down not just by bushels of coffee or boxes of bananas; nor do they depart to dozens of countries that buy some days and don't on others.]

Arias Sánchez, a major proponent of CAFTA-DR,[7] emphasizes the development of his country's economy toward greater global integration. Together these varied examples of Costa Rica's place in the global economy, as well as of the endurance of its national identity, render an image of a Central American homeland's beneficial differences (e.g., lower pay, tropical weather, etc.) and similarities with or parallels to the North.

Costa Rican intellectual Carlos Cortés delves more deeply than Arias Sánchez into accepted perceptions of Costa Rican-ness, explaining Costa Ricans' views of themselves:

> Somos diferentes porque naturalmente, somos diferentes: sin indios, sin violencia, sin clases sociales, sin ejército, por un lado; con una población blanca, con una estabilidad democrática, con educación para todos, con paz, por el otro.[8]

> [We're different because, naturally, we are different: without Indians, without violence, without social classes, without a military, on the one hand; on the other, with a white population, with democratic stability, with education for all, with peace.]

Cortés lists a series of markers of Central American-ness, and more broadly a version of Latin American-ness, that according to official views do not apply to Costa Rica: indigenous and mestizo populations, high levels of poverty, armed (and continual) internal conflicts, and militarized societies.[9] Cortés's critique of Costa Rican exceptionalism responds to a tradition of unquestioned acceptance of an *idiosincrasia tica* (Costa Rican idiosyncrasy), the myth, reviewed by fellow Costa Rican Giovanna Giglioli, of a particular unchanging Costa Rican personality and temperament.[10] Costa Ricans' difference from "lo otro, lo no-costarricense" [the other, the not-Costa Rican] is founded on three "factores determinantes de la realidad costarricense" [determining factors of Costa Rican reality]: racial homogeneity, isolation from other colonies during colonization, and the use of the *meseta central* (central highlands) as a metaphor for the entire country to the exclusion of other regions.[11] In her analysis of treatises on Costa Rican-ness, Giglioli tracks the ideological twists and turns that support and promulgate the "truth" of her compatriots' idiosyncrasy and, thus, their difference from their conflict-happy neighbors. She explains that repeatedly affirming their Hispanic ancestry (vs. an indigenous one) not only highlights their "cultural originality" but also the fact that life in the *meseta central* is a "negación de lo centroamericano caracterizado por la presencia perturbadora del mundo indígena y la violencia deshumanizante de su vida política" [negation of that which is Central American, characterized by the perturbing presence of the indigenous world and the dehumanizing violence of its political life].[12] The Costa Rican press and both popular and official rhetoric echo the beliefs Costa Rican intellectuals criticize. For instance, in the recent documentary

NICA/ragüense about Nicaraguan immigrants in Costa Rica, several *josefinos* (inhabitants of San José) interviewed by the Nicaraguan and U.S. filmmakers unabashedly describe *nicas* as violent, dark-skinned, and uneducated. They opine that, as a group, these *nicas* do not contribute in any way to Costa Rican society other than to abuse its (state) generosity.[13]

Such reactions to Nicaraguan immigration demonstrate the impact of Costa Rican-ness on national rhetoric. As noted, government officials and business leaders actively propagate the appropriateness of their country for investment. Government institutions (including schools) and the press also assist in the dissemination of hegemonic representations of Costa Rica. Yet more critical, and cynical, readers of Costa Rica, such as the aforementioned Carlos Cortés and Giovanna Giglioli, see their shared homeland differently. The two poems by Costa Rican poet Luis Chaves (1969) that open this chapter recreate a home that in its salient features reminds us of the homes defiled and loved in contemporary Salvadoran and Nicaraguan texts. Readers aware of popular perceptions of Costa Rican exceptionalism may be surprised by similarities between these literary representations of the local. While Chaves's poems cited above do not explicitly engage with current Costa Rican social reality, they do present fragments of a world dissimilar from the imagined "Arcadia tropical, isla de paz, utopía natural" [Tropical Arcadia, island of peace, natural utopia] that Costa Rica is purported to be.[14] In fact, much like Sobalvarro's poems and Hernández's short stories, the fragmentary or fragmented San José imagined in these two short poems echoes Reguillo's contention that "perhaps today fragmentation is just the only available alternative to try to grasp the complex, multiple and contradictory meanings through which Latin America acquires its meanings."[15] This estimation tarnishes official imagery of Costa Rica as a tropical globalizing Eden with a national "character" as stable as its coat of arms.[16]

Luis Chaves poetically challenges belief in Costa Rican stability and exceptionalism in many texts from his various poetry collections, including *Historias Polaroid* [*Polaroid Stories*] (2000), *Chan Marshall* (2005) and *Asfalto: un road poem* [*Asphalt: A Road Poem*] (2006).[17] In this chapter's first epigraph, "Heredades" ["(Inherited) Estates"] from *Historias Polaroid*, instead of an Arcadia situated far away from its conflictive neighbors, Chaves depicts a homeland's deteriorated landscape. The only object left intact to attest to the existence of former inhabitants is a toilet. It is also the only visible inheritable item. Speaking from a distance and with an unemotional and disaffected tone, the poetic speaker reduces the house's past and the memory of it to the white toilet. This reduction of human experience to its base level communicates a pessimistic view of daily living. The toilet functions as a multifaceted metonymy. It is a piece, or synecdoche, of the house that once sat upon the empty lot. In a more complex series of images, it also metonymically represents the waste it transports and the sewers to which it leads. Through relations of contiguity, but without Sobalvarro's directness, Chaves's poem represents his home's empty and decayed spaces. Chaves's indirectness skirts the feelings of disgust and rejection that chapter 3's texts elicit with their explicit portrayals of waste and the homeland's deterioration. Instead, Chaves's poetry remains on the surface of things and generally refrains from getting dirty. This chapter's second epigraph also helps to highlight the tonal and attitudinal differences between Chaves and the writers discussed in the previous chapter. While in Sobalvarro disillusionment and boredom lead the poetic I to thoughts of death and images of malodorous decay, Chaves's poetic speaker remains unmoved by his surroundings and simply reports his observations as he spies a dismantled house through a rusted hole in a metal fence ("Heredades") or a "temporary" family in a bar's mirror. "Leaving 'El Caracas,'" from the more recent *Chan Marshall* (2005), speaks in a more personal but still distant poetic voice about dissatisfaction with life, ennui, and a sense of alienation by describing the you's inability to connect with either "esta ciudad" [this city] or his family, who might as well consist of fellow bar patrons. The poetic I views alienation from others and home with no distress. He accepts the distance as a matter of fact and does not look for the "fissures" (Sobalvarro) that keep one separated from others. He is an onlooker, or bystander, uninterested in the place(s) and inhabitants before him, unwilling to invest himself but willing, however, to photograph and thus commemorate what he observes as he tours home.

At a distance, Chaves's poetic speakers position themselves as tourists in their own homeland. The tourist is a temporary other in a foreign locale. The images s/he comes upon are opportunities to photograph her/his temporary present. "¿Tan rápido llegó el 2002?" ["2002 Already?"], also from the award-winning *Chan Marshall*,[18] describes the passage of time, the loss of intimacy, and the distancing of family through short, (apparently) disconnected anecdotes told by a "tourist." The poetic speaker poses as an external viewer, not as a resident, of home as he rolls through images of daily life. From the beginning, the poem's context is delimited to an intimate but removed home space where interior and exterior sounds are easily confused and conflated:

El sonido de los refrigeradores
arrulla a las familias
y creen que es la lluvia
o vice versa.
Para los turistas,
esto que es tu casa
será un video amateur
de palomas que llegan a comer de sus manos.

[The sound of refrigerators
lulls the families (to sleep)

and they think it's the rain
or vice versa.
For tourists,
your house
will be an amateur video
of pigeons that eat out of their hands.] (1–8)

The first few lines set the action in a rainy, "modern" (refrigerators) place and introduce the reader to sleeping protagonists who, according to the second half of the stanza, are photographable. The poetic speaker moves easily from an interior view of vulnerable, sleeping residents to an exterior one of peering, camera-wielding tourists. The back and forth movement between inside and outside, plus the inability to discern between the sound of rain (outdoors) and an appliance (indoors), form the foundation of the entire poem.

The exoticization of home via the poetic speaker's outsider position calls to mind the fact that tourism is a primary contributor to the Costa Rican economy and that Costa Rica's reputation as Central America's Switzerland—and "¡*Pura vida!*" ["Life to the core!"], a popular *tico* motto—is key to its allure.[19] Furthermore, the stock image of tourists feeding pigeons details the Costa Rican home's identity as tourist spot and also speaks volumes about the poetic I's view of, and relationship to, the homeland.

Photogenic Costa Rica attracts photo-hungry tourists.[20] In Chaves's poems, however, that allure does not manage to captivate its national citizens. The poetic speaker's close-ups of compatriots' personal lives depict imperceptive, isolated people who lack deep relationships with or understanding of their home. Instead, Costa Ricans, including the poetic speaker, play specific and limited roles in the homeland. Their lives are like a film in which they play only extras, as the third stanza reads:

Del cine salen los electores
a vivir una película
en que todos son extras
y nada hay en eso de dramático,
como tampoco nada excepcional
en el charco de diesel tornasolado
donde los niños escupen para divertirse.

[Electors come out of the cinema
to live the movie
in which they're all extras
and there's nothing dramatic about that,
like there's nothing exceptional
about the iridescent diesel puddle
kids spit in for fun.] (15–21)

The poetic speaker imagines that his and his compatriots' experience as "electors" in Costa Rican society (and by allusion, democracy) holds nothing more substantial than do the films they watch at the cinema. For their experience as electors is only a celluloid performance, as is life in their un-dramatic homeland (18).[21] Again, in this image of ineffectual citizenship, Chaves's poetry contests hegemonic images of Costa Rican society, in this case specifically politics, and lumps Costa Rica together with its neighbors whose hold on democratic procedures is tenuous at best.[22] In fact, the poetic speaker hammers the point even further by emphasizing citizens' ultimate unimportance: they are not protagonists of their homeland nor even bit players but rather simply extras. For tourists, Costa Ricans are metaphorically mere pigeons flocking in plazas—nothing but photo opportunities and postcard images. In the stanza's closing lines, Costa Ricans, represented by the children, only "play" at modernization by spitting in the "diesel tornasolado" (20). As do the poor Managuan children who play in Lake Xolotlán, in their daily lives Costa Ricans view the residue of modernization from its outskirts. Even in Costa Rica, the living illustration of its less modern neighbors' potential, there is nothing "exceptional" (19). In short, Chaves takes agency away from his compatriots and belittles their role in their globalizing, democratic society.

The exterior view of family and home stands out in these two stanzas from "¿Tan rápido llegó el 2002?" In contrast, the poem's six other stanzas speak in the first person, and the poetic speaker integrates himself into his interlocutor's world. The second stanza, for instance, defines the people as a we who used to sleep without dreaming and whose feet touched as they slept: "No hace mucho tiempo / dormíamos sin soñar / mientras nuestros pies se tocaban" [Not too long ago / we slept without dreaming / and our feet touched] (10–12). The eleventh and twelfth lines quoted here appear again later as the poem's closing verses. The poem ends by revealing that the sleeping people who in the first stanza cannot differentiate the sound of rain from the hum of the refrigerator and who play the "natives" in tourists' videos used to share moments of physical intimacy and dreamless sleep. This loss of physical contact, repeated in many of Chaves's poems, bespeaks changes in interpersonal solidarity and community.[23] The calm, unperturbed sleep signals previously uncomplicated lives (primitives). This primitivity, however, may just be what the poetic speaker-tourist wants us to see, for the subjects of the video consider themselves and their world "developed" or "modern": "Sin duda los primitivos / encontrarían aquí un significado" [Undoubtedly the primitives / would find meaning here] (13--14).[24] Their modernity, symbolized by the diesel puddle (20), differentiates them from the so-called primitives that preceded them and draws a nuanced illustration of daily life in the poetic speaker's world. His is a world both of relative wealth (Costa Rica compared to its neighbors) and relative poverty (Costa Rica compared to the North).

Once the poet has undone the image of home as a welcoming place from which tourists keep souvenirs, the poem digs more deeply into the pasts of the house and its inhabitants. Unlike chapter 2's nostalgic poems, though, the revelations that fill Chaves's poems do not possess the same emotional and visual potency. Rather, they are quick snapshots with short captions that expose what lies behind front doors. For instance, in this poem's fourth stanza, the reader learns that the house of the poem's you no longer exists and that the family's mementos are also gone: "Allá donde fue tu casa / ya no está la foto blanco y negro / de la hija de un alcohólico" [Over there where your house was / the black and white photo / of the daughter of an alcoholic is gone] (22–24). The black-and-white photograph serves to hide the father's alcoholism and simplify complex family relations. The poetic speaker, intent on uncovering the "truth" about the you and the we, brings to light both the disease and the implications of living with an alcoholic father. His *paseo* through these lives amounts to a recounting of the ways in which daily life has marked the inhabitants and how, in turn, the inhabitants have attempted to leave a mark on the material world. The black-and-white photo, along with a carving on a tree, "tiene dos iniciales encerradas / en un poliedro / que debió ser corazón" [it has two initials / in a polyhedron / that should have been a heart] (26–28), recall past (loving) relationships and imperfectly drawn, permanent tattoos.

Narrating from afar, the poetic speaker then breaches the distance between himself and the subjects of his snapshots and re-enters the poem, moving from we to I. The poem's last three stanzas draw the reader further into a family's far-off quotidian reality in which even calling each other by name is as much an event as it would be in "esas películas para intelectuales" [those movies for intellectuals] (32). Again, film poetically represents home life, in this case those "intellectual" films in which protagonists' names, identities, or characteristics are not clearly depicted, spoken, or enacted. The family Chaves portrays is an other at home and in its interpersonal interactions. This silence and lack of communication is reiterated throughout and emphasized with this filmic comparison as well as in the following stanza:

> Herencia de mi madre es hablar poco,
> el resto no es culpa de nadie.
> Vivo en la que fue su casa
> como un turista
> y es mi padre ese señor
> que alimenta a las palomas.
>
> [Speaking little is inherited from my mother,
> the rest is no one's fault.

I live in what was her house
like a tourist
and that gentleman
feeding the pigeons is my father.] (33–38)

Finally, in the second to last stanza, the poetic speaker confesses that the videotaped house of the opening verses belongs to his own uncommunicative family and that the taped image of his father will be tourists' easily replicated and "authentic" souvenir. Chaves's representation of the tourists' way of seeing the poetic speaker's homeland coincides with one of sociologist John Urry's characterizations of tourist social practices:

> The tourist gaze is directed to features of landscapes and townspeople which separate them off from everyday experiences. Such aspects are viewed because they are taken to be in some sense out of the ordinary.... People linger over such a gaze which is then normally visually objectified or captured through photographs, postcards, films, models and so on. These enable the gaze to be endlessly reproduced and recaptured.[25]

The pigeon-feeding father, "es mi padre ese señor" (37), pulls the reader back to the first stanza's declaration that the you's house is the backdrop for the filming of pigeons eating out of tourists' hands. In the second mention of this stock Western tourist image, the father behaves like a tourist as defined by Chaves's poem and thus becomes a tourist. Even more strikingly, the poetic speaker also recognizes himself as a tourist in his own house, thereby reiterating the distanced view of home, house, and hearth. This purposeful separation between the protagonists (the I, the father, etc.) and the occupied, viewed landscape animates the movement away from "home" to an *elsewhere*. At the same time, the familial relationship between the different interlocutors and protagonists reminds us that the influence of heredity (and "natural" connections) cannot be completely discounted and that the inherited "hablar poco" [speaking little] (33) has historical and cultural consequences. By extension, family members' removed relationships represent their separation from their compatriots—the inexistence of solidarity locally[26] or of a sentiment of "horizontal comradeship."[27] Local and familial disconnections in the poem also demonstrate the mobility and instability of the roles of "native" and tourist and the changeable landscape that the globalizing home(land) is.

Chaves concludes "¿Tan rápido llegó el 2002?" by returning to the poem's opening words and images. He contradicts the mobility and changeability noted in the previous stanza by attempting to secure meanings and places in the closing lines. He tells the reader his family opts to believe that it is the rain, and not the refrigerator, that lulls it to sleep. Such a reading connotes a peaceful coexistence with nature that the rest of the poem questions and even denies. It recalls Belli's exilic view of

Costa Rica as "demasiado plácida" [too placid].[28] And as if to force this "placid" image of the family to be so, Chaves's poetic speaker insists, "pero es cierto / que dormíamos sin soñar / y que nuestros pies se tocaban" [but it's true / that we slept without dreaming / and our feet touched] (41–43). This ventured return to a more intimate and less chaotic past,[29] together with the recognition of the importance of inherited traits, lends the poem movement. It allows the meaning of home, defined as both a place and a sentiment of belonging, to shift around for its inhabitants. As surely as the closing lines try to draw disparate images together, the preceding stanzas resist "es cierto"'s (41) fixity.

Movement and change are apt ways to begin to see how Luis Chaves and other contemporary writers look *elsewhere* for a home to replace, overlap, and create a palimpsest over their geographical, national, and cultural homes that even in a globalized world remain put and at the same time continually shift. While the I and his family age, the house (or at least its parts) and memories of it remain (e.g., the toilet in "Heredades" and the initials on the family's tree). These visible, material remnants or synecdoches of the imagined or remembered whole can only be conjured fragmentarily. At the same time that they convince us of the homeland's solidity, they also convince us of its imaginariness. This paradoxical duality helps foster its inhabitants' experience of ambivalence. Patricia Yaeger writes about the precariousness of place. In reference to a reaction to the 1995 bombing of the Federal building in Oklahoma City, but with wider implications, Yaeger asserts that

> first, a sense that place is too brittle—that neither her apartment nor the surrounding city can be reproduced in real time or space; and second, an intimation that materiality is not just solid but also imaginary—that *place only persuades us because it is made out of reiterated stories and objects that produce a constant, pervasive sense of locatability* (italics added).[30]

In Chaves's poem the photographable aspect of the home—his father feeding pigeons—certifies the existence of the home from which the poetic speaker- and his father-turned-tourist distance themselves.[31] Thus are they granted the possibility of being in one place ("on tour" or "*de paseo*") and having yet another place where they are at home. As Pezzullo summarizes in *Toxic Tourism*, "[F]or the tourist, the existence of a home implies the possibility that a tourist is not *from there* and, therefore, can exercise the power to visit and to leave" (italics in original).[32] The poetic speaker and his father are able to gaze at the place they inhabit as if tourists or outsiders, rather than as residents or insiders. This freedom to change positions vis-á-vis their home robs them of stability but not of place. Home maintains its "pervasive sense of locatability."[33] The fact that being a tourist carries with it negative connotations stigmatizes Chaves's protagonists and poetic speakers. Conventional tourists themselves often want not to be perceived as such. As Dean MacCannell writes,

> [Tourists] are reproached for being satisfied with superficial experiences of other peoples and other places. . . . The tourist critique of tourism is based on a desire to go beyond the other "mere" tourists to a more profound appreciation of society and culture.[34]

In these poems, though, Chaves's poetic speakers and interlocutors are insiders who willingly take on the role of outsiders: "tourism and participation in the other modern alternatives to the everyday makes a place for unattached individuals in modern society."[35] Chaves's declaration that he inhabits his parents' home as a tourist releases him from ties that bind him locally. As a tourist, it is his choice to stay or leave. This choice is unburdened by the responsibilities of "natives." Unlike unattached figures we see in poems by Marta Leonor González, Susana Reyes, and others, however, in Chaves the unattached only pretend to be outsiders. They are not those who inhabit the social and economic margins. By choice are they outside and in search of a replacement home. MacCannell's characterization of tourism leads the reader to conclude that Chaves rebels poetically against the implication that, as nontourists, he and his compatriots should practice "profound appreciation"[36] of home and "know" their home better. Instead, many of his poems present poetic speakers who gladly live at a distance, as the opening lines of Chan Marshall's "Los otros" ["The Others"] illustrate: "San José no fue más / que luces a la distancia" [San José was no more / than lights at a distance] (1–2). In this touristic look from afar at the place of residence (San José, Costa Rica) and at family, Chaves's poetic speakers sightsee. Their tourism helps them organize and glimpse their own lives "as an orderly series of formal representations, like snapshots in a family album";[37] or, in *Asfalto: un road poem*'s terms, as "Todo en pasado, recuerdos, como video clips extranjeros" [Everything in the past, memories, like foreign video clips] (26) rather than as their own lived and felt quotidian experiences.

Chaves's poetic speakers and protagonists accept and cynically enjoy their touristic experience of home, the place they "should" know. Meanwhile, other writers' texts portray the alienation from home more viscerally and less rationally or intellectually. In Chaves's poems discussed earlier in this chapter, subjects in relation to the geography of home, people, and place are unfixed and mutable. The reader witnesses movement away from belonging *here* to existing in an *elsewhere* whose geography is unclear. Salvador Canjura's 1997 short story, "El vaho" ["Fog"], from *Prohibido vivir* [*Living Prohibited*], imagines this *elsewhere* as a frightening experience of dislocation or misplacement ("extravío").[38] In "El vaho," Canjura (El Salvador, 1968) visualizes a city that is untourable. It can easily be read as San Salvador or any other Latin American city in the "tropics" (62), populated by plazas honoring long-forgotten national heroes, a National Theater, billboards (69), coffee shops (70), and train service (70-71). The city is a recognizable urban space that slowly disappears under an enveloping fog and icy cold air. The fog functions as the parchment of a palimpsest: the underlying city becomes the almost effaced manuscript. Eventually the fog, as text, replaces the city's landmarks. Its people are left to read and navigate their home without them. They become unwilling urban tourists in a newly illegible geography. In turn, the city itself risks losing its place-ness, its solidity, as it becomes locatable only through its inhabitants' memories.

Canjura's protagonist, a real estate agent named Ricardo, does not pay attention to the fog until the day he climbs into his car and visibility is less than thirty feet (62). Unlike Hernández's protagonists, who suffer from and then glory in their homeland's catastrophic "tropical rain," Ricardo and his fellow citizens are unable to fulfill their daily obligations because of the omnipresent fog that eventually makes the city impassable (67). The only one able to navigate the city is an old blind man who uses his sense of hearing to orient himself. The rest of the citizenry travels blindly through the city, fearful of running into traffic or into a wall (65) and arriving at their destinations only by stroke of luck (68). When Ricardo first encounters the blind man, who is nameless throughout the story,[39] he is fascinated by his ability to find his way where sighted people cannot. In fact, Ricardo follows the blind man unaware that the object of his fascination knows he is being followed. Soon Ricardo becomes the blind man's companion as he takes one last walking tour of the city: "Como ya le he dicho, desearía caminar por algunas calles, entrar a unos cafés y edificios de los que guardo muy buenos recuerdos. ¿Podría hacerme el favor de ir conmigo?" [As I've told you, I'd like to walk through some streets, go into a few cafés and buildings of which I have some fond memories. Can you indulge me and come along with me?] (69).

Most interesting about Canjura's story are some narrative details that highlight its connections to this chapter's poetry. Ricardo is a real estate agent who reacts to the blind man's request for companionship: "Ricardo pensó en su empleo, en el absurdo de presentarse en la oficina. '¿A quién le interesan los bienes raíces en este momento?'" [Ricardo thought about his job, about how absurd it would be to show up at the office, "Who's interested in real estate right now?"] (70). Ricardo sells property, which now that the fog has blanketed the city only the blind man can locate. The irony of this is not that the blind man can "see" with his ears. Rather, Ricardo, who as a realtor should have little trouble guiding himself around the city, can no longer find the houses he must sell in order to earn a living. He cannot even find his own way home. Even before the fog finds its way indoors, it incapacitates Ricardo and his fellow citizens. Upon the blind man's departure for his daughter's home, Ricardo stumbles through the city like a robot. Somehow he makes his way home. By next morning, once the fog has swallowed his home (71), Ricardo has lost all sense of locatability. He cannot escape the power of the feeling of "extravío" [misplacement] (71) that torments the city's inhabitants. This "misplacement" leads Ricardo to a clearly desperate decision and radical action: self-mutilation.

Believing that only blindness can save him from the overwhelming sensation of disorientation and from the urban chaos rendered by the fog, Ricardo turns off the light and calmly gouges out his now useless eyes (70). Such a drastic solution points to the significance of locatability and belonging in and to a place, a home, a refuge. In "El vaho" the loud bustling chaos of cities like San Salvador, Managua, or San José is at the same time hushed and heightened by the all-encompassing, blinding fog. The protagonist's self-mutilation shocks the reader. Perhaps, though, the severity of it and its permanence is realistic in the story's world: "Todos estamos ciegos ahora, Ricardo—dijo el anciano—el problema es que nadie quiere aceptarlo" [We are all blind now, Ricardo—said the old man—the problem is that no one wants to accept it] (68). This literal and figurative blindness relocates the I and you away from home. For Ricardo, the removal of his own eyes promises an end to the fog's oppression.[40] It also promises to develop other senses that will allow him to get his bearings as he travels through the city. By mutilating himself, Canjura's protagonist strives to *become* the old blind man and survive in his transformed city by recreating a mental map of home, memories of the geography of home, and feelings of belonging that evaporate with the increasing fog (68, 70). The fog succeeds in making Ricardo's home strange, in distancing him from it while he still inhabits it. Unlike Chaves's poetic speakers, however, Ricardo desperately wants to save himself from impending doom and become an urban dweller like "el ciego" [the blind man], one who retains his home within him, in his bones. The blind man offers Ricardo hope to experience the city otherwise (not visually) and somewhere else (not as what it has visibly become). Canjura narratively presents the anxiety of misplacement that Chaves's unsentimental poetic speakers seem to elude.

The loss of "locatability,"[41] the irremediable "extravío" that Canjura's protagonist suffers when he can no longer *see* his home, is quite different from Chaves's poetic speakers who play sightseers, photographers, and videotapers of home. In both cases, though, home is a movable, shifting space, and place. Protagonists and poetic speakers are in search of alternative homes; homes unlike yet like the ones they inhabit every day. At their core both perceptions and representations of home and desire for an *elsewhere* are recognizable to the reader. For instance, Chaves's poetic speakers recognize parallels between the bar patrons and their families, and Canjura's protagonist knows that his city lies beneath the fog. At the same time, though, while they are located somewhere and locatable, these poetic speakers and protagonists position or place themselves nowhere. The sentiment of being nowhere impels them to look for another place that belongs to them and to which they belong.

The search for a place of belonging is dramatized briefly in Chaves's "Esperando el bus de regreso" ["Waiting for the Return Bus"], the closing poem from *Asfalto: un road poem*.[42] There the couple—whom we have accompanied on a tour of Costa Rica throughout the previous poems of the collection—wait for different buses to take them to their respective homes. In this final snapshot, as if to present both protagonists as mirror images engaged in the same activity separately and unbeknownst to each other, Chaves does not specify the subject:

> Viento en contra. Las manos en el bolsillo. Una juega con monedas de cien y cincuenta, el encendedor y dos clips que no recuerda cómo terminaron ahí. La otra, más pausada, busca algo que, por no ser un objeto concreto, nunca encontrará en ese lugar.
>
> [Upwind. Hands in pockets. One plays with a 100 (colón) and a 50 (colón) coin, the lighter and two clips, s/he doesn't remember how they ended up there. The other, moving more slowly, looks for something that, because it isn't a concrete object, s/he will never find in that place.] (67)

In this scene, narrated as stage directions, the you feels around for an intangible "it." Like Canjura's Ricardo, who owns a car, Chaves's protagonists have access to transportation home, but they do not know what home is or how to get there. Clearly, home or belonging is not geographically delimited, it is not "un objeto concreto" (67).

Throughout *Asfalto*'s prose poems, a third person poetic speaker narrates the couple's progress across the Costa Rican homeland. This speaker privileges the reader to the traveling couple's distance from each other and from their surroundings as well as their reliance on pop music (mostly U.S. and British) to fill "la distancia sideral que los reunía" [the sidereal distance that brought them together] (5).[43] Adrift even as they travel through their own home, Chaves's couple sarcastically takes note of their lived experiences in that place. In a poem relating the couple's stay in a roadside motel, the poetic speaker notes, "Es la época del año que los entendidos llaman *estación lluviosa*, porque invierno es un término demasiado primer-mundo para esta parte del planeta" [It's the time of year those in the know call the *rainy season* because winter is too first-world for this part of the planet] ("Moteles, lluvia, trenes, etc." ["Motels, Rain, Trains, etc."], 19).

Even though Chaves's couple travels Costa Rica as tourists might (specific vacation spots are named), the two local vacationers demonstrate little enthusiasm. For example, in the opening poem "Macrocosmos a 90 kilómetros por hora" ["Macrocosm at 90 KPH"] the poetic speaker describes their emotional detachment and "silencio cósmico" [cosmic silence] (5). The contrast between our travelers and tourists is further emphasized later in a poem that narrates a stop by a fruit stand along the way. Our travelers get out of the car to stretch. The woman wanders over to the stand but walks away, the poetic speaker tells us, upon hearing the vendor's prices. She then blends in easily with the pale tourists looking at a scenic view. What makes her stand out from the foreigners is that she does not partake of the stand's tropical fruit. Neither does she share their awed reactions to the isthmus's "prodigious" nature. Instead, in "Todo esto será tuyo" ["All This Will Be Yours"], her assessment of the vista is simultaneously distant and melancholic:

> Algunos turistas, casi todos pálidos como los lugareños, se acercan, frutas tropicales en mano al mirador que ofrece la manida pero siempre portentosa vista panorámica de los valles y montañas centroamericanas (¡incroyable!, wonderful!, ¡cabrón, güey!). Ella, confundida entre los extraños, se inclina sobre la baranda de plywood, echa un vistazo allá abajo, al paisaje, y dice para sí unas palabras que la baja temperatura convierte en nubecitas transitorias:
> —La pregunta no es si algún día la vida será más justa con todo esto. La pregunta es si esto se lo merece.
>
> [Some tourists, almost all of them pale like the locals, with tropical fruits in hand, approach the scenic overlook with its well-worn but still prodigious panoramic vista of Central American valleys and mountains (incredible!, wonderful!, son of a bitch, dude!). She, confused amid the strangers, leans on the plywood railing, glances below at the landscape, and says a few words to herself that become fleeting clouds in the cold climate:
> —The question is not if one day life will be more just with all of this. The question is if it deserves it.] (53–54)

Like the pigeon-feeding father, "ella," an unrecognizable local among tourists, plays a tourist in her homeland. While she does express awe, she questions the value and future of the landscape in front of her. Although she is "there" viewing the place that both she and the tourists have traveled to survey, she makes no attempt to connect with it or to see it. She is incapable of being present for an in-person experience of the local nature of her homeland. This "natural" distance between the locals and their surroundings—as well as the devaluation of what tourists see as Costa Rican patrimony—is also noticeable midway through the "road poem." After picking up a hitchhiking *díllei* (deejay), in "Tres tripping tigres" ["Three Tripping Tigers"][44] and partaking of hallucinogens he offers, the car "brinca pesadamente" [jumps heavily] (27). The three Costa Ricans assume the cause to be a rock, a pothole, or a bottle. While the traveling companions do not give the incident a second thought, the poetic speaker ends his account of this leg of the road trip by saying, "Atrás arrollado sobre el asfalto, el cadáver de otra especie endémica en vías de extinción" [Behind them, run over on the asphalt, the cadaver of another endemic species on its way to extinction] (27). The touring *ticos'* disregard for their homeland echoes anthropologist Erve Chambers's retelling of a conversation with a Costa Rican counterpart: "He pointed out that many rural Costa Ricans fail to see the significance of these [national] parks in the same way as foreign visitors."[45] While tourists (and perhaps tourist guides) may think Costa Rica's natural places should be protected and preserved for posterity, locals may see them as places that should be "conquered" or exploited for economic growth.[46] Or, like Chaves's road trippers, locals may not appreciate their cultural and ecological value.

In the poetic images discussed above, local travelers exist separately from the places they observe and through which they travel. Chaves's "road poem" functions like a tourist brochure that invites the reader and viewer to imagine her/himself in a tourist destination:

> A lot of tourism leaflets suggest this deflection, this reversal of the gaze, by offering the would-be traveler advance images of curious or contemplative faces, solitary or in groups, gazing across infinite oceans, scanning ranges of snow-capped mountains or wondrous skylines: his own image in a word, his anticipated image, which speaks only about him but carries another name (Tahiti, Alpe d'Huez, New York). The traveller's space may thus be the archetype of *non-place*.[47]

The displacement experienced by Augé's tourist is mediated by images of the place visited. It allows the gazer to look at her/himself rather than inhabit the place. Augé uses the term "non-place" to describe spaces of transit (highways, airports, hotel chains, etc.), supermarkets, and even cable networks. He sees non-places as history-less spaces of "supermodernity" that intersect and are entangled with their opposite, "anthropological places." As do Augé's would-be travelers, Chaves's locals know their homeland has "remarkable feature[s]"[48] but they do not care to connect to the places they visit or with the local residents they encounter. As they traverse the homeland by car they are content in "the mere knowledge" of their homeland's "prodigious" nature, satisfied to remain in the "space of non-place," which "creates neither singular identity nor relations; only solitude, and similitude."[49] The interactions of *Asfalto's* road trippers with their compatriots are limited to their drug-infused encounter with the hitchhiking *díllei* and her brief flirtation with this same companion. Both interactions represent the couple's efforts to inhabit alternate places. By the end of their trip, *Asfalto's* travelers have not connected with each other or with the homeland they traverse. Even more, they have failed to appreciate their homeland's difference; the difference that makes it, and them, photographable. As they tour home together they find themselves alone, distant from each other and from their road trip experience. Similarly, in Canjura's short story, Ricardo struggles against the fog that has erased the landmarks that mark the city's distinctive, or in Augé's terms, anthropological, places.

The narrowing of differences between individuals and places may be necessary for the successful entry of Central American countries into the globalized world touted by such figures as Costa Rica's Óscar Arias Sánchez and other ardent proponents of CAFTA-DR. As noted at the beginning of this chapter, it is Costa Rica's perceived similarity to the United States and other countries of the North that have given it the upper hand in international business. At the same time, the isthmus's progressive preparation to participate more fully and more equally in globalization is replacing, absorbing, and covering up its places that make it a Costa Rican, Nicaraguan, or Salvadoran home. In part, what writers like Luis Chaves and Salvador Canjura contemplate is the result of this leveling off of their homeland's physical and human geography. Their texts highlight the distancing of the poetic speakers and protagonists from the places they inhabit, severing the sense of belonging *somewhere* and leaving them *extraviados* (misplaced) and in search of an *elsewhere*. An *elsewhere* that could be called "home," but is now just another tourist option among many.

The purposeful, metaphorical blindness displayed in Chaves and Canjura is an intermediary positioning between local tourists skimming the surface of the homeland and life in media images that we will see in the next chapter. In chapter 4, Central Americans view home from afar, mingling and becoming interchangeable with and confused among visiting, camera-toting tourists. They take for themselves the tourist's prerogative of remaining unattached while they travel.[50] They experience home as just another (visited) locale that may make a good photograph or postcard image or anecdote. This aloofness vis-à-vis Central American homelands is heightened in chapter 5. There, poetic speakers and narrators create their identities from global images that distance them from a homeland that physically holds them in place. They transport themselves through these images to virtual, global everydays without ever leaving local homelands. They wrap themselves in a global "otherness" that protects them from local identities that threaten to tether them down, "porque uno está caído en tierra / pero no sembrado" [because one is fallen on earth / but is not planted] (2–3).[51] The rootlessness and unlocatability of an *elsewhere* sought out by traveling locals in this chapter is found virtually in chapter 5.

NOTES

1. Amy Barrett, "Costa Rica: Cultural Similarities Make It an Outsourcing Favorite," *BusinessWeek*." February 13, 2009. http://www.businessweek.com/print/smallbiz/content/feb2009/sb2009029_672165.htm (accessed July 8, 2009).

2. Ibid.

3. Ibid.
4. See http://www.costaricaisit.net/portal/page/menucostaricaisIT/whycostarica.html.
5. Arias Sánchez was president of Costa Rica for a second time from 2006 through 2010. He also held the presidency from 1986 to 1990.
6. Óscar Arias Sánchez, cited in "Boletín de la Cámara de Tecnología de Información y Comunicación": http://www.camtic.org/boletinclic/detalle.php?id_item=572&boletin=65.
7. Costa Rica is the only Central American country in which the ratification process involved a long negotiation with the populace. The free trade agreement was put to a popular referendum and approved by over half the voters in October 2007. See Costa Rica's *El País* for details: http://www.elpais.com/articulo/internacional/Costa/Rica/aprueba/ratificacion/TLC/EE/UU/elpepuint/20071008elpepuint_4/Tes.
8. Carlos Cortés, *La invención de Costa Rica y otras invenciones* (San Jose: Editorial Costa Rica, 2003), 39.
9. The 1948 abolition of the military is a major point of pride and used as proof of Costa Rican distinctiveness.
10. Giovanna Giglioli, "¿Mito o idiosincrasia?: Un análisis crítico de la literatura sobre el carácter nacional," in *Identidades y producciones culturales en América Latina*, comp. Marta Salvadora (San Jose: Editorial de la Universidad de Costa Rica, 1996), 168, 169.
11. Ibid., 167, 170.
12. Ibid., 202.
13. *NICA/ragüense*, dir. Julia Fleming and Carlos Solís, 2005, DVD. For an analysis of and response to Costa Rican exceptionalism by Nicaraguans living in Costa Rica, see Carlos Sandoval García's *Otros amenazantes: los nicaragüenses y la formación de identidades nacionales en Costa Rica* (San Jose: Editorial de la Universidad de Costa Rica, 2002).
14. Cortés, *La invención de Costa Rica*, 40.
15. Rosanna Reguillo, "Latin America: A Story in Three Movements," *Radical History Review* 89 (Spring 2004): 42.
16. Arias Sánchez, cited in "Boletín de la Cámara de Tecnología de Información y Comunicación."
17. In the past couple of years, Chaves has published two books of prose, *300 páginas: prosa* [*300 Pages: Prose*] (San Jose: Ediciones Lanzallamas, 2010) and *El mundial 2010—apuntes* [*Notes on the 2010 World Cup*] (San Jose: Editorial Germinal, 2010), and two more of poetry, *Monumentos ecuestres* [*Equestrian Monuments*] (San Jose: Editorial Germinal, 2011) and *La máquina de hacer niebla* [*The Fog Machine*] (Seville: Ediciones de la Isla de Siltolá, S. L., 2012). Chaves also blogs at http://www.luischaves.com/
18. Luis Chaves, *Chan Marshall* (Madrid: Visor Libros, 2005). Chaves won the III Premio de Poesía Fray Luis de León with this poetry collection. Winners of this award (given by the Diputación de Cuenca) win a cash award (15,000 euros in 2011) and are published by Visor Libros (Madrid). The title of the collection is the stage name of U.S. indie-rock singer and songwriter Cat Power and includes a list of explanatory notes about some of its musical references. *Chan Marshall* is divided into three sections: "Fallas de origen" ["Manufacturer Error"], "Grandioso bingo (ventitrés fragmentos)" [Grandiose Bingo (Twenty-Three Fragments)], and "Bonus Track." The second and third sections include only one text each.
19. Costa Rica is a "world leader in ecotourism" and also attracts "'3S tourism'— shorthand for sun, sea, and sand." John Davenport and Edward L. Jackiewicz, "Spaces of Tourism" in *Placing Latin America: Contemporary Themes in Human Geography*, ed. Edward L Jackiewicz and Fernando J. Bosco (Lanham, MD: Rowman & Littlefield, 2008), 101, 106.
A casual observer might notice as s/he flies to San José that most fellow travelers are from the United States or other foreign countries. When flying to San Salvador or

Managua the case tends to be different: the overwhelming majority of fliers are immigrants (and their foreign-born children) returning home to visit family and old friends.

20. In "Spaces of Tourism," Davenport and Jackiewicz also comment on newer areas of cultural urban tourism, including metropolitan centers for sex tourism and "to gaze on the region's vast impoverishment" by paying for guided tours through shantytowns (e.g., through Rocinha, a favela in Rio de Janeiro) (108). There are hotels in the cultural center of San José known as friendly to sex tourists. Prostitution is legal in Costa Rica, but pimping is illegal. The Costa Rican police aggressively patrol area schools in response to harassment of schoolchildren by pedophilic sex tourists. In 2004, the tourist industry, along with children's rights organizations, spearheaded a national campaign to spread the message: "No es buena idea ayudar a los turistas a buscar menores para tener sexo" [It isn't a good idea to help tourists find underage people for sex]. A private foundation, Paniamor, teaches tourism workers about sexual exploitation and how to denounce sexual tourists searching for children, "Costa Rica contra el turismo sexual" (June 20, 2004) in *BBCMundo*: http://news.bbc.co.uk/hi/spanish/misc/newsid_3823000/3823817.stm.

21. Chaves's portrayal agrees with Gioconda Belli's of Costa Rica as too placid to inspire expressive passion (chapter 1).

22. A case in point is the June 28, 2009, Honduran military coup against elected President Manuel Zelaya.

23. In her essay "¿Mito o idiosincracia?," Giglioli contradicts the accepted view that *ticos'* isolation is a positive character trait. She faults *ticos* for not fostering feelings of solidarity among each other, "pobre en sentimientos de solidaridad" [poor in sentiments of solidarity] (193).

24. With Mary Louise Pratt's "contact zone," a space in which peoples encounter each other "usually involving conditions of coercion, radical inequality, and intractable conflict," the reader can conceptualize the strained contact among locals and between locals and tourists that Chaves portrays. Mary Louise Pratt, *Imperial Eyes: Travel Writing and Transculturation*. (New York: Routledge 1992), 6.

25. John Urry, *The Tourist Gaze: Leisure and Travel in Contemporary Societies* (London: Sage Publications, 1990), 3.

26. Giglioli, "¿Mito o idiosincrasia?," 193.

27. Benedict Anderson, *Imagined Communities: Reflections on the Origins and Spread of Nationalism*, rev. ed. (London: Verso, 1991), 7.

28. Gioconda Belli, *El país bajo mi piel* (New York: Vintage Books, 2003), 199.

29. Such a static image of the homeland also alludes to the tourist's practice of collecting signs. Urry cites Jonathan Culler on this practice, "tourists are fanning out in search of the signs of Frenchness, typical Italian behavior, exemplary Oriental scenes" (3). Jonathan Culler, "Semiotics of Tourism," *The American Journal of Semiotics* 1 (1981): 127.

30. Patricia Yaeger, "Introduction: Narrating Space," in *Geography of Identity*, ed. Patricia Yaeger (Ann Arbor: University of Michigan Press, 1996), 20.

31. This sentiment recalls Didion's conceptualization of and reaction to El Salvador in *Salvador*. See introduction.

32. Phaedra C. Pezzullo, *Toxic Tourism: Rhetoric of Pollution, Travel, and Environmental Justice* (Tuscaloosa: University of Alabama Press, 2007), 33.

33. Yaeger, "Introduction," 20.

34. Dean MacCannell, *The Tourist* (New York: Schocken Books, 1976), 10.

35. Ibid., 15.

36. Ibid., 10.

37. Ibid., 15. Another example of Chaves's use of photography to represent unintimate daily family life is the two-line poem from *Chan Marshall*, "México D.F.": "Esa foto donde ninguno sonríe: / ¿quién nos creerá que fue de la época buena" [That photo where no one smiles: who'd believe it was of the good times?].

38. Salvador Canjura, *Prohibido vivir* (San Salvador: Istmo Editores, 2000). Canjura recently published his second short story collection, *Vuelo 7096* (San Salvador: DPI, 2012). He also maintains a blog: http://tierradecollares.blogspot.com/.

39. Note the similarity to Chaves's suggestion that being named is out of the ordinary ("¿Tan rápido llegó el 2002?").

40. Removing his eyes can also be read as a metaphor for dealing with state repression.

41. Yaeger, "Introduction," 20.

42. Luis Chaves, *Asfalto: un road poem* (San Jose: Ediciones Perro Azul, 2006).

43. There is ample evidence in Chaves's poetry collections (*Historias Polaroid, Chan Marshall*, and *Asfalto: un road poem*) of music as the soundtrack to daily life and memories, "la música tonta que mi memoria agrega / como banda sonora" [the silly music my memory adds / like a soundtrack] ("1985/2002 [El tonto comprende poco, el necio comprende mal"] [1985/2002 (*Stupid Understands Little, Stubborn Misunderstands*)]) (*Chan Marshall*, 4–5). Along with the repeated use of film and photography, Chaves's poetry is full of musical references. A case in point is *Chan Marshall*, in which Chaves riffs on songs by Cat Power, Gary Glitter, and cover band Dr. Elephant; he also translates an "unreleased" Chan Marshall song.

44. Note the allusion to the tongue twister and, perhaps, to Cabrera Infante's *Tres tristes tigres* [*Three Trapped Tigers*] (1967).

45. Erve Chambers, *Native Tours: The Anthropology of Travel and Tourism* (Long Grove, IL: Waveland Press, 2000), 74.

46. Ibid., 74–75.

47. Marc Augé, *Non-places: Introduction to an Anthropology of Supermodernity*, trans. John Howe (London: Verso, 1995), 86.

48. Ibid., 97.

49. Ibid., 97, 103.

50. MacCannell, *The Tourist*.

51. Juan Sobalvarro, Untitled, *Unánime* (Managua: Nuevo Signo Fondo Editorial INC, 1999).

FIVE

Almost Home

Central America in a Virtual World

Pero todo está claro.
El volumen ensordecedor es lo único
que nos obliga a acercarnos.

[But everything is clear.
The deafening volume is the only thing
that forces us to get closer.]
—Chaves, "La máquina de hacer niebla"

Becoming a tourist at home is a self-distancing ploy that allows texts and their narrators to continue to portray home with their feet still touching its soil or concrete. By maintaining and/or recognizing the "soil" underfoot, or by hearing the sound their feet make on pavement (Canjura), the texts in chapter 4 do not completely uproot themselves as they search for other places to inhabit. The conscious awareness of staying put but not belonging to or no longer perceiving home as home counters the ubiquitous imagery of roots in meditations on national and cultural identity. As Liisa Malkki observes, descriptions of refugees' experience are commonly arboreal or botanical: "people are often thought of, and think of themselves, as being rooted in place and as deriving their identity from that rootedness. The roots in question here are not just any kind of roots; very often they are specifically arborescent in form."[1] As members of a homeland "tree," a genealogy, individuals are tied to their place of birth because this tree "evokes both temporal continuity of essence and territorial rootedness."[2] And while the poets and writers discussed in this and the previous chapters are not political refugees, they do live in the homeland as uprooted or transplanted noncitizens[3] with "[v]iolated, broken roots signal[ing] an ailing cultural identity and a damaged nationality":[4]

> Ni este lugar me pertenece
> porque uno está caído en tierra
> pero no sembrado
> y adónde te llevan, los años,
> tus colegas. Nadie te conoce.
> No hay casa para el hombre
> sólo amenaza.[5]
>
> [Not even this place belongs to me
> because one is fallen on earth
> but is not planted
> and where do (they) take you, the years,
> your colleagues.
> No one knows you.
> There is no house for man
> only threats.] (1–7)

In this untitled poem from his 1999 poetry collection, Juan Sobalvarro's poetic speaker denies belonging to the land he inhabits (2) by differentiating between "caído" [fallen] and "sembrado" [planted]. "Fallen," he lies on a specific "tierra" [earth, land, or soil], yet is not "planted" there with any sense of permanence.[6] Outside forces manipulate and relocate him, "y adónde te llevan" (4). Regardless of where he lands, he is certain that he remains homeless, "no hay casa" (6). This Sobalvarro poem recalls and contradicts César Vallejo's "XXVIII," *Trilce* (1922).[7] Imagining a meal that will never be because his mother is gone and there is "nonada"[8] to eat and nowhere to eat it, Vallejo's poetic speaker laments the loss of home and family. For Sobalvarro, setting the table and sharing a meal (8, 10), for which Vallejo's poetic I desperately yearns, does not create the sentiment of belonging. Vallejo wishes his dead mother were there to ask him to take a seat and eat, but in Sobalvarro's post-conflict Nicaragua that is a useless, unproductive desire to have. He writes:

> Pero uno que es incómodo
> que no quiere el asiento
> ni que le sirvan comida,
> ni saluda porque da pereza
> —y nada se pierde y ni sirve de algo (saludar)—.
>
> [But one who is uncomfortable
> who doesn't want a seat
> nor to be served food,
> and who can't be bothered to greet anyone,
> —and nothing is lost and it's no use (to greet anyone) —.] (19–23)

These lines express certainty that sitting at the dinner table and greeting those around you is useless. They contradict the assumption, as iterated by Vallejo in "XXVIII," that home and family are spiritual sustenance. They contradict the assumption of the hearth as welcoming. Sobalvarro's poetic speaker instead refuses to plant his feet where he has landed or to integrate himself as a member of a (family) tree. In fact, unlike Canjura's protagonist and Chaves's local tourists, here Sobalvarro's poetic speaker wants to wander and remain unattached to (but in) Managua.[9] This free-floating, perhaps nomadic poetic speaker resists the feelings of belonging to home that political ideals (chapter 1), nostalgia (chapter 2), disgust (chapter 3), or even displacement (chapter 4) might arouse.

The life of the nomad, or of the "global soul" as Iyer puts it,[10] may be glamourized in a global world. But it is less tangible or concrete than that of lost local tourists searching for home in their pockets (Chaves) or beneath a dense fog (Canjura). In Deleuze and Guattari's parlance, the nomad inhabits an "open space," a space without obstacles, a space that is "localized" but not "limited."[11] This chapter's protagonists, narrators, and poetic speakers "do not want to leave. . . . They move while seated."[12] Rather than travel Deleuze and Guattari's steppes, deserts, and seas, they move (un)attached across a landscape unlike that of previous chapters. In the Central American texts I explore in this chapter, the homeland is a(n) (im)material landscape without limits, a background more celluloid, aural, or virtual than physical or material, "[M]iraba las imágenes que fluían por el techo corredizo como si ese agujero rectangular fuera un / televisor: la pantalla horizontal donde se transimitía un largometraje diferente al del parabrisas" [(He) looked at the images that flowed through the sun roof as if the rectangular hole were a / television set; the horizontal screen showing a different feature film from the windshield].[13] This poetic speaker speeding through the Costa Rican countryside is unable or unwilling to view his surroundings as different from the "orgasmic flow"[14] of media images that make up today's daily life. In the enclosed space of his car, Chaves's local tourist resides in a virtual place wherein the present is only a series of images played on a movie or television screen, a virtual world that may be more easily digested and livable than the tangible landscape, the "striated"[15] space of the roadway on which he is driving.

Using media to make sense of daily life at home and in the homeland is part and parcel of the effects of modernization on the formation of local and national identities.[16] Jesús Martín-Barbero, in an essay on culture industries and identities in Latin America, acutely posits:

> Whereas lettered cultures are associated with language and territory, electronic, audiovisual, and musical cultures go beyond this, producing new *communities* that respond to new ways of *being together*, of perceiving and narrating identity. We are facing new, less long-term

identities, more precarious but also more flexible, capable of amalgamating ingredients from very diverse cultural universe (italics in original).[17]

In Chaves and other writers, Martín-Barbero's distinct separation of lettered and current "electronic, audiovisual, and musical cultures" is not clear cut. Their texts blur the line between "lettered" texts and other media. Chaves's *Asfalto: un road poem* and earlier poetry collections integrate mass media into poetic discourses and demonstrate the blurring of different "universes" in the creation and writing of new, more flexible, and malleable identities in Central America. Thus, while the displaced poetic speakers and narrators of chapter 4 feel around for an *elsewhere* far afield from a home where they may anchor themselves, in the texts that follow poetic speakers and protagonists inhabit an electronic, audiovisual, virtual world.

Luis Chaves's poem "Ringside," from *Historias Polaroid*,[18] takes the reader to an *elsewhere* inhabited by his family and a television screen.[19] This television both encapsulates the family's reality while at the same time expanding its universe by connecting it to the diverse global culture of the 1970s. In the poem, which opens the poetry collection,[20] that diverse global culture is represented by the "Rumble in the Jungle," the historic boxing match that took place in Zaire (now the Democratic Republic of the Congo) in October 1974. George Foreman, the heavyweight world champion, was favored to beat the older Muhammad Ali. Ultimately, after Foreman tired himself out, Ali beat Foreman by knockout in the eighth round.[21]

Before arriving at the poem's surprise left hook, if you will, the poetic speaker sets the scene with a quotidian anecdote of a boy and his father watching a boxing match. As the poem develops, the parents are transposed onto the figures on the screen. Ali and Foreman and their bout become the televised version of the poetic I's home life.

> Fue la mejor pelea de Alí
> o de Cassius Clay, como él lo llamaba,
> negándose a aceptar
> su recién adquirido nombre musulmán.
>
> Ese negro levantaba los guantes
> y convertía el cuadrilátero
> en una pista de baile.
> Años después comprendí
> que ese fue mi encuentro inicial con la poesía.
>
> Entre el quinto y sexto round
> papá bajó su guardia por primera y última vez,
> sin dejar de ver la tv dijo:
> no me iba a casar con su mamá

aunque usted ya había nacido,
estaba enamorado de otra.

En el álbum familiar
tengo un viejo fotoposter de Alí
justo cuando noqueaba a Foreman en Zaire.
Es mi foto preferida de mamá.

[It was Ali's best fight,
or Cassius Clay, as my father called him,
refusing to accept
his newly acquired Muslim name.

That Black man would raise his gloves
and would turn a boxing ring
into a dance floor.
Years later I understood
that was my first encounter with poetry.

Between the fifth and sixth rounds,
Dad lowered his guard for the first and last time,
without looking away from the TV, he said:
I wasn't going to marry your mother
even though you had already been born,
I was in love with someone else.

In the family album
I have an old poster of Ali
just as he knocked out Foreman in Zaire.
It's my favorite picture of Mom.]

Following the action on the poem-screen, we too are ringside spectators of the "Rumble in the Jungle" and of the poetic speaker's active retelling of his virtual encounter with boxing and poetry. Here, as in poems discussed in the previous chapter, Chaves's poetic speaker plays a spectator, one who should be close enough to be spattered by the boxers' blood and sweat. But the poetic I does not focus on the violence of the boxing match. Instead, he watches Ali as he "dances" in the ring, surely sparring verbally with Foreman. For the poetic speaker, Ali is a poet gliding on the screen, "float[ing] like a butterfly and sting[ing] like a bee" (Muhammad Ali).

In the third stanza the poem's focus moves away from the fight as the father momentarily takes his mind, but not his eyes, off of the television and addresses his son. Perhaps, like Foreman between the fifth and sixth rounds, exhausted from throwing punches, the father gives the mother (read from the son's perspective as Ali) an opening. The image of the father we see in the first and second stanzas is one of a stubborn, perhaps prejudiced man. In the third stanza we come to know him as someone who, when deciding whether or not to abandon the poetic I's pregnant mother, chooses to behave conventionally—honorably in his context—instead of leaving her to marry the woman he is in love with. If in this analogy the father is Foreman, then the figure on the receiving end of the father's metaphorical punch, his revelation, is the poetic speaker. We do not see or hear him react, however, even though it seems to have been a secret.[22]

The poem's closing stanza, in which the poetic speaker celebrates his mother (Ali's championship) by telling us his favorite photo of her in the family album is a poster of Ali knocking out Foreman, complicates the entire poem's apparently simple anecdote. The mother as boxer makes visual the tension at home implied by the father's affirmation that he married the mother even though he did not love her. By imagining his mother as Ali, the poetic speaker empowers her (like Ali, she starts out as the underdog).[23] It also inserts her into a father-son activity. The poem's final image reimagines the poetic speaker's parents and his home. The poem's initial anecdote about a son watching a boxing match on television with his father becomes a commentary on the replacement of belonging at home with belonging in television and other media images. After all, the poetic speaker keeps a photo of Ali and Foreman, not of his parents, in his family album.

Despite its surface simplicity and everydayness, "Ringside" is formally complex. It conflates three diverse images viewed by the poetic speaker: he watches Ali beat Foreman; he observes his parents' marriage; and, he looks at a still of Ali's knockout punch. In each viewing, the poetic speaker remains outside the action. As in poems from the previous chapter, Chaves's poetic speaker does not act upon the landscape that surrounds him or contains him. Television (as appliance and medium) mediates the relationship between the two spectators. The father and son literally do not see eye to eye. Neither do they attempt to interact with each other. And yet the Ali-Foreman fight somehow impels the father's utterance, as if the fighters on the screen spur the father onward to explain his relationship with his wife to their son. The father's sudden statement pushes the poetic I to revisualize his progenitors' marriage and his and his parents' place in their family album and in family life.

The predominant image in the poem is of Muhammad Ali in the boxing ring, an image that enthralls both the poetic I and his father. As if to mitigate the effects of his father's opening up, the poetic speaker wraps the revelation in several layers of imagery that both diminish and heighten the importance of the moment. The foregrounding and layering of the Ali images on top of the father's disclosure highlights the poetic speaker's nearness to media images and his distance from his family. Like the life "sound track" that music provides in other Chaves poems, here the Ali-Foreman fight provides stand-ins for his parents and an imaginary home (the boxing ring). Chaves's poetic I creates an alternative space to inhabit that looks like a television screen and feels like home to him. In this television home, the poetic speaker can sit, watch, be entertained, and react to news of his parents' marriage without having to interact with the principal actors.

In the poetic I's quasi-tragic family situation, television is a habitable *place* that Jesús Martín-Barbero and Germán Rey have deemed

> un 'lugar' neurálgico donde en alguna forma se da cita y encuentra el país [Colombia], en escenario de perversos *encuentros* . . . entonces la televisión tiene bastante menos de instrumento de ocio y diversión que de escenario cotidiano de las más secretas perversiones de lo social, y también de imaginarios colectivos desde los que las gentes se reconocen y representan lo que tienen derecho a esperar y desear (italics in original).[24]

> [a neuralgic 'place' where the country (Colombia) somehow makes a date and meets, a scene of perverse *encounters* . . .thus television is less an instrument of leisure and entertainment and more the daily setting of the most secret perversions of the social, and also of collective imaginaries in which people recognize themselves and represent what they have a right to expect and desire.]

In "Ringside," television is the device that uncovers the "secretas perversiones" of the parents' relationship. Television provides the son with a device to assimilate his father's revelation. It allows him to respond, without seeming to, to his father's representation of his marriage by saving the fotoposter and using it to re-envision his mother's and father's relationship as Ali knocking out Foreman, "Es mi foto preferida de mamá" (19). The poetic I, like his mother in this and other poems, enacts his desire for an everyday home life away from home. In this case, home lies in memories of a television transmission and a mass-produced image of famous boxers. In turn, these images form the poem itself, attesting to his disclosure that "ese fue mi encuentro inicial con la poesía" (9). In the poetic speaker's home, television links family members and contextualizes memories of family life.

At the same time, the poem's appropriation of the story and imagery of the "Rumble in the Jungle" provides it with an alternative setting for the narration of a "home" story. The scene that the poem's speaker occupies straddles and blurs the local (that space in front of the television set) and the global (the international broadcast of the Ali-Foreman bout), thus creating an intermediary "glocal" space whose setting is nowhere. This nowhere represents the poetic speaker's desire to de-anchor himself from the place he inhabits and to re-place himself where he feels he belongs, somewhere that feels unattached and nowhere to him. As Martín-Barbero and Rey explain, television images effect changes in the ways in which viewers apprehend space and time:

Del *espacio*, profundizando el *desanclaje* que produce la modernidad por relación al *lugar*, desterritorialización de los modos de presencia y relación, de las formas de percibir lo próximo y lo lejano que hacen más cercano lo vivido "a distancia" que lo que cruza nuestro espacio físico cotidianamente (italics in original).[25]

[From *space*, deepening the *detachment* produced by modernity in relation to *place*, deterritorialization of the modes of presence and relation, of the forms of perception of the near and the far that make what's lived "at a distance" closer than what physically comes across us daily.]

This de-mooring from home while at home is facilitated by television and electronic media that make daily life seem virtual and the world on the screen seem like lived experience:

Como si lo que tenemos
cada día frente los ojos
fuera aquel viejo televisor coreano,
esperamos que aparezca en el borde inferior
el mensaje de *falla de origen* (italics in original).[26]

[As if what we have
in front of our eyes every day
were that old Korean television set
we expect the message *manufacturer's error*
will appear at the bottom of the frame.]

The consumption of mass media frames daily life and creates a skewed perception of it that causes it to lose its "realness" and become as virtual as the images on screen. The everyday thus becomes disposable ["desechable"] and gains the veneer of being resettable.

The inhabitants of this virtualized, disposable everyday exist between the physical space in which they live and the invented virtual one in which they "live." Their stance on the ground beneath their feet is not based on the reality of their home but rather on the "global" ground they are constantly (re)inventing as real. Their experiences of home, as well as of the global world, are ambiguous, untethered, in between. Theirs is a self-enacted de-mooring at home and an attempted mooring in a virtual world. Following Deleuze and Guattari in *A Thousand Plateaus*, this virtual Central American life is a nomadic existence on an electronic steppe with urban nomads looking for temporary shelter in the flow of an electronic assemblage that fascinates them.

One problem with this voluntary detachment from the local in favor of a nomadic existence is that it assumes the disappearance of the home and homeland that lies beneath the fog (Canjura) of globalization. It also fails to fulfill the desire, even if latent, for human connection, for intimacy with something other than a screen overflowing with electronic images. "Ringside" exemplifies both of these problems. First, the act of placing the Ali-Foreman fotoposter in his photo album demonstrates the poetic speaker's urge to hold home close and to recognize ties to something or someone beyond electronic images, even if those bonds are represented by mass-produced, global images. Second, the image of the boxers that the poetic speaker transposes over that of his parents neither disappears them nor erases his memory of watching the international boxing bout locally in his family's home. Despite his attempts, Chaves's poetic speakers cannot cast off their experiences of home and its *"fallas de origen"* ("Coda"), but they can and do find momentary refuge virtually.

In contemporary Central America where, historically, "cosmopolitan liberals'" worst fear has been not being up-to-date or stylish, this inhabited, disposable, virtual everyday is conjoined to disposable identities.[27] One result of this junction is the constant desire of elites to inhabit a verifiably global isthmus, "nuestros políticos suspiran por ver a Costa Rica [read Central America] globalizada" [our politicians yearn to see a globalized Costa Rica].[28] This desire aids in the proliferation of images of globality *in situ* surrounded by the impoverished majority, as Sobalvarro so graphically depicts in his representations of Xolotlán's lakefront and Managua's cosmetic modernity. This spread of global and globalizing images, the invention of blurred, grainy alternative identities and homelands are tightly connected. Eunice Shade (Nicaragua, 1980) uses photography to illustrate the artifice employed by the Managuan intelligentsia to invent more attractive and global, less provincial identities. In "Tal vez 1600 Asas" ["Maybe 1600 ASAs"],[29] a short story about young, artsy Managuans who attend a photography exhibit and end the night by getting drunk and high at a local bar, Shade introduces protagonists looking for places to inhabit away from but without leaving home. Her well-traveled, well-read protagonists see their city as inadequate and thus consume foreign commodities to replace and invent global identities for themselves. Unlike Chaves's, Shade's re-creation of home drips with sarcasm and, perhaps, resentment. She explicitly portrays educated, "rickety" Managuans and mocks their desire to be something, somewhere, and/or someone else. Their search for belonging in a more cosmopolitan world harkens back to the nineteenth century when independent Nicaragua's earliest prose writers worked diligently to create in local intellectuals the sense that they were members of a much broader lettered community.[30] Shade's intellectuals wear their "inherited" "Creole nobility" (14) as badges of honor, proof of their elite status. This proof, however, must be updated periodically to reflect how the world defines elites.[31] As Kinloch Tijerino asserts, ideas about progress and social betterment, such as the myth that there are models of perfection for humans to follow ("mito del modelo o prototipo de perfección de la especie"), seduce Nicaraguans, lead them to "copiar los estilos de vida de las sociedades industrializadas del llamado Primer Mundo" [copy the lifestyles of the industrialized societies of the so-called First World].[32]

"Tal vez 1600 Asas" repeatedly portrays the allure of the foreign and the certainty of the local's inferiority. The story has five sections in which the reader is acquainted with the proclivities and limitations of Managuan intellectuals and artists. In the passage below, the narrator paints a telling picture of the dissembling intellectuals who attend opening night of a German-Nicaraguan photographer's (Josefina Kiesler) show disguised as hippies, rock stars, and revolutionaries:

> Las calles de Añil empezaron a llenarse de carros, todos lustrados y apretados. Desfiló raquítico el cuerpo letrado de Managua. La fotógrafa rubia estrechó manos periodistas, poéticas, pintoras, musicales. Algunos olían bien. Bañaditos y heladitos por el aire acondicionado. Según ellos herederos de la nobleza criolla. ¡Joder! Otros se encubrían de ropajes post- hippies- punk- rock- stars. Según ellos los herederos de Joplin-Ginsberg-Cobain-etc-. Tampoco faltaron los y las fans de Silvio Rodríguez, los dijes del Ché [sic], las camisas de Víctor Jara…la cultura fetichista managüense.
>
> [Añil's streets began to fill up with cars, polished and packed together. Managua's rickety learned preened. The blonde photographer shook journalistic, poetic, painterly, musical hands. Some smelled good. Bathed and cooled by the air conditioning. Heirs to Creole nobility, they like to think. Hell! Some covered themselves with post-hippy-punk-rock-star clothes. Heirs, too, of Joplin-Ginsberg-Cobain-etc. Abundant Silvio Rodríguez fans, Che charms, Víctor Jara shirts…Managuan fetishist culture.] (14)

Visually this panoramic snapshot severely criticizes the protagonists and their environs. The young Managuan intellectuals it captures inform the reader of the narrator's perspective on the narrated scene. The learned elite's attempts at cleaning ("bañaditos") and dressing ("se encubrían de ropajes") themselves up as iconic Latin American and U.S. figures stress their efforts to blur barriers between Managua's reality and the global imagery they hope to incarnate. The commingling of Latin American, or "local," and U.S., or "global," countercultural and revolutionary iconography stands out in a text set in Nicaragua, a nation with its own homegrown rebel icons. Florence Babb's book on postrevolutionary tourism interprets the recent popular consumption of Che images as a "safer, more remote, and non-Nicaraguan radicalism" as well as a more authentic pre-Pact Sandinismo.[33] But in Shade's cynical depiction of post-conflict Nicaragua, images of Che represent a decontextualized, inactive revolutionary ethos transformed into Managuan hipness. In fact, the Argentine, Cuban, and Chilean revolutionary figures that adorn Nicaraguan intellectuals' bodies represent fashion and consumption trends, not leftist politics.[34] Shade's fetish-carrying intelligentsia dodge the heroes whom Cardenal and others memorialize and come off as both obsessive and superstitious in their belief in the potential of iconic objects to transport them away from Managua's "tránsito escándaloso, gases tóxicos" [loud traffic, toxic gases] to the virtual "avenidas extranjeras" [foreign avenues] they imagine occupying (7). Their decontextualized fetish objects are backstage passes they hope will provide them access to a transnational elite whose identities are "global," or northern, not local. Further, the narrator subtly juxtaposes the urgency of the exhibit attendees to perform ultramodern-ness with the photographer's penchant for black-and-white photography. Kiesler refuses to relinquish her Leica M3 for a digital camera. The narrator explains the photographer's preference by alluding to various photojournalists and their pioneering documentary work. In particular, she focuses on photojournalist Raoul Shade's "realismo interpretativo" [interpretative realism] (16),[35] which posits that black-and-white photography "deciphers" objective reality,[36] to explicate Kiesler's own photographic philosophy. Thus readers are drawn to "sophisticated" aesthetic questions and away from the banal lives of "este peculiar círculo de celebridades" [this peculiar celebrity group] (20) that happened upon Kiesler's exhibit.

The story begins where Managua's local intellectuals began: Avenida Universitaria, a very busy avenue that travels between the National (Universidad Nacional Autónoma de Nicaragua—UNAN-Managua) and the Jesuit (Universidad Centroamericana—UCA-Managua) universities. According to the narrator, "Prescinde de fuentes y jardines imposibles, tiene en común con avenidas extranjeras personas divagando con mochilas y libros decorativos" [It does without fountains and impossible gardens, what it shares with foreign avenues is people wandering around with backpacks and decorative books] (7). Into the urban setting, the narrator incorporates street vendors, cab drivers, copy shops, and, most importantly, a (pricey) well-known bookstore, El Parnaso. It is here where the story's two principal characters meet for the first time: Martín Mulligan (of Irish-American descent) and Fiorella Cassirer (of Italian descent). Martín is a graduate student and "Poeta"[37] back home in Managua before he returns to France to complete a dissertation on Arthur Rimbaud (20–21). Fiorella is a "reader" (22) and an avid admirer of two of Nazi-sympathizer Leni Riefenstahl's most controversial films, *Triumph of the Will* and *Olympia* (12), a fact she only reveals after several drinks and hits of PCP-laced marijuana (25). Martín is also planning a trip to New Delhi to "rediscover" Rimbaud[38] and take photos with a camera from his school days. They meet again when each, independently of the other, decides to attend "Mitos humanos de Josefina Kiesler" ("Josefina Kiesler's Human Myths") after reading the exhibit announcement in the newspaper. The exhibit and its aftermath form the core of the short story.

In the third and fourth sections of the story, Shade portrays a cast of *intelectualoides* [so-called intellectuals] engaged in one-upmanship, petty arguments, illicit drug use, and sex. As the purveyors and defenders of Managua's "cultura fetichista" (14) arrive at Galería Añil, the reader hears the debates over Kiesler's photography and listens to the intelligentsia's many disagreements about Nicaraguan art. The opening reception's presenter (Natalia Orange, "esthete") and a documentarian (Tamara Montenegro) argue about the aesthetic value of Kiesler's work. Tamara, famous for films on indigenous peoples, argues that "no podés obviar la tecnología, es inútil" [you can't ignore technology, it's useless] (14). In response, Natalia defends Kiesler's right to produce "trabajo artesanal" [artisanal work] (14) which to some—like the documentarian—does not constitute art. Later this "intellectual" debate about the aesthetics of digital media devolves into a bar brawl between Tamara and Josefina (26).[39] Because "en el fondo todos preferían el relax" [deep down they all preferred to hang out] (27), the fight does not stop the party. The night of debauchery progresses, and the narrator constructs the Nicaraguan learned as petty dabblers in cultural issues, a portrayal that diametrically opposes the prevailing image of Central American writers' serious political commitment to their homelands. The "cat-fight," idle gossip, and drugged sexual encounters mock renowned Nicaraguan literati whose exploits before and during the Sandinista revolution and regime are important elements of dominant images of Central American authorship.[40]

In the midst of a meandering story of drunk, belligerent intellectuals, we also contemplate a couple of photographs taken by the German-Nicaraguan photographer that question the significance of "bruma" [fog], "sombra" [shadow], "distorsión" [distortion], "borroso" [blurriness], and "humo" [smoke] not just in photography but also in life in the city of Managua. As noted earlier, Kiesler's innovation is precisely her rejection of new, more technologically advanced ways of photographing. She remains committed to crafting her images in the "antiquated" dark room (17) and, as she screams at Tamara, "jamás renunciaría a su técnica por una propuesta vulgar como la de Kodak" [(she) would never give up her technique for one so common as Kodak's] (26). At her exhibition's opening, Kiesler describes her "modus operandi" (17) as focusing on three elements: "contrastes entre luces y sombras, la creación de espacios u objetos y en algunos casos la alteración técnica del contenido en la foto" [light and shadow, the creation of spaces and objects, and in some cases the technical modification of the content of a photograph] (17). Kiesler's emphasis on her role as photographer, or operator of the camera, and on the produced photograph evidences Susan Sontag's assertion that

> despite the presumption of veracity that gives all photographs authority, interest, seductiveness, the work that photographers do is no generic exception to the usually shady commerce between art and truth. . . . In deciding how a picture should look, in preferring one exposure to another, photographers are always imposing standards on their subjects.[41]

These reflections on photographic techniques, on the possibility of "representing" a subjectivity even in photographs, highlights Shade's "supuestos letrados del tercer mundo" [false Third World literati] (18) in their attempts to pose as cultured, globalized people. Kiesler wields the power of composition and representation unambiguously. We see this, for instance, in her artist's statement and in the instructions she gives the waiter who is cajoled into snapping a photo of the group at the local bar (31). But as Roland Barthes reminds us, photographic subjects also have agency. Barthes's reaction to being photographed elucidates the relation between Shade's protagonists' posing and photographer's photographing. He confesses, "I constitute myself in the process of 'posing,' I instantaneously make another body for myself, I transform myself in advance into an image."[42] In Shade's story, the protagonists work hard at forming saleable images of themselves, images that demonstrate their seduction by and consumption of globality. They are acutely aware that "Todos compran pasado y revenden futuro" [Everyone buys the past and resells the future] (7). But these posed images, like the two photos the narrator describes, are grainy and unfocused—snapshots of the protagonists' fleeting grasp of their local and virtual home places.

The first photographic image that appears is one of Kiesler's black and white photos of a woman staring intently at the Thames. The photo of a lone woman features an image antithetically "definidamente borrosa" [clearly blurry], "Una escala de grises; el blanco en movimiento del negro en cámara lenta endureciendo las arrugas grises" [A scale of grays: white moving from black in slow motion hardening the gray wrinkles] (18). It functions as a visual depiction of the shadowy, unfocused characters who live in Shade's provincial Managua. The aforementioned photo, the one Kiesler composes of the intellectuals after her fight with the documentarian, stresses the protagonists' "blurry" daily existence and identities. It communicates and commemorates the group's arrogant stance and temporary intimacy all "en el estilo de Robert Cappa (sic)" [in the style of Robert Capa],

> ligeramente fuera de foco, como si se desintegraran, aunque los bordes de sus figuras estuvieran delineados con precisión por el color negro que parecía fijar sus espíritus en el tiempo o en el papel fotográfico que ella [Josefina] revelaría en su cuarto oscuro días después.
>
> [slightly out of focus, as if they were disintegrating, although the borders of their figures were outlined with precision in black which seemed to fix their spirits in time or on the photographic paper that she (Josefina) would develop in her dark room in the coming days.] (32)

The comparison to Capa is intriguing. While Capa is certainly known for the aesthetic detailed above, his legacy rests on war photography, his photos' "quality of immediacy ... by a participant taking his chances,"[43] and the intimacy his battlefield subjects reveal.[44] The concrete references in "Tal vez 1600 Asas" to Capa and other photojournalists challenge and foreground the unrooted, self-centered natures of the characters. The allusions to well-known photojournalists bring to mind photos of authenticity, whether of the events photographed or of the subjects and their sentiments. In contrast, the story's characters revel in artifice both in their appearance as well as their interactions with each other. In this sense, Kiesler's photo of the group's memorable night also exemplifies Sontag's reading of family photos: "As photographs give people an imaginary possession of a past that is unreal, they also help people to take possession of space in which they are insecure."[45] The photo's subjects position themselves as they hope to be read, with love in their eyes (Martín and Fiorella) or with looks of arrogance (the older male intellectuals) (31). They, as Sontag asserts, stake their claim on a desirable past and place. But the photographic image's lack of focus also betrays their insecurity. Besides "representing" (Barthes) in the photo, Shade's characters' bravura is bolstered and heightened by marijuana; they are "tocado[s] por la magia de la hierba" [touched by the magic of grass] (26). The photo's blurriness, in addition to the smokiness of the setting, signals the unstable ground on which the characters stand. The poses they assume—in their interpersonal interactions and in the photo—do not secure them to the ground that their feet touch but rather to an imaginary place they would rather inhabit. As Shade writes, in "Cosas raras de Pili, Mili y Lili" ["Strange things about Pili, Mili, and Lili"], a story from *El texto perdido* about superficial Managuans obsessed with U.S. pop music, movies, and "el chat," "Inventaban un estatus que no tenían, un dinero que no tenían, un estilo de vida inexistente en nuestro país" [They invented a status they didn't have, money they didn't have, a lifestyle that's nonexistent in our country] (73). Pili and Mili share with the *intelectualoides* the ardent desire to forget "el pecado de una identidad" [the sin of an identity] that signifies, especially to non-Nicaraguans, war and poverty (73). To escape this vision of their homeland and compatriots, Shade's characters attach themselves to global images in the hopes of distancing themselves from their unphotogenic homeland and of convincing the world of their globality.

This purposeful invention of virtual realities based on global media images or trends helps place texts outside of the local geography. The virtualization of daily life, or the transformation of media images into lived experience, not only tears at the connection between inhabitants and the homeland but also between inhabitants. In "Tal vez 1600 Asas," the marijuana and Chilean whiskey the Nicaraguan intellectuals ingest blunt their aggressive competitiveness and ease them into the "Jamaican" atmosphere—"electrifying" music and "floating" sensuality (25)—of the night. Thus soothed and entertained, they feel at peace and as if they belong that night and in that bar. As a Chaves poem set in a nightclub hints, however, such moments of belonging and connection are temporary constructions, poorly built bridges between the disconnected. "La máquina de hacer niebla" ["The Fog Machine"], from *Historias Polaroid*, illustrates interpersonal disconnections and the hollowness of belonging virtually or being virtually home:

> A dos centímetros de mi oído
> sus labios casi gritan
> "le hacés daño a la gente".
> La luz estroboscópica revela
> en acelerados intervalos
> la escencia tribal del baile.
> Las paredes vibran
> y desde un extremo del bar
> vemos películas de Tura Satana
> sin poder escuchar los diálogos.
> Una máquina hace niebla
> mientras busco mi defensa
> y ella se inclina hacia donde estoy,
> esperando ese argumento.
>
> [Two centimeters from my ear
> her lips almost yell
> "you hurt people."
> The strobe light reveals
> at fast intervals
> the tribal essence of the dance.
> The walls vibrate
> and from one end of the bar
> we see Tura Satana movies
> without being able to hear the dialogue.
> A machine makes fog
> while I think up my defense
> and she leans toward where I am,
> waiting for that argument.] (1–14)

Chaves re-creates the ambience of everyday (urban) living. The overload of sensory material is easy to imagine: too loud music, strobe lights, "tribal" dancing, vibrating walls, video monitors, artificial fog. It reverberates through the Tura Satana[46] films being screened. The images on the video screens go undescribed by the poetic speaker, but the reference to Satana brings to mind frenetic movement, violence, sex, death, and the performance of multiple gender and sexual identities. The arguing couple, though, sits immobile in the center of the poem and the nightclub. The argument's opening strain, "le hacés daño a la gente" (3), is put on pause as the poetic speaker fills in the background. The pause allows the reader to visualize, hear, and understand the couple's dynamics. During the pause, the poetic speaker tries to think up his "defense" (12). Meanwhile the woman moves nearer her counterpart in order to hear him. The setting for this potentially heated conversation questions the couple's interest in communication and intimacy. The constant movement and talking bodies amid a "foggy" space where it is hard to hear and speak and be heard concisely represents the Central American global experience. Far from the concrete city, Central Americans ramble nomadically through digital communities, unable to communicate even in the environment of global souls, a supposed "communication utopia." As Martín-Barbero writes,

> En la hegemonía de los flujos y transversalidad de las redes, en la heterogeneidad de sus tribus y la proliferación de sus anominatos, la ciudad virtual despliega a la vez el primer terrritorio sin fronteras y el lugar donde se avizora la sombra amenazante de la contradictoria "utopía de la comunicación."[47]
>
> [In flows' hegemony and webs' transversality, in tribes' heterogeneity and the proliferation of its anonymities, the virtual city simultaneously unfolds the first territory without borders and the place in which the threatening shadow of the contradictory "communication utopia" lies in wait.]

The experience of globality, as seen in Central American texts, is arrayed with more technical or electronic tools than before, but manifests fewer links between compatriots and less belonging in "real" life. In the foggy homeland of strobe lights and vibrating bodies, as in Chaves's and Shade's texts, belonging is standing alone in a crowd. The technological advances tasked with facilitating a borderless expanse of open global communication show their seams in unattached, displaced subjects. Physical proximity fails to draw together inhabitants of a virtual home. As the second stanza of "La máquina de hacer niebla" bears out:

> Pero todo está claro.
> El volumen ensordecedor es lo único
> que nos obliga a acercarnos.[48] (15–17)

The couple's forced nearness speaks volumes about the misplaced's inability to foster affection or sentiments of attachment and belonging. The artificially produced fog and deafening sounds blur the two immobile yet free-floating bodies. But the technology that surrounds and draws them closer cannot fabricate intimacy. It cannot root them except temporarily and insecurely.

Security and belonging are highly valued commodities in a globalizing Central America. Chaves's hipsters and Shade's *intelectualoides* outwardly disdain the homeland where they find themselves "fallen" (Sobalvarro), yet they continue to move toward each other in search of closeness. Intimates only virtually, via media images of iconic figures or posed snapshots, Central Americans like Chaves's and Shade's (poetic) narrators float randomly. With the homeland in sight, they choose to hover above it, simultaneously fearing and desiring to alight and find home, a home more real and risky than virtual.

NOTES

1. Liisa Malkki, "National Geographic: The Rooting of Peoples and Territorialization of National Identity among Refugees and Scholars," *Cultural Anthropology* 7, no. 1 (February 1992): 27.
2. Ibid., 28.
3. This use of arboreal metaphors is obvious in Claribel Alegría (chapter 1).
4. Malkki, "National Geographic," 34.
5. Juan Sobalvarro, *Unánime* (Managua: Nuevo Signo Fondo Editorial INC, 1999).
6. In fact, unplanted seeds remain dormant and may rot.
7. César Vallejo, *Trilce*, 2nd ed. (Buenos Aires: Editorial Losada, 1967)
8. "Nonada" is one of *Trilce*'s numerous neologisms. In "XXVIII," the term negates the presence of food in the poetic speaker's imaginary meal. It is a union of two negatives that adds to the list of "no"s in the poem.
9. The Managua from *Unánime*'s "Boceto desvelado de Managua" ["Sleepless Outline of Managua"], is unloved, "gritan que nadie quiere ciudad" [they scream that no one wants the city] (12), and nothing more than "un nombre de índole remota" [a name of a distant nature] (22).
10. Pico Iyer, *The Global Soul: Jet Lag, Shopping Malls, and the Search for Home* (New York: Knopf, 2000).
11. Gilles Deleuze and Felix Guattari, *A Thousand Plateaus: Capitalism and Schizophrenia*, trans. Brian Massumi (Minneapolis: University of Minnesota Press, 1987), 381–82.
12. Ibid., 381.
13. Luis Chaves, "Macrocosmos a 90 kilometros por hora," *Asfalto: un road poem* (San Jose: Ediciones Perro Azul, 2006), 5.
14. Allusion to Beatriz Sarlo. Jesús Martín-Barbero, "Identities: Traditions and New Communities," trans. Zilkia Janer, *Media, Culture, and Society* 24, no. 5 (2002): 638.
15. Deleuze and Guattari, *A Thousand Plateaus*, 381.
16. Benedict Anderson, *Imagined Communities: Reflections on the Origins and Spread of Nationalism*, rev. ed. (London: Verso, 1991). As mentioned earlier, Anderson explores in detail the pivotal role of newspapers in the formation of nationhood and national identities.
17. Jesús Martín-Barbero, "Transformations in the Map: Identities and Culture Industries," trans. Zilkia Janer, *Latin American Perspectives* 27, no. 4 (July 2000): 34.
18. Luis Chaves, *Historias Polaroid* (San Jose: Ediciones Perro Azul, 2000).
19. Recall Howard Cosell's role in *Bananas* as commented on in the introduction.
20. *Historias Polaroid*'s opening poem forms part of "Todo lo que no vuela" ["Everything that Doesn't Fly"] which itself forms about two-thirds of the collection. At the end of this book, Chaves tells the reader that the title is a variation of the lyrics of the Charly García song "Love is Love" from *La hija de la lágrima* [*The Tear's Daughter*] (1994). The second section of this poetry collection consists of prose poems and is titled "Documentos falsos" ["False Documents"].
21. For an in-depth look at this bout, see Leon Gast's award-winning documentary film *When We Were Kings* (1996).
22. In a companion piece to this poem in *Historias Polaroid*, "Nócaut" ["Knockout"], the son remembers the father's amateur boxing matches and his desire (unfulfilled) to be carried on his father's shoulders after a victory. The memory arises from a message left on his answering machine by his mother requesting a letter of reference for his father for a "cursillo religioso" (a short course on Christianity to train lay people to be

leaders in their congregations). According to the poem, a couple of snapshots and an old pair of boxing gloves are all the son has left from that time he shared with his father. All the father has is his son's willingness to write the requested letter: "De aquello a él sólo le queda / un hijo que escribe / una nota impersonal / y la envía por fax" [All that he has left is / a son who writes / an impersonal note / and faxes it] (15–18). Note the insistence on emotional and physical distance aided and abetted by technology.

23. To beat the younger, stronger Foreman, Ali used his "rope-a-dope" strategy. Ali allowed himself to be pushed up against the ropes, which helped him absorb Foreman's punches. When Foreman tired, Ali knocked him out.

24. Jesús Martín-Barbero and Germán Rey, *Los ejercicios del ver: hegemonía visual y ficción televisa* (Barcelona: Editorial Gedisa, 1999), 17.

25. Ibid., 24.

26. Luis Chaves, "Coda," *Chan Marshall* (Madrid: Visor Libros, 2005).

27. Magda Zavala, "Ciudades secundarias en la aldea global: desde San José de Costa Rica," in *Las ciudades latinoamericanas en el nuevo [des]orden mundial*, coords., Patricio Nava and Marc Zimmerman (Mexico City: Siglo XXI, 2004), 313.

28. Ibid., 315.

29. In addition to the collection in which this story was published, *El texto perdido* (Managua: Amerrisque, 2007), Shade also published a poetry collection in 2008, *Escalera abajo* [*Stairway Down*] (Managua: Editorial MA), and a collection of essays, *Espesura del deseo* [*The Denseness of Desire*] (Managua: Editorial Zorrillo) in 2012.

30. Bravo and Miranda write that in their "historia[s] patria[s]" [national histories] Tomás Ayón and José Dolores Gámez had the specific goal of "Crear en los educados la conciencia que pertenecen a una comunidad mucho mayor que las localidades donde viven" [Creating in the educated the consciousness of belonging to a much larger community than the local places where they live]. Alejandro Bravo and Nelly Miranda, "Literatura, identidad y conciencia nacional," in *Nicaragua en busca de su identidad*, ed. Frances Kinloch Tijerino (Managua: Instituto de Historia de Nicaragua, Universidad Centroamericana, 1995), 122.

In a broader context, Benedict Anderson asserts that it was "pilgrim creole functionaries and provincial printmen [who] played the decisive historic role" in the development of a "new consciousness" in the Americas (*Imagined Communities*, 65).

31. In his article on the development and endurance of authoritarianism in Central America, historian Acuña Ortega writes that the dominant and middle classes and *ladinos* share "una profunda alienación respecto de su propio entorno natural, histórico, social y cultural. Este llamado síndrome del 'homeless mind' parece ser un rasgo característico de tales sectores desde por lo menos hace más de un siglo y es posible que tenga su origen en los códigos de discriminación étnica elaborados en el periodo colonial" [profound alienation from their own natural, historical, social and cultural milieu. This so-called 'homeless mind' seems to have been characteristic of such sectors for at least the last century and it's possible that it originated in the Colonial period's codes of ethnic discrimination]. Osvaldo Acuña Ortega, "Autoritarismo y democracia en Centroamérica: La larga duración (siglos XIX y XX)," in *Nicaragua en busca de su identidad*, ed. Frances Kinloch Tijerino (Managua: Instituto de Historia de Nicaragua, Universidad Centroamericana, 1995), 551.

32. Frances Kinloch Tijerino, "Civilización y barbarie: Mitos y símbolos en la formación de la idea nacional," *Nicaragua en busca de su identidad*, ed. Frances Kinloch Tijerino (Managua: Instituto de Historia de Nicaragua, Universidad Centroamericana, 1995), 272.

33. Florence Babb, *The Tourism Encounter: Fashioning Latin American Nations and Histories* (Palo Alto, CA: Stanford University Press, 2011), 62. Also, see the introduction for a brief overview of the pact between Ortega's FSLN and the Liberal party.

34. In contrast, Babb finds that in postrevolutionary Nicaragua, Che images are "broad symbols of cultural and political opposition" (*The Tourism Encounter*, 62).

While Shade's intellectuals do hold themselves above and against local culture, their political positions are ambiguous.

35. Besides Raoul Shade, the narrator mentions several other photojournalists known for their war and street photography: Cartier-Bresson, Eugene Smith, Ara Guler, Brassai, Joseph Koudelka, Robert Capa.

36. Shade quotes Raoul Shade as theorizing that, "A diferencia de la fotografía a color, el blanco y negro no imita la realidad objetiva en su afán de precision, sino que la desentraña, porque es secundario su papel de reproducción fidedigna" [Unlike color photography, black and white photography doesn't imitate objective reality by attempting to be precise, it deciphers it because faithful reproduction is secondary to it] (16).

37. In Nicaragua, in particular, "Poeta" is an important yet often common honorific.

38. The perceived conceit of Martín's plans is duly noted by Nacho Oveja, the group's "periodista farandulero" [celebrity journalist] (18), "Atrasar su tesis Doctoral para encontrar a Rimbaud quién sabe donde [sic]...en los putales seguramente y en cantinas de mala muerte. ¡Qué Dios le ayude! Esta gente no entiende. ¡Cómo se le ocurre que el alma de un gran poeta va a estar esperándolo en semejante centros de corrupción! [To delay his doctoral thesis to find Rimbaud who knows where...surely in whorehouses and sketchy bars. May God help him! These people don't understand. How could he think that the soul of a great poet would be waiting for him in such centers of corruption!] (21).

39. The narrator's description of the two women's fight is stereotypical: "Ambas, como buenas gatas callejeras dieron inicio a un combate ante los ojos atónitos del resto...Pelos de punta, arañazos, gritos, mejillas sonrojadas y sudor" [Both of them, like good female street cats started combat before the amazed eyes of the group...Hair on end, scratches, screams, flushed cheeks, sweat] (26).

40. Gioconda Belli, Sergio Ramírez, and Ernesto Cardenal have all produced memoirs in which they commemorate their and their comrades' roles in the Sandinista revolution.

41. Susan Sontag, *On Photography* (New York: Farrar, Strauss and Giroux, 1977), 6.

42. Roland Barthes, *Camera Lucida: Reflections on Photography*, trans. Richard Howard (New York: Farrar, Strauss, and Giroux, 1981), 10.

43. Ana Winand, "Capa, Robert," in *Contemporary Photographers*, 2nd ed., ed. Colin Naylor (Chicago: St. Martin's Press, 1988), 155.

44. Max Weintraub, "Robert Capa," in *Encyclopedia of Twentieth-Century Photography*, vol. 1, ed. Lynne Warren (New York: Routledge, 2006), 239.

45. Sontag, *On Photography*, 9.

46. Satana is "Varla" in Russ Meyer's cult pornographic film *Faster, Pussycat! Kill, Kill!* (1965).

47. Jesús Martín-Barbero, "Mediaciones urbanas y nuevos escenarios de comunicación," in *Las ciudades latinoamericanas en el [des]orden mundial*, coord. Patricio Nava and Marc Zimmerman (Mexico City: Siglo XXI Editores, 2004), 82.

48. See chapter epigraph for translation.

Conclusion

Walker (1987),[1] the Alex Cox film which is said to have blacklisted the British director from Hollywood,[2] tells the tragicomic story of Tennessee filibuster[3] William Walker, who served as president of Nicaragua from 1856 to 1857 and was executed by Honduras in 1860 after a repeat, ill-fated attempt to take over the isthmus. Cox's Walker, played by U.S. actor Ed Harris, is an uncompromising man of limitless, blind ambition that borders on insanity. He and his "Immortals," a small ragtag crew of California filibusters, are spurred on to the isthmus by the offer of large land grants as well as by Nicaraguan Liberals, who upon losing power to the Conservatives requested assistance from U.S. business. Rudy Wurlitzer's script mostly follows the chronology of events that led to Walker's presidency and eventually his loss of power.[4] *Walker*, however, is anything but a straight biopic. It is the biography both of Walker and of U.S. imperialism and interventionism as told and acted by a crew seemingly high on psychotropic drugs. Yet it is also a serious political satire with an acute sense of irony and of purpose.[5] The film's express goals are clear: to use Walker's unbridled assault on Nicaraguan sovereignty as a historical metaphor for U.S. interventionism in Latin America and Vietnam;[6] and, to criticize the U.S.'s fundamental role in the Contra War and the undermining of the 1980s Sandinista regime.

The cinematographic means to these political ends are far from direct. The film manipulates time, skewing historical events and, most significantly, incorporating anachronisms. These anachronisms layer on a sense of lunacy and lend black humor and critique to the film. For some critics, Cox exploits "magical realism."[7] Others interpret the film's bizarre characters and plot more aptly for this book: "[M]any Central Americans [as opposed to U.S. viewers] may simply nod their heads in recognition."[8] This difference in perspective—U.S. viewers' interpretation of filmic lunacy as "outlandishly unbelievable"[9] as opposed to Central Americans' knowing nods—reminds us that *Walker*, as are *Bananas* and *Salvador*, is an outsider's perspective of the vicissitudes of Central American history. The William Walker episode, mostly forgotten in the United States but well-remembered in the isthmus, provided Cox and his retinue the opportunity to indulge in the serious and humorous irony of filming in a country of strategic interest to imperialists. But the more important issue for this book is what can Central Americans recognize about their homelands and themselves in this outwardly outlandish film?

Ed Harris's Walker is a nineteenth-century, slightly more competent, and much more ambitious version of Woody Allen's Fielding Mellish. Walker repeatedly declaims that his goal is to liberate the country from oppression and exploitation ("God, Science, and Hygiene"), and to bring democracy and civilization to his "fellow" Nicaraguans (almost immediately upon arriving in the country he declares himself and the "Immortals" to be Nicaraguans). In short, Walker strives to convince Nicaraguans, as well as the audience, that he has only the best intentions in mind. As Walker gains power, however, his focus narrows to the avid exercise and maintenance of that power. Vivified by scenes of the Immortals' frenetic fighting and by the manic music of the Clash's Joe Strummer, as the film progresses Walker's hold on reality dissolves.

Initially, the populace meets Walker's arrival in Nicaragua with impassivity. As Walker and his army arrive in Rivas, the first town he is to take for his Liberal collaborators, the camera pans across bored children and mildly unsettled adults. To the Immortals' surprise, however, as soon as they enter a depopulated street, Conservative forces attack. The camera captures blood spurting from many U.S. and Nicaraguan bodies. This scene sets the pattern for other battle scenes in which Walker, perfectly dressed in black and with a black cowboy hat, marches without firing a shot and impervious to the violence and death around him. Heightening the arrogance of Walker's sense of fearlessness and immortality are two conversations he has the night before the attack on Rivas. The company's drummer asks to trade the war drum for a firearm because the only images of drummers he has ever seen are of dead drummers lying beside their drums. Walker assures him that he will be safe if he stays by his side. The second conversation is with one of his favorite lieutenants, Timothy. Timothy comes to Walker worried that the Immortals do not understand for what or whom they are fighting. Walker's response is that they are fighting for their Liberal friends against their Conservative enemies. Timothy confesses that the Immortals cannot tell the difference between the two sides. Tellingly Walker advises him that neither he nor his comrades-in-arms need to concern themselves with that small issue, that fundamentally their cause (whatever that may be) is "righteous."

Both the drummer and Timothy are killed in the ensuing battle. The drummer falls quickly and becomes the image he feared. Shortly after that, unmoved by the carnage surrounding him, Walker marches by a mortally wounded Timothy. Dying, Timothy manages to call him a "dumbshit" for getting everyone killed. Walker, unflappable, responds, "Then we'll be together again." Eventually Walker's men rouse him from his trance-like state, and under heavy fire they all take cover in a house. While the Immortals battle their opponents, their leader sings and plays the piano. To save themselves, the army creates a diversion, escapes through the back of the house, and following Walker's orders, leaves the wounded to fend for themselves. This battle sequence concludes with a Liberal sympathizer screaming in melodramatic agony amid bloody bodies strewn about the street. He chastises his countrymen for not recognizing that Walker and his men are purveyors of peace, democracy, and liberty; as well as of much needed civilization and development.[10] This sequence brings forth several important, repeated elements of Walker's filmic characterization. Throughout, he demonstrates inflexibility and an inflated sense of self and superiority over and above Nicaraguan elites and the general population he easily dominates. He fully buys into the press's epithet for him, "the grey-eyed man of destiny," and believes totally and completely in his own virtues and historical relevance. As he tells his men, "Unless a man believes that there is something great for him to do, he can do nothing great."

Walker's behavior in the battle for Rivas, as well as in the movie's opening scenes of the war for Sonora,[11] sets the framework for his character's devolution. He goes from being an idealistic, loving man overcome with grief at the loss of his fiancée to a megalomaniac willing to eliminate any dissent and to abandon all principles for the sake of power, and finally to a maniac. Following his military victories he quickly ascends to the presidency—after having the president executed for treason. Walker "elects" himself president by publishing the headline, "Walker is elected president."[12] He immolates Granada, his own seat of power, when it comes under siege by the city's elite who have plotted a Central American war against him. As Granada burns, he play-acts a surgeon in a make-shift hospital[13] and greedily takes a bite from a patient's organ. In the background a U.S. soldier's wife plays the piano and Nicaraguan children and prisoners sing. Amid the insanity, two of his men interrupt Walker's cannibalism by insisting they leave Granada immediately. The Colonel, however, will not be hurried. He climbs to the pulpit and, as if giving the homily, reiterates the righteousness of his mission to bring "Progress and Democracy" to Latin America.[14]

Paralelling Walker's devolution is the film's own, in pacing and in its spectacular unraveling from realism to the fantastical to the absurd. The film begins as a traditional biopic, a "true story," narrated, slow, and encompassing. We then see Walker march unscathed through hails of bullets that bring down everyone, it seems, around him. Later we see Granada's elite, as they flee the city in a stagecoach, flipping through copies of *Newsweek* whose cover is graced by Walker's picture and the tagline: "Nicaragua's Liberator." Their stagecoach is passed by a Mercedes Benz.[15] At the end of the movie, while Walker marches his army out of the cathedral singing the late-nineteenth century hymn "Onward Christian Soldiers," U.S. Marines arrive in a Soviet military helicopter[16] to rescue the besieged Walker and his Immortals.[17]

In Cox's scenario, Nicaragua is but the place William Walker chooses to play out his fantasies of owning a country and holding ultimate power, thus fulfilling his destiny of greatness. As Walker gains control of Nicaragua, it becomes a place in which to refashion a version of the U.S. South, complete with its power and racial structures and the relegalization of slavery.[18] In this way, despite its leftist credentials and collaboration with INCINE,[19] as well as its discredit of interventionism, the film narrates Nicaraguans as simple placeholders for powerful outsiders rather than subjects with personal agency and in control of their homeland's future. The United States "will be back," Walker reassures his audience while Granada burns, because even in their own homeland Nicaraguans need to be guided and controlled. Furthermore, the media accounts of Walker's presidency in *El Nicaragüense* (a newspaper founded by Walker), *Newsweek*, and *Time* serve to erase Nicaraguans from their homeland. In the movie's fight for Nicaragua, even, Nicaraguans are mostly dead extras. Despite its many historical inaccuracies,[20] *Walker's* fantastical narrative is grounded in fact and offers Central American viewers a plausible, yet external, vision of the isthmus.

Walker, as does *Bananas*, contemplates Latin America from afar with cameras at the ready. Both films stress the importance of the media in the proliferation of a Latin American image—an image whose focus rests on foreigners' missions on the continent as purveyors of "progress," not on Latin Americans as thinking, active subjects. This is obvious in *Bananas*. The San Marcos episodes play second fiddle to the representation and development of Fielding Mellish's neuroses. The film, like so many of Woody Allen's movies, is really about the main character's failure as a man. Nevertheless, Latin America provides a significant backdrop to Mellish's experiences. Woody Allen's Latin America is a conflict-filled, comic place where, to deal with the scarcity of food in the hardscrabble "mountains," for instance, the guerrilla leadership sends Mellish with a long list of sandwich orders to a local New York–style delicatessen. San Marcos holds the audience's attention because of its comedic absurdities, its comic possibilities.

In *Walker's* case, the ravages of war are everywhere and dictatorial edicts are taken seriously. The camera crew that records the Immortals' rescue at the end of the film reminds viewers of the opening scene of *Bananas*, yet there is nothing sporting or humorous in Cox's disturbing scene. Blood spurts everywhere. Injured, screaming Nicaraguans and other non-U.S. citizens are left to die in Granada as it burns. Similarly, Walker's decree of English as Nicaragua's official language (as opposed to the declaration of Swedish as the official language of San Marcos) and the hunger his army endures while under siege serve up a taste of *Bananas'* sense of irony, but not its lightheartedness or playfulness. Nonetheless, *Bananas's* imagined Latin America is recognizable in *Walker's* Nicaragua. As in *Bananas*, the U.S. interloper dominates the action. In *Walker*, the filibuster's fate, not that of a destroyed Nicaragua, lies at its core: "[I]t was all about Walker."[21] *Walker's* critique of U.S. intervention in the developing world is earnest, though satirical. It sets itself up as a potential trigger for sociopolitical consciousness, not hearty laughter, in its non-Nicaraguan viewers.[22] It is, after all, a film made by outsiders for outsiders (but with the support of elite Sandinista insiders).

The film's portrayal of the media in its contemporary incarnation and of the historical William Walker's quest for publicity also exposes Walker's self-invention. The filibuster was written up in the popular press for his (mis)adventures abroad. His was perceived as both a "grand cultural" and "military crusade" in which he embodied the U.S.' racial (white) and cultural (Western) superiority.[23] In addition, Walker's *The War in Nicaragua*, written expressly to collect financial support for his civilizing expeditions on the isthmus,[24] added to his mystique. As a celebrity hound, Walker prefigures more current modes of media-produced subjectivities. To re-create and legitimize himself and his intentions for the isthmus, Walker invents (and accepts) an oath of loyalty to Nicaragua. Further, the Immortals recite the oath as a sign of their commitment to their leader's enterprise. Walker's actions demonstrate his supposition that not only can one choose places of attachment but one can also change them. He and his men can become "Nicaraguan" while maintaining their U.S. superiority. Ed Harris's Walker legitimizes his own brand of Nicaraguan-ness by simply proclaiming it as such and professing selfless devotion to the country's "regeneration." He projects a newly created "progressive" or regenerated Central American-ness, a U.S.-fabricated Central American-ness. Clearly, however, proclamations of progress and "patriotic" democracy do not endow him or his men with a "nica" perspective. Instead they give Walker just enough rope to hang himself, for his stubborn waving of a pseudo-Nicaraguan flag leads to his abandonment by the U.S. Marines and his subsequent execution. Yet, Walker's new identity delegitimizes Nicaraguans' intimate relationship to their homeland. This external version of Central American subjectivity is utterly contrary to the isthmus's view of Walker and of the many ensuing interventions and occupations. In fact, on the isthmus Walker represents the unified, successful expulsion and defeat of the U.S., not its economic or cultural power. The downfall of the "grey-eyed man of destiny" exemplifies Central Americans' potential, unrealized power over their own destinies.

The effortlessness with which Harris's Walker takes on a Central American nationality offers an instructive contrast to contemporary Central Americans' own complex perceptions of belonging in and to the place of their birth. The film brings to the fore the ways in which Central America and its inhabitants are fodder for outsiders' political and economic projects. Nicaraguan elites, in their lust for power and money, invite Walker in. Their willingness to wheel and deal, to make a "trato" [deal], keep him there. In *Walker*, Nicaragua (and, by extension, the isthmus) is a place to be recast in the image of the conqueror, a place to be made productive, a place to become by force more than "a tiny fucked-up country somewhere south of here [the U.S.]" (magnate Cornelius Vanderbilt in *Walker*) that can be taken over as necessary for business and/or ideology. The film also draws and projects Central Americans in silhouette. Walker—U.S.' culture promises to "fill-in" empty Central Americans who lack personal agency to practice sovereignty or to exercise power over their own lives. This emptiness allows Walker to fill it in with an alternate and self-generated national identity.

In contrast to Walker's falsified Central American-ness, Central American texts explore the tense relationships that exist between isthmian subjectivities. The texts I study in this book carefully negotiate isthmian identities and (dis)placements at home and demonstrate their waxing and waning in the cycles of post-conflict globalization processes. A short entry from Ed Harris's production journal contests the silence to which *Walker*, *Bananas*, and *Salvador* relegate Central American subjects. He writes, "I ain't got it in me to wax poetic about this country and its people. They do that themselves."[25] Instead, this quote acknowledges Central American subjectivities. In his journal, Ed Harris reflects on Nicaragua as poetic muse and confesses his inability to poeticize it. His enigmatic statement reveals that the surrounding physical and human geography resist observers' assessments of it and poetry-making about it. When Harris looks around, in the lines that precede the excerpt, he sees people of all ages working hard early in the morning—people who are not "lazy."[26] He appreciates the aesthetic potential of his surroundings, but rather than position himself to speak of and for the Nicaraguan homeland and its inhabitants, Harris leaves poetic production about Nicaraguan-ness to Nicaraguans. Speaking from the perspective of an outsider, the actor acknowledges the *there-ness* of the Nicaraguan landscape. More significantly, though, he discerns its distinctive *here-ness* in the experience of its local inhabitants. In other words, the quotation prioritizes insiders' over outsiders' experiences of Nicaraguan and Central American "ineffability"[27] and tangibility. In refusing to poeticize Nicaragua, Harris metaphorically suggests the inaccessibility of the homeland's depths, especially to someone on the outside looking in. It infers that the homeland is branded not only by tangible landmarks and monuments but also by the indentations and scars of the past. The journal entry perceives the unseen, lived histories of the homeland's inhabitants. As Whisnant, in reference to the Nicaraguan custom of designating addresses based on landmarks rather than building numbers, notes, "[W]hatever the superficial character of the landscape, it is the landscape of the mind that matters most—not things as they are, but things as they have been."[28] Harris's observation prods Central Americans to realize their places and responsibilities at home, a home that has often seemed up for grabs to foreign powers, a home whose past is consciously and too easily eluded.

Conclusion

Throughout this book, we have been guided through diverse versions of past, present, and future Central American homes. In this book's poetry and short stories, the poetic speakers and narrators roam about the literary, sociohistorical, and digital landscapes collecting materials to aesthetically reproduce their experiences of home and homeland. No matter our routes or modes of transportation (poetry or short fiction), the sense of belonging and dis- and misplacement in the homeland palpitate throughout. We began with revolutionaries leading the way, creating alternate homelands and new patriotic heroes. The likes of Dalton, Cardenal, and Rugama dreamed of belonging in and to a new homeland that incorporated the social margins or peripheries. These were utopias that would never be, as recent history tells us. Post-conflict writers represent the destruction of the physical homeland as well as of the dreams of its inhabitants and contemplate what can possibly come after. Some feel nostalgia for their pasts and retrace their histories through imagined versions of home looking for ways to continue to live in homelands where the past is erased by practiced forgetfulness and overwritten by new "globalized" landmarks. For nostalgics, the new does not assuage the desire for the old. More cynical, and less outwardly hopeful, are writers who cannot see past the detritus that dots their quasi-globalized homelands as they stroll through it sweaty and hungry in the tropical heat. The waste left by modernization efforts and years of war simultaneously overwhelm yet attach Central Americans to the homeland. Those who cannot get away physically, but do not easily tolerate their Central American-ness, fashion themselves tourists at home. They live as if permanent vacationers misplaced in the homeland, tiptoeing through it. This light tread—and virtual tourism through the homeland—achieves a tenuous separation in this book's final chapter. There, Central Americans who still reside at home reshape subjectivities that place them in a realm (virtually) far from the vicissitudes of everyday Central America. These homelands are thoroughly imagined, visual, and aural but, nevertheless, tangible. While all the texts in this book experience home and belonging as paradoxically concrete and impalpable, in chapter 5 the concrete fades until it almost disappears from sight and touch.

What is it that keeps even nomadic Central Americans from cutting the cord that binds them home? Chaves's traveling *tica* questions whether Costa Rican nature, a lure for foreign visitors and their money, is worth saving; yet she remains home and continues traversing her homeland. Similarly, Reyes's scarred Salvadorans stay put in a highly violent post-conflict San Salvador that is hardly recognizable and which, in Canjura's story, disappears under a heavy fog. Even an environmentally devastated lake awakens a twisted sense of belonging in contemporary Central American writers. In each of these examples, the Central American homeland conjures affection. It manages to evoke and maintain the affective attachment of its inhabitants despite its post-conflict scars and the throbbing pustules left by modernization's fits and starts. Affection for and sentiments of solidarity with compatriots feed writers' constructions of imaginary yet locatable places to inhabit on the isthmus. These writers demonstrate that the desire for *locatability* and belonging at home is not fulfilled by "global" citizenship. Be they as "global" as is possible in contemporary Central America, they still hunger for *local* attachments. Images on a screen cannot manufacture the warmth of the "papaíto país" or of the *guanaco*, *pinolero*, or *tico* next door. The local home breeds a sense of belonging that survives the homeland's political and economic chaos. Despite frequently overt gestures toward a "global" identity, this book's Central American writers exercise their personal agency to produce *glocal* Salvadoran, Nicaraguan, and Costa Rican subjectivities. These are subjectivities in which they find virtual, memory-filled paths out of the homeland while remaining astride the isthmus. They occupy a contradictory space: at once rootless and rooted locally.

Local history and cultural change are fundamental to the experience of rooted rootlessness of Salvadoran, Nicaraguan, and Costa Rican subjects and texts discussed in these pages. At the same time, the search for belonging at home is not limited to these three Central American homelands. An exploration of the conflicts and tensions surrounding notions of belonging to and at home in contemporaneous Honduran and Guatemalan texts, for example, would certainly be a fruitful endeavor. One potential area of research is the production of a Honduran identity vis-à-vis its relationship with the United States during the region's armed conflicts. The Soccer War could be an excellent starting point to study, for instance, hybrid Salvadoran-Honduran identities and the appropriation and creation of identity markers. One example of the complexity of transisthmian affection for and attachment to the local is the aforementioned debate around the origin of the *pupusa* (see the introduction). While this debate may seem an example of an "ignorant" and misplaced nationalism, it does point to the everyday significance of home, belonging, and meaning-making to Central Americans. In my view, a study of home in post-conflict Guatemala would necessarily involve researching the destruction of indigenous peoples' physical homes and symbols of home and belonging (for instance, the military's systematic desecration of *milpas* and its creation of postmassacre model villages) during the government's genocidal campaigns against the Maya. A comparative study of Maya and *ladino* literary representations of Guatemala as home and the construction of national-ethnic subjects would take on the challenge posed by Mayan fiction, to "disrup[t] the myth of a homogenous nation-state" and explore "new ways of producing national identities, and the tense negotiations of multiculturalism in Central American countries."[29] This complex study of contemporary post-conflict views of the homeland would also take into account transformations of Mayan cosmogony in contemporary practice.

Rooted rootlessness takes on a new meaning when discussing the pull of the isthmus as it extends beyond its geographical borders. In reality, the yearning for contact with the homeland and a sense of belonging, in whatever form it takes, is passed on to younger generations of Central American-Americans who claim a subjectivity rooted in the isthmus even if they have never lived there. In the case of El Salvador, U.S.-born Salvadorans inherit from their immigrant parents imagined visions of the Salvadoran homeland. Nostalgic diasporic and transnational imaginaries of El Salvador present Salvadoran-Americans with conventional notions of Salvadoran-ness. These notions conceive of Salvadorans as hard-working, wily, and persevering against all odds both in and away from the homeland. The continued, constant flow of people (to the United States) and remittances (back home) seems to support the idea of the United States as both the place in which to "make it" and in which to remake or reimagine the lost Salvadoran homeland. Sociological studies of Salvadoran immigration to the United States as well as poetry and fiction by Salvadoran-Americans demonstrate the power of the sentimental, often conflicted, ties between the faraway family homeland and the U.S. home. These ties are also renegotiated among other Latin Americans and U.S. Latinos, as scholars of Central American immigration and U.S. Central Americans demonstrate.[30] As on the isthmus, the diaspora's finding home and enjoying a sense of belonging entails a continual refashioning of subjectivities and experiences.

Home is tangible and intangible. It is a place that occupies a physical space and an emotional one. Even as we criticize the places we come from and create distance between us, a part of them and a part of us remain connected. The texts in this book repeatedly depict the transformation and destruction of homelands and homes and the endurance of home affections. Amid the clatter of globality, it is still possible to discern home calling to us. It is the soundtrack that plays in the background of our memories; the remembrances that anchor us to places. These are places we possess and that possess us. If only we also remembered that to value home is also to be responsible for its survival.

NOTES

1. *Walker*, dir. Alex Cox, written by Rudy Wurlitzer, booklet by Graham Fuller, Linda Sandoval and Rudy Wurlitzer (1987; The Criterion Collection, Universal Studios, 2007), DVD.

2. "Interview: Alex Cox," by Simon Abrams. *Slant Magazine*. March 1, 2011. http://www.slantmagazine.com/film/feature/interview-alex-cox/254. Among other instances, in this 2011 *Slant* interview Cox alleges that he was blacklisted from Hollywood for making *Walker* in collaboration with the Nicaraguan Sandinista government. In the comments section, a poster contradicts Cox and asserts that his blacklisting was a result of Cox being a scab during a 1988 screenwriters' strike.

3. Filibuster in this context refers to adventurers on unlawful military expeditions in support of revolutions in foreign countries. They were also called "freebooters" (*Concise Oxford Dictionary*).

4. Ralph Lee Woodward, Jr., *Central America: A Nation Divided*. 2nd ed. (New York: Oxford University Press, 1985); James Dunkerley, *Power in the Isthmus: A Political History of Modern Central America* (London: Verso, 1988); Héctor Pérez-Brignoli, *A Brief History of Central America*, trans. Richard B. Sawrey A. and Susan Stretti de Sawrey (Berkeley: University of California Press, 1989); Lynn V. Foster, *A Brief History of Central America* (New York: Facts on File, 2000); Albert Z. Carr, *The World and William Walker* (New York: Harper & Row, Publishers, 1963); Brady Harrison, *Agent of Empire: William Walker and the Imperial Self in American Literature* (Athens: The University of Georgia Press, 2004); William Walker, *The War in Nicaragua*, foreword by Robert Houston (Tucson: University of Arizona Press, 1985). Woodward details Walker's life as a filibuster and the effects of his (un)successful power grabs on Central American Conservative-Liberal struggles and, long term, on U.S.-Nicaragua relations. He, as others do (Dunkerley, Pérez-Brignoli, Foster), notes that the "National War," or "National Campaign," waged by Central American governments against the filibuster represents a rare moment of isthmian unity. Nicaraguan Liberals' invitation of U.S. intervention also discredited them and their ideas of progress and helped Conservatives hold power longer than they would have otherwise. Also see book-length studies on Walker (Carr, Harrison) and Walker's own narrative of his filibustering.

5. As Cox tells it in *X Films: True Confessions of a Radical Filmmaker* (Brooklyn, NY: Soft Skull Press, 2008), it was difficult to secure funding and distribution, with the Sandinista government's support of the film via INCINE (Instituto Nacional de Cine Nicaragüense) [National Institute of Nicaraguan Film] adding to the financial drama. David E. Whisnant criticizes INCINE's decision to help fund *Walker* and, implicitly, then Vice President of Nicaragua Sergio Ramírez's approval of the script. For Whisnant, the Walker episode could have served to explain Nicaraguan history and culture and attracted a "popular" audience but "neither potential was realized; the film was in most respects a disaster" (217). David E. Whisnant, *Rascally Signs in Sacred Places: The Politics of Culture in Nicaragua* (Chapel Hill: University of North Carolina Press, 1995).

6. Harrison, *Agent of Empire*; Sumiko Higashi, "*Walker* and *Mississippi Burning*: Postmodernist Versus Illusionist Narrative," in *The Historical Film: History and Memory in Media*, ed. Marcia Landy (New Brunswick: Rutgers University Press, 2001), 218-231. Harrison and Higashi consider *Walker*'s critique of the U.S. in the Vietnam War.

7. Jeremiah Kipp, review of *Walker*, *Slant Magazine*, February 13, 2008.

8. Vincent Canby, review of *Walker*, *New York Times*, December 4, 1987.

9. Ibid.

10. In *X Films*, Cox recounts that this speech was the brainchild of a Nicaraguan actor, Roberto López Espinoza, a Sandinista who believed the views of pro-U.S. Nicaraguans (e.g. Contras) should be presented. The actor wanted to introduce the idea of "culture" and "progress" as "gifts donated to us by our betters" (153). Cox calls this scene the film's "most authentic 'Nica' moment" (153).

11. Walker's initial foray into Latin America was to Baja California and Sonora in 1853. There, following the dictates of "Manifest Destiny," he and his cohort hoped to establish a colony that would subsequently be annexed to the U.S. He was defeated by Mexico.

12. Woodward, *Central America*, 140. In fact, Walker was elected president after his puppet president Patricio Rivas deserted.

13. Filmed in Managua's cathedral, unusable since the 1972 earthquake.

14. He also ominously warns his audience that the U.S. will never leave the isthmus alone and that the Nicaraguan homeland will never be their own because the U.S. will always intervene. Walker speaks as the U.S. and justifies the occupation as fate: "because it is our destiny to be here. It is our destiny to control you people. So no matter how much you fight, no matter what you think. . . .we'll be back time and time again."

15. The speeding Mercedes is an anachronistic reminder of the Somozas' infamous car fleets.

16. Cox, *X Films*, 160; *Walker*, Booklet by Graham Fuller, Linda Sandoval, and Rudy Wurlitzer, 37-38, 2007, DVD. Ironically, the Russian-made helicopter had recently been in combat against U.S.-sponsored Contras.

17. A "company man" (read CIA) and a camera crew arrive with the Marines to evacuate all U.S. citizens. Walker's bedraggled soldiers immediately pull out their U.S. passports and climb into the helicopter. Walker, however, unperturbed and standing perfectly erect as usual, responds to the challenge, "Your nationality, sir," with "I am William Walker, President of the Republic of Nicaragua." He is left behind. The film's final scene is of Walker's 1860 execution. As credits roll, a newsreel plays contemporary images of Ronald Reagan's defense of U.S. intervention in Central America and of the casualties of the Contra War. If the viewer somehow missed the film's anti-interventionist message, the final scenes hammer it home.

18. Slavery was abolished in Mexico and Central America shortly after the winning of independence (1821) from Spain.

19. See note 5.

20. See Higashi, "*Walker* and *Mississippi Burning*," on *Walker*, history, and postmodern filmmaking.

21. Cox, *X Films*, 146.

22. The *Walker* DVD includes a short documentary on the making of the film. In it we see interviews with young U.S. *sandalistas* who played extras in the film. *Sandalistas* were sandal-wearing foreign activists who went to Nicaragua to support the Sandinista revolution. In addition, Tomás Borge, one the FSLN's founders and Minister of the Interior during the first Sandinista regime, makes an appearance. He is filmed "directing" one of the Nicaraguan extras.

23. Whisnant, *Rascally Signs*, 76-79. In addition, in *The World and William Walker* Carr writes in detail about *El Nicaragüense*'s influence on U.S. journalistic views and on the creation and maintenance of Walker's image. As Whisnant notes, two celebratory musicals also popularized Walker's escapades (79).

24. Houston, foreword to *The War in Nicaragua* by William Walker (Tucson: University of Arizona Press, 1985), 9.

25. Rudy Wurlitzer, *Walker* (New York: Harper & Row, Publishers, 1987), 16. This journal entry is also reproduced in the booklet that accompanies the *Walker* DVD.

26. Wurlitzer, *Walker*, 16.

27. Joan Didion, *Salvador* (New York: Washington Square Press, 1983).

28. Whisnant, *Rascally Signs*, 448.

29. Arturo Arias, *Taking Their Word: Literature and the Signs of Central America* (Minneapolis: University of Minnesota Press, 2007), 79.

30. For example, see Arias, *Taking Their Word*; Nora Hamilton and Norma Stoltz Chinchilla, *Seeking Community in a Global City: Guatemalans and Salvadorans in Los Angeles* (Philadelphia: Temple University Press, 2001); Cecilia Menjívar, *Fragmented Ties: Salvadoran Immigrant Networks in America* (Berkeley: University of California Press, 2000); and, Ana Patricia Rodríguez, *Dividing the Isthmus: Transnational Histories, Literatures, and Cultures* (Austin: University of Texas Press, 2009).

Bibliography

Abrams, Simon. "Interview: Alex Cox." *Slant Magazine*. March 1, 2011. http://www.slantmagazine.com/film/feature/interview-alex-cox/254.
Acuña Ortega, Osvaldo. "Autoritarismo y democracia en Centroamérica: La larga duración (siglos XIX y XX)." In *Nicaragua en busca de su identidad*, edited by Frances Kinloch Tijerino, 535–571. Managua: Instituto de Historia de Nicaragua, Universidad Centroamericana, 1995.
Ahmed, Sara. *The Cultural Politics of Emotion*. New York: Routledge, 2004.
Alegría, Claribel. *Anillo de silencio*. Mexico City: Ediciones Botas, 1948.
———. *Esto soy: Antología poética*. San Salvador: Dirección de Publicaciones e Impresos, 2004.
———. *Flowers from the volcano*. Translated by Carolyn Forché. Pittsburgh: University of Pittsburgh Press, 1982.
———. *Luisa en el país de la realidad*. San Salvador: UCA Editores, 1997.
———. *Mágica tribu*. 2nd ed. San Salvador: Índole, 2008.
———. *Saudade*. 2nd ed. San Salvador: Dirección de Publicaciones e Impresos, 2000.
———. *Sobrevivo*. Havana: Casa de las Américas, 1978.
———. *Soltando amarras/Casting Off*. Translated by Margaret Sayers Peden. Willamantic, CT: Curbstone Press, 2002.
———. *Umbrales*. 2nd ed. San Salvador: Dirección de Publicaciones e Impresos 1997.
Alegría, Claribel, and Darwin J. Flakoll, *Cenizas de Izalco*. Barcelona: Seix Barral, 1966.
—and Darwin J. Flakoll, eds. and trans. *On the Frontline: Guerrilla Poems of El Salvador*. Willamantic, CT: Curbstone Press, 1989.
Alvarenga, Luis. *El ciervo perseguido: Vida y obra de Roque Dalton*. San Salvador: Dirección de Publicaciones e Impresos, 2002.
Anderson, Benedict. *Imagined Communities: Reflections on the Origins and Spread of Nationalism*, rev. ed. London: Verso, 1991.
Aparicio, Frances R., and Susana Chávez-Silverman, eds. *Tropicalizations: Transcultural Representations of Latinidad*. Hanover, NH: University Press of New England, 1997.
Aparicio, Yvette. "Literary Convention and Revolution in Roque Dalton's *Taberna y otros lugares*." *Revista de estudios hispánicos* XXXII, no. 1–2 (2005): 169–181.
———. "Negotiating Politics and Aesthetics: The Poetry of Claribel Alegría, Ernesto Cardenal and Roque Dalton," PhD diss., University of California, Irvine, 2000.
———. "Poesía nicaragüense escrita después de Darío, de Cardenal, de la Revolución." In *Literatura y otras artes en América Latina: Actas del XXXIV Congreso del Instituto Internacional de Literatura Iberoamericana*, edited by Daniel Balderston, et al. 151–157. Iowa City: University of Iowa, 2004.
———. "Reading Social Consciousness in Claribel Alegría's Early Poetry." *Cincinnati Romance Review* 18 (1999): 1–6.
Araya Jiménez, María del Carmen. "El lado oscuro de San Jose: Miedos de comunicación y construcción de pánicos morales." In *El lado oscuro: ensayos sobre la violencia*, edited by Anacristina Rossi and Nora Garita, 61-113. San José: Uruk Editores, S.A., 2007.
Arellano, Jorge Eduardo. "Presentación: Managua en el tiempo." *Revista de la Academia de Geografía e Historia de Nicaragua* (Segunda época) LXV (2007): 7–10.
Arias, Arturo. *Gestos ceremoniales, narrativa centroamericana, 1960-1990*. Guatemala City: Artemis-Edinter, 1998.

———. *Taking Their Word: Literature and the Signs of Central America*. Minneapolis: University of Minnesota Press, 2007.
———, ed. *The Rigoberta Menchú Controversy*. Minneapolis: University of Minnesota Press, 2001.
Arnove, Robert F. "Education as Contested Terrain in Nicaragua." *Comparative Education Review* 39, no. 1 (1995): 28–53.
Atwood, Roger. "Gringo iracundo: Roque Dalton and His Father." *Latin American Research Review* 46, no. 1 (2011): 126–49.
Augé, Marc. *Non-places: Introduction to an Anthropology of Supermodernity*. Translated by John Howe. London: Verso, 1995.
Babb, Florence. *The Tourism Encounter: Fashioning Latin American Nations and Histories*. Palo Alto, CA: Stanford University Press, 2011.
Baker-Cristales, Beth. "Los ausentes siempre presentes: Inmigrantes salvadoreños como actores políticos transnacionales." In *Transnacionalización de la sociedad centroamericana: Visiones a partir de la migración*, compiled by FLACSO Programa El Salvador, 139–156. San Salvador: FLACSO Programa El Salvador, 2005.
———. *Salvadoran Migration to Southern California: Redefining El Hermano Lejano*. Gainesville: University of Florida Press, 2004.
Balderston, Daniel, ed. *Literatura y otras artes en América Latina: Actas del XXXIV Congreso del Instituto Internacional de Literatura Iberoamericana*. Iowa City: University of Iowa, 2004.
Bananas. Directed by Woody Allen. United Artists, 1971. VHS.
Bandes, Susan A., ed. *The Passions of the Law*. New York: New York University Press, 1999.
Barbas-Rhoden, Laura. *Writing Women in Central America: Gender and the Fictionalization of History*. Athens: Ohio University Press, 2003.
Barthes, Roland. *Camera Lucida: Reflections on Photography*. Translated by Richard Howard. New York: Farrar, Strauss and Giroux, 1981.
Batres-Márquez, S. Patricia, Helen H. Jensen, and Gary W. Brester. "Salvadoran Consumption of Ethnic Foods in the United States." Working Paper 01-WP 289, Center for Agricultural and Rural Development, Iowa State University, Ames, October 2001.
Bell, Daniel M., Jr. *Liberation Theology After the End of History: The Refusal to Cease Suffering*. London: Routledge, 2001.
Belli, Gioconda. *El país bajo mi piel*. New York: Vintage Books, 2003.
Benedetti, Mario. *Los poetas comunicantes*. Montevideo: Biblioteca de Marcha, 1972.
Benz, Stephen. "Through the Tropical Looking Glass: the Motif of Resistance in U.S. Literature on Central America." In *Tropicalizations: Transcultural Representations of Latinidad*, edited by Frances R. Aparicio and Susana Chávez-Silverman, 51–66. Hanover, NH: University Press of New England, 1997.
Beverley, John. *Testimonio: On the Politics of Truth*. Minneapolis: University of Minnesota Press, 2004.
Beverley, John, and Marc Zimmerman. *Literature and Politics in the Central American Revolutions*. Austin: University of Texas Press, 1990.
Billig, Michael. *Banal Nationalism*. London: Sage Publications, 1995.
Booth, John A., Christine J. Wade, and Thomas W. Walker. *Understanding Central America: Global Forces, Rebellion, and Change*. 5th ed. Boulder, CO: Westview Press, 2010.
Boschetto-Sandoval, Sandra M., and Marcia Phillips McGowan, eds. *Claribel Alegría and Central American Literature: Critical Essays*. Athens: Ohio University Center for International Studies, 1994.
Bouvier, Virginia M. *The Globalization of U.S.-Latin America Relations: Democracy, Intervention and Human Rights*. Westport, CT: Praeger, 2002.
Boym, Svetlana. *The Future of Nostalgia*. New York: Basic Books, 2001.

Bravo, Alejandro, and Nelly Miranda. "Literatura, identidad y conciencia nacional." In *Nicaragua en busca de su identidad*, edited by Frances Kinloch Tijerino, 117–135. Managua: Instituto de Historia de Nicaragua, Universidad Centroamericana, 1995.
Briante, Susan. Introduction. "Hybrid Cultures: The Prose Poem in Spanish." *Sentence: A Journal of Prose Poetics* 2 (2004): 47–51.
Calderón, Esthela. *Soplo de corriente vital (Poemas etnobotánicos)*. Managua: Ediciones 400 Elefantes, 2008.
Calhoun, Craig. *Nationalism*. Minneapolis: University of Minnesota Press, 1997.
Calle 13. *Entren los que quieran*. Sony BMG US Latin, 2010.
Canby, Vincent. Review of *Walker*. *New York Times*, December 4, 1987.
Canjura, Salvador. *Prohibido vivir*. San Salvador: Istmo Editores, 2000.
Cardenal, Ernesto. *Antología*. Managua: Nueva Nicaragua-Monimbó, 1983.
———. *Apocalypse and Other Poems*. Edited and selected by Robert Pring-Mill and Donald D. Walsh. Introduction by Robert Pring-Mill. Translated by Thomas Merton, Kenneth Rexroth, Mireya Jaimes-Freyre, and the editors. New York: New Directions, 1977.
———. *Epigramas*. Mexico City: Universidad Nacional Autonóma de México, 1961.
———. *El estrecho dudoso*. Madrid: Ediciones Cultura Hispánica, 1966.
———. *Flights of Victory / Vuelos de Victoria*. Edited and translated by Marc Zimmerman with Ellen Banberger and collaboration of Mirta Urróz. Willamantic, CT: Curbstone Press, 1988.
———. *Homenaje a los indios americanos*. Leon: Universidad Nacional Autónoma de Nicaragua, 1969.
———. *Salmos*. Medellin: Ediciones Universidad de Antioquia, 1964.
———. *La santidad de la revolución*. Salamanca: Ediciones Sígueme, 1976.
———. *Zero Hour and Other Documentary Poems*. Edited and selected by Donald D. Walsh. Translated by Paul W. Borgerson, Jr., Jonathan Cohen, Robert Pring-Mill, and Donald D. Walsh. Introduction by Robert Pring-Mill. New York: New Directions, 1980.
Carr, Albert Z. *The World and William Walker*. New York: Harper & Row, Publishers, 1963.
Castellanos Moya, Horacio. *El asco: Thomas Bernhard en San Salvador*. San Salvador: Arcoiris, 1997.
Castillo, Otto René. *Let's Go*. Translated by Margaret Randall. Willamantic, CT: Curbstone Press, 1995.
Chambers, Erve. *Native Tours: The Anthropology of Travel and Tourism*. Long Grove, IL: Waveland Press, 2000.
Chaves, Luis. *Asfalto: un road poem*. San Jose: Ediciones Perro Azul, 2006.
———. *Chan Marshall*. Madrid: Visor Libros, 2005.
———. *Historias Polaroid*. San Jose: Ediciones Perro Azul, 2000.
———. *La máquina de hacer niebla*. Seville: Ediciones de la Isla de Siltolá, S. L., 2012.
———. *Monumentos ecuestres*. San Jose: Editorial Germinal, 2011.
———. *El mundial 2010—apuntes*. San Jose: Editorial Germinal, 2010.
———. *300 páginas: prosa*. San Jose: Ediciones Lanzallamas, 2010.
Clark, Walter Aaron, ed. *From Tejano to Tango: Latin American Popular Music*. New York: Routledge, 2002.
Classen, Constance. "The Odor of the Other: Olfactory Symbolism and Cultural Categories." *Ethos* 20, no. 2 (June 1992): 133–166.
Corbin, Alain. *The Foul and the Fragrant: Odor and the French Social Imagination*. Cambridge, MA: Harvard University Press, 1986.
Cortés, Carlos. *La invención de Costa Rica y otras invenciones*. San Jose: Editorial Costa Rica, 2003.
Cortez, Beatriz. *Estética del cinismo: Pasión y desencanto en la literatura centroamericana de posguerra*. Guatemala City: F & G Editores, 2010.

———. "Estética del cinismo: La ficción centroamericana de posguerra." *Áncora: Suplemento Cultural La Nación*. March 11, 2001. http://wvw.nacion.com/ancora/2001/marzo/11/historia3.html

Cox, Alex. *X Films: True Confessions of a Radical Filmmaker*. Brooklyn, NY: Soft Skull Press, 2008.

Craft, Linda. *Novels of Testimony and Resistance from Central America*. Gainesville: University Press of Florida, 1997.

Cruz, Mirian, Carlos López Cerdán, and Claudia Schatan. "Pequeñas empresas, productos étnicos y de nostalgia: oportunidades en el mercado internacional: los casos de El Salvador y México." Serie Estudios y Perspectivas, no. 17. Mexico City: Sede Subregional de la CEPAL en México, Unidad de Desarrollo, Naciones Unidas, 2004.

Culler, Jonathan. "Semiotics of Tourism." *American Journal of Semiotics* 1 (1981): 127–140.

Dalton, Roque. *Las historias prohibidas del Pulgarcito*. 11th ed. Mexico City: Siglo XXI Editores, 1997.

———. *Miguel Mármol: Los sucesos de 1932 en El Salvador*. San Salvador: UCA Editores, 1993.

———. *No pronuncies mi nombre: Poesía completa*. 3 vols. Compilation, Introduction, and Poem Index by Rafael Lara Martínez. San Salvador: Dirección de Publicaciones e Impresos, 2005 and 2008.

———. *Pobrecito poeta que era yo*. San Salvador: UCA Editores, 2005.

———. *Taberna y otros lugares*. San Salvador: UCA Editores, 1995.

———. *El turno del ofendido*. San Salvador: UCA Editores, 2000.

Darío, Rubén. *Poesías completas*. 9th ed. Edited, Introduction, and Notes by Alfonso Méndez Plancarte. Madrid: Aguilar, 1961.

Davenport, John, and Edward L. Jackiewicz. "Spaces of Tourism." In *Placing Latin America: Contemporary Themes in Human Geography*, edited by Edward L. Jackiewicz and Fernando J. Bosco, 97–113. Lanham, MD: Rowman & Littlefield, 2008.

Dawes, Greg. *Aesthetics and Revolution: Nicaraguan Poetry, 1979-1990*. Minneapolis: University of Minnesota Press, 1993.

Day, Graham, and Andrew Thompson. *Theorizing Nationalism*. Edited by Jo Campling. Basingstoke, UK: Palgrave Macmillan, 2004.

Deleuze, Gilles, and Felix Guattari. *A Thousand Plateaus: Capitalism and Schizophrenia*. Translated by Brian Massumi. Minneapolis: University of Minnesota Press, 1987.

Delgado Aburto, Leonel. *Márgenes recorridos: Apuntes sobre procesos culturales y literatura nicaragüense del siglo XX*. Managua: Instituto de Historia de Nicaragua y Centroamérica: Universidad Centroamericana, 2002.

Delville, Michel. *The American Prose Poem: Poetic Form and the Boundaries of Genre*. Gainesville: University of Florida Press, 1998.

Didion, Joan. *Salvador*. New York: Washington Square Press, 1983.

Dunkerley, James. *Power in the Isthmus: A Political History of Modern Central America*. London: Verso, 1988.

Escudos, Jacinta. *A-B-sudario*. Guatemala City: Alfaguara, 2003.

———. *Crónicas sentimentales*. Guatemala City: F & G Editores, 2010.

———. *Cuentos sucios*. San Salvador: Dirección de Publicaciones e Impresos, 1997.

———. *El desencanto*. San Salvador: Dirección de Publicaciones e Impresos, 2001.

———. *El diablo sabe mi nombre*. San Jose: Uruk Editores, 2008.

Fernández, Jesse. *El Poema en prosa en Hispanoamérica: Del modernismo a la vanguardia (Estudio crítico y antología)*. Madrid: Ediciones Hiperión, 1994.

Fernández Retamar, Roberto. *Para una teoría de la literatura hispanoamericana*, rev. ed. Havana: Editorial Pueblo y Educación, 1984.

FLACSO Programa El Salvador. *Transnacionalización de la sociedad centroamericana: Visiones a partir de la migración*. San Salvador: FLACSO Programa El Salvador, 2005.

Foro Nicaragüense de la Cultura, *Foro movimientos culturales y la política cultural del estado nicaragüense. Análisis crítico y propositivo: Memoria*. Managua: Foro Nicaragüense de la Cultura, COSUDE and RENIES, 2007.

Foster, Lynn V. *A Brief History of Central America*. New York: Facts on File, 2000.
Fowler, William R., Jr. "Ethnohistoric Sources on the Pipil-Nicarao of Central America: A Critical Analysis." *Ethnohistory* 32, no. 1 (Winter 1985): 37–62.
Friedman, Thomas L. *The World is Flat: A Brief History of the Twenty-First Century*. New York: Farrar, Strauss and Giroux, 2005.
Gammage, Sarah. "Viajeros y viajeras en El Salvador: Enlazando mundos, estrechando vínculos." In *Transnacionalización de la sociedad centroamericana: Visiones a partir de la migración*, compiled by FLACSO Programa El Salvador, 61-100. San Salvador: FLACSO Programa El Salvador, 2005.
García Canclini, Néstor. *Consumers and Citizens: Globalization and Multicultural Conflicts*. Translated and Introduction by George Yúdice. Minneapolis: University of Minnesota Press, 2001.
Giglioli, Giovanna. "¿Mito o idiosincrasia?: Un análisis crítico de la literatura sobre el carácter nacional." In *Identidades y producciones culturales en América Latina*, compiled by Marta Salvadora, 167–206. San Jose: Editorial de la Universidad de Costa Rica, 1996.
González, Luis Armando. "Implicaciones culturales de la globalización." *Revista de Estudios Centroamericanos (ECA)* 62, no. 703–704 (May–June 2007): 377–396.
González, Marta Leonor. *Casa de fuego*. Managua: 400 Elefantes, 2008.
———. *Huérfana embravecida*. Managua: Ediciones de Bolsillo 400 Elefantes, 1999.
Goodwin, Robin, and Duncan Cramer, eds. *Inappropriate Relationships: The Unconventional, the Disapproved, and the Forbidden*. Mahwah, NJ: Lawrence Erlbaum Associates, 2002.
Haas, Nadine. "Representaciones de la violencia en la literatura centroamericana." German Institute of Global and Area Studies (GIGA) Working Papers, Institute of Latin American Studies, GIGA, Hamburg, Germany, October 2010.
Hagerty, Richard A., ed. *El Salvador: A Country Study*. Federal Research Division. Washington, DC: Sup. of Documents, U.S. G.P.O., 1990.
Hall, Carolyn, and Héctor Pérez Brignoli. *Historical Atlas of Central America*. Cartography by John V. Cotter. Norman: University of Oklahoma Press, 2003.
Hamilton, Nora, and Norma Stoltz Chinchilla. *Seeking Community in a Global City: Guatemalans and Salvadorans in Los Angeles*. Philadelphia: Temple University Press, 2001.
Harlow, Barbara. *After Lives: Legacies of Revolutionary Writing*. London: Verso, 1996.
Harrison, Brady. *Agent of Empire: William Walker and the Imperial Self in American Literature*. Athens: The University of Georgia Press, 2004.
Hernández, Claudia. *De fronteras*. Guatemala City: Editorial Piedra Santa, 2007.
Hernández-Aguirre, Mario. "La nueva poesía salvadoreña: 'La generación comprometida.'" *Revista Cultura*, no. 20 (April-June 1961): 77–99.
Higashi, Sumiko. "*Walker* and *Mississippi Burning*: Postmodernist Versus Illusionist Narrative." In *The Historical Film: History and Memory in Media*, edited by Marcia Landy, 218–231. New Brunswick, NJ: Rutgers University Press, 2001.
Houston, Robert. Foreword to *The War in Nicaragua*, by William Walker. Tucson: University of Arizona Press, 1985.
Huezo Mixco, Miguel. *La perversión de la cultura: Artículos y ensayos*. San Salvador: Editorial Arcoiris, 1999.
Iffland, James. *Ensayos sobre la poesía revolucionaria de Centroamérica*. San Jose: EDUCA, 1994.
Íncer, Jaime. "El Lago de Managua (historia, geografía y geología)." *Revista de la Academia de Geografía e Historia de Nicaragua* (Segunda época) LXV (2007): 232–237.
Iyer, Pico. *The Global Soul: Jet Lag, Shopping Malls and the Search for Home*. New York: Knopf, 2000.
Jackiewicz, Edward L., and Fernando J. Bosco, eds. *Placing Latin America: Contemporary Themes in Human Geography*. Lanham, MD: Rowman & Littlefield, 2008.
Jauregui, Carlos A. *Canibalia: Canibalismo, calibanismo, antropofagia cultural y consumo en América*. Madrid: Iberoamericana-Vervuert, 2008.

Johnson, Lyman. Introduction. In *Death, Dismemberment, and Memory: Body Politics in Latin America*, edited by Lyman Johnson, 1–26. Albuquerque: University of New Mexico Press, 2004.
Johnson, Lyman, ed. *Death, Dismemberment, and Memory: Body Politics in Latin America*. Albuquerque: University of New Mexico Press, 2004.
Kinloch Tijerino, Frances. "Civilización y barbarie: Mitos y símbolos en la formación de la idea nacional." In *Nicaragua en busca de su identidad*, edited by Frances Kinloch Tijerino, 257-276. Managua: Instituto de Historia de Nicaragua, Universidad Centroamericana, 1995.
Kinloch Tijerino, Frances, ed. *Nicaragua en busca de su identidad*. Managua: Instituto de Historia de Nicaragua, Universidad Centroamericana, 1995.
Kip, Jeremiah. Review of *Walker*. *Slant Magazine*, February 13, 2008. http://www.slantmagazine.com/film/review/walker/3389
Küppers, Gaby. "Provisiones creativas de energía para un futuro que, con esfuerzo, debe establecerse fuera del caos reinante." Translated by Marisol Batres, 113–122. In *De fronteras*, by Claudia Hernández. Guatemala City: Piedra Santa, 2007.
Landy, Marcia, ed. *The Historical Film: History and Memory in Media*. New Brunswick, NJ: Rutgers University Press, 2001.
Lara Martínez, Rafael. *La tormenta entre las manos: Ensayos sobre literatura salvadoreña*. San Salvador: Dirección de Publicaciones e Impresos, 2000.
Lindo-Fuentes, Héctor, Erik Ching, and Rafael Lara Martínez. *Remembering a Massacre in El Salvador: The Insurrection of 1932, Roque Dalton, and the Politics of Historical Memory*. Albuquerque: University of New Mexico Press, 2007.
Lungo, Mario, and Roxana Martel, "Ciudadanía social y violencia en las ciudades centroamericanas." In *Estudios culturales centroamericanos en el nuevo milenio*, edited by Marc Zimmerman and Gabriela Baeza Ventura, 265–282. Houston: LACASA Publications, 2007.
Malkki, Liisa. "National Geographic: The Rooting of Peoples and the Territorialization of National Identity among Scholars and Refugees." *Cultural Anthropology* 7, no. 1 (February 1992): 24–44.
MacCannell, Dean. *The Tourist*. New York: Schocken Books, 1976.
Marcus, George, ed. *Rereading Cultural Anthropology*. Durham, NC: Duke University Press, 1992.
Martín-Barbero, Jesús. "Identities: Traditions and New Communities." Translated by Zilkia Janer. *Media, Culture and Society* 24, no. 5 (2002): 621–641.
———. "Mediaciones urbanas y nuevos escenarios de comunicación." In *Las ciudades latinoamericanas en el nuevo [des]orden mundial*, coordinated by Patricio Navia and Marc Zimmerman, 73–84. Mexico City: Siglo XXI Editores, 2004.
———. "Transformations in the Map: Identities and Culture Industries." Translated by Zilkia Janer. *Latin American Perspectives* 27, no. 4 (July 2000): 27–48.
Martín Barbero, Jesús, and Germán Rey. *Los ejercicios del ver: Hegemonía visual y ficción televisa*. Barcelona: Editorial Gedisa, 1999.
McClintock, Cynthia. *Revolutionary Movements in Latin America: El Salvador's FMLN & Peru's Shining Path*. Washington, D.C.: United States Institute of Peace Press, 1998.
McGowan, Marcia Phillips. "Closing the Circle: An Interview with Claribel Alegría." In *Claribel Alegría and Central American Literature: Critical Essays*, edited by Sandra Boschetto-Sandoval and Marcia Phillips McGowan, 228–245. Athens: Ohio University Center for International Studies, 1994.
Menjívar, Cecilia. *Fragmented Ties: Salvadoran Immigrant Networks in America*. Berkeley: University of California Press, 2000.
Miller, William Ian. *The Anatomy of Disgust*. Cambridge, MA: Harvard University Press, 1997.
Monsiváis, Carlos. "De la sociedad tradicional a la sociedad postradicional." In *Imaginarios de nación: Pensar en medio de la tormenta*. Cuadernos de nación, coordinated by Jesús Martín-Barbero, 31–46. Bogota: Ministerio de Cultura, 2001.

Bibliography

Navia, Patricia, and Marc Zimmerman, coords. *Las ciudades latinoamericanas en el nuevo [des]orden mundial*. Mexico City: Siglo XXI Editores, 2004.

Nica/ragüense. Directed by Julia Fleming and Carlos Solís. 2005. DVD.

Nobus, Dany. "Over My Dead Body: On the Histories and Cultures of Necrophilia." In *Inappropriate Relationships: The Unconventional, the Disapproved, and the Forbidden*, edited by Robin Goodwin and Duncan Cramer, 171–189. Mahwah, NJ: Lawrence Erlbaum Associates, 2002.

Nussbaum, Martha. "Secret Sewers of Vice: Disgust, Bodies and the Law." In *The Passions of the Law*, edited by Susan A. Bandes, 19–62. New York: New York University Press, 1999.

Omang, Joanne. "El Salvador and the Topography of Terror." Review of *Salvador*. Washington *Post*. March 13, 1983, final ed., Book World sec.: 1. *Newsbank, Inc.* (accessed 21 March 2011).

Orantes, María Cristina. *Paso leve que el polvo avanza*. San Salvador: Alkimia Libros, 2005.

———. *El grito hacia adentro*. San Salvador: Dirección de Publicaciones e Impresos, 2012.

Oyamburu, Jesús, coord. *Visiones del sector cultural en Centroamérica*. San Jose: Embajada de España, 2000.

Palmer, Steven. "Getting to Know the Unknown Soldier: Official Nationalism in Liberal Costa Rica, 1880–1900." *Journal of Latin American Studies* 25 (1993): 45–72.

Pérez-Brignoli, Héctor. *A Brief History of Central America*. Translated by Richard B. Sawrey A. and Susan Stettri de Sawrey. Berkeley: University of California Press, 1989.

Pezzullo, Phaedra C. *Toxic Tourism: Rhetoric of Pollution, Travel, and Environmental Justice*. Tuscaloosa: The University of Alabama Press, 2007.

Poesía y más, *El libro de los conjuros*. By Carmen González Huguet, Claudia Hérodier, María Cristina Orantes, and Susana Reyes. San Salvador: Poesía y más, 2001.

Pratt, Mary Louise. *Imperial Eyes: Travel Writing and Transculturation*. New York: Routledge, 1992.

Pring-Mill, Robert. Introduction to *Apocalypse and Other Poems*, by Ernesto Cardenal. Edited and selected by Robert Pring-Mill and Donald D. Walsh. Translated by Thomas Merton, Kenneth Rexroth, Mireya Jaimes-Freyre, and the editors. New York: New Directions, 1977.

Ramírez, Sergio. *Hatful of Tigers: Reflections on Art, Culture and Politics*. Translated by D. J. Flakoll. Willamantic, CT: Curbstone Press, 1995.

Reguillo, Rosanna. "Latin America: A Story in Three Movements." *Radical History Review* 89 (Spring 2004): 36–48.

Reyes, Susana. *Historia de los espejos*. San Salvador: Dirección de Publicaciones e Impresos, 2004.

———. *Los solitarios amamos las ciudades*. San Salvador: Índole Editores, 2009.

Robinson, William I. *Latin America and Global Capitalism: A Critical Globalization Perspective*. Baltimore: Johns Hopkins University Press, 2008.

———. *Transnational Conflicts: Central America, Social Change, and Globalization*. London: Verso, 2003.

Rodgers, Dennis. "A Sympton Called Managua." *New Left Review* 49 (Jan.–Feb. 2008): 103–120.

Rodríguez, Ana Patricia. *Dividing the Isthmus: Transnational Histories, Literatures, and Cultures*. Austin: University of Texas Press, 2009.

———. "Wasted Opportunities: Conflictive Peacetime Narratives of Central America." In *The Globalization of U.S.-Latin America Relations: Democracy, Intervention and Human Rights*, edited by Virginia M. Bouvier, 227–247. Westport, CT: Praeger, 2002.

Rodríguez, Ileana. *Women, Guerrillas, and Love: Understanding War in Central America*. Translated by Robert Carr. Minneapolis: University of Minnesota Press, 1996.

Rossi, Annacristina, and Nora Garita, eds. *El lado oscuro: Ensayos sobre la violencia*. San Jose: Uruk Editores, S.A., 2007.

Rugama, Leonel. *La tierra es un satélite de la luna / The Earth is a Satellite of the Moon*. Translated by Sara Miles, Richard Schaaf, and Nancy Weisberg. Willamantic, CT: Curbstone Press, 1985.

———. "La tierra es un satélite de la luna." In *Poetry Like Bread: Poets of the Political Imagination by Curbstone Press*, edited by Martín Espada, exp. ed., 218, 220. Willamantic, CT: Curbstone Press, 2000.

Salvadora, Marta, comp. *Identidades y producciones culturales en América Latina*. San Jose: Editorial de la Universidad de Costa Rica, 1996.

Sánchez Ramírez, Roberto. *Breve historia de la navegación en el Lago Xolotlán*. Managua: PAVSA, 2008.

Sandoval García, Carlos. *Otros amenazantes: Los nicaragüenses y la formación de las identidades nacionales en Costa Rica*. San Jose: Editorial de la Universidad de Costa Rica, 2002.

Sanford, Victoria. *Buried Secrets: Truth and Human Rights in Guatemala*. New York: Palgrave Macmillan, 2003.

Santillán, Diana. "Renegociar las identidades nacionales: Los vínculos transnacionales, los discursos de las diásporas y las comunidades pan étnicas." In *Transnacionalización de la sociedad centroamericana: Visiones a partir de la migración*, compiled by FLACSO Programa El Salvador, 101–138. San Salvador: FLACSO Programa El Salvador, 2005.

Schwartz, Richard A. *Woody, From Antz to Zelig: A Reference Guide to Woody Allen's Creative Work, 1964–1998*. Westport, CT: Greenwood Press, 2000.

Scruggs, T. M. "Socially Conscious Music Forming the Social Conscience: Nicaraguan *Música Testimonial* and the Creation of a Revolutionary Movement." In *From Tejano to Tango: Latin American Popular Music*, edited by Walter Aaron Clark, 41–69. New York: Routledge, 2002.

Shade, Eunice. *Escalera abajo*. Managua: Ediciones MA, 2008.

———. *Espesura del deseo*. Managua: Editorial Zorrillo, 2012.

———. *El texto perdido*. Managua: Amerrisque, 2007.

Sobalvarro, Juan. *Agenda del desempleado*. Managua: 400 Elefantes, 2007.

———. *El dueño de la pelota*. Managua: 400 Elefantes, 2012.

———. *¿Para qué tanto cuento?* Managua: 400 Elefantes, 2000.

———. *Perra vida: Memorias de un recluta del Servicio Militar*. Managua: Lea Grupo Editorial, 2005.

———. *Unánime*. Managua: Nuevo Signo Fondo Editorial INC, 1999.

Sontag, Susan. *On Photography*. New York: Farrar, Strauss and Giroux, 1977.

Spence, Jack. *War and Peace in Central America: Comparing Transitions Toward Democracy and Social Equity in Guatemala, El Salvador, and Nicaragua*. Electronic book. Brookline, MA: Hemisphere Initiatives, November 2004. www.hemisphereinitiatives.org.

Stewart, Kathleen. "Nostalgia—a Polemic." In *Rereading Cultural Anthropology*, edited by George E. Marcus, 252–266. Durham, NC: Duke University Press, 1992.

Stewart, Susan. *On Longing: Narratives of the Miniature, the Gigantic, the Souvenir, the Collection*. Durham, NC: Duke University Press, 1993.

Strehle, Susan. *Transnational Women's Fiction: Unsettling Home and Homeland*. Basingstoke, UK: Palgrave Macmillan, 2008.

Tenorio, María, and Miguel Huezo Mixco. *Resultados consolidados del diálogo nacional por la cultura*. San Salvador: CONCULTURA, 2007.

Tilley, Virginia Q. *Seeing Indians: A Study of Race, Nation, and Power in El Salvador*. Albuquerque: University of New Mexico Press, 2005.

Trigo, Abril. *Memorias migrantes: Testimonios y ensayos sobre la diáspora uruguaya*. Rosario, Argentina: B. Viterbo Editora / Montevideo: Ediciones Trilce, 2003.

Turcios, Roberto. "*Made in* Posguerra." *Visiones del sector cultural en Centroamérica*, coordinated by Jesús Oyamburu, 223–231. San Jose: Embajada de España, 2000.

Urry, John. *The Tourist Gaze: Leisure and Travel in Contemporary Societies*. London: Sage Publications, 1990.

Vallejo, César. *Trilce*. 2nd ed. Buenos Aires: Editorial Losada, 1967.

Viroli, Maurizio. *For Love of Country: An Essay on Nationalism and Patriotism*. Oxford: Clarendon Press / New York: Oxford University Press, 1995.
Walker. Directed by Alex Cox. Written by Rudy Wurlitzer. 1987. Booklet by Graham Fuller, Linda Sandoval, and Rudy Wurlitzer. The Criterion Collection. Universal Studios, 2007. DVD.
Walker, William. *The War in Nicaragua*. Foreword by Robert Houston. Tucson: University of Arizona Press, 1985.
Weintraub, Max. "Robert Capa." In *Encyclopedia of Twentieth-Century Photography*, edited by Lynne Warren, vol. 1, 236–240. New York: Routledge, 2006.
When We Were Kings. Directed by Leon Gast. Gramercy Pictures, 1996. DVD.
Whisnant, David E. *Rascally Signs in Sacred Places: The Politics of Culture in Nicaragua*. Chapel Hill: University of North Carolina Press, 1995.
Wicks, Robert. *Modern French Philosophy: From Existentialism to Postmodernism*. Oxford: One World Publications, 2003.
Williams, Tamara. "Reading Ernesto Cardenal Reading Ezra Pound: Radical Inclusiveness, Epic Reconstitution, and Textual Praxis." *Chasqui: Revista de literatura latinoamericana* 21, no. 2 (November 1992): 43–52.
Winand, Anna. "Capa, Robert." In *Contemporary Photographers*, 2nd ed., edited by Colin Naylor, 153–155. Chicago: St. James Press, 1988.
Woodward, Jr., Ralph Lee. *Central America: A Nation Divided*. 2nd ed. New York: Oxford University Press, 1985.
Wurlitzer, Rudy. *Walker*. New York: Harper & Row, Publishers, 1987.
Yaeger, Patricia. "Introduction: Narrating Space." In *The Geography of Identity*, edited by Patricia Yaeger, 1–38. Ann Arbor: University of Michigan Press, 1996.
Yaeger, Patricia, ed. *The Geography of Identity*. Ann Arbor: University of Michigan Press, 1996.
Zavala, Magda. "Ciudades secundarias en la aldea global: Desde San José de Costa Rica." In *Las ciudades latinoamericanas en el nuevo [des]orden mundial*, coords. Patricio Nava and Marc Zimmerman, 311–317. Mexico City: Siglo XXI, 2004.
Zimmerman, Marc. "Introduction: Ernesto Cardenal After the Revolution." In *Flights of Victory / Vuelos de Victoria*, by Ernesto Cardenal. Edited and translated by Marc Zimmerman with Ellen Banberger and collaboration of Mirta Urróz et al., ix–xxxii. Willamantic, CT: Curbstone Press, 1988.
Zimmerman, Marc, and Gabriela Baeza Ventura, eds. *Estudios culturales centroamericanos en el nuevo milenio*. Houston: LACASA Publications, 2007.

Index

Acahualinca, 33, 34–35, 37, 41, 77
affection, 6–8, 13, 16, 50, 52, 68, 70, 82, 94, 109, 136, 145, 147–149
Agenda del desempleado (Sobalvarro), 78–79, 94, 98n35
"Agenda del desempleado" (Sobalvarro), 79–80
Ahmed, Sara, 86
Alegría, Claribel, 12, 52–56, 57, 59, 70, 73n27, 73n29, 73n30, 74n40
Ali, Muhammed (Cassius Clay), 2, 138n23; "Rumble in the Jungle", 124–126, 127
Allen, Woody, 1–3, 4, 5, 17n3, 142, 144
"El alma nacional" (Dalton), 29–30, 31
Anderson, Benedict, 7, 18n20, 29, 30, 31, 138n30
Anillo de silencio (Alegría), 53
Apollo Space Program, 33, 34, 35, 46n50
Araya Jiménez, María del Carmen, 84–85, 98n33, 98n40
Arias, Arturo, 12–13, 148
Arias Sánchez, President Óscar, 102–103, 117, 118n5
armed conflicts, Central America, 2, 10, 25, 36, 38, 41, 49, 51, 52, 91, 103, 148
Asfalto: un road poem (Chaves), 104, 111, 114–116, 124
attachments. *See* affection
Augé, Marc, 74n46, 116

Babb, Florence, 97n21, 130, 138n34
Bananas (Allen), 1–2, 3, 17n6, 137n19, 141, 144, 146
"El barco del poeta" (González), 55
Barthes, Roland, 133
Belize, 9
Belli, Gioconda, 12, 26, 43n15, 52, 109, 119n21, 139n40

belonging, 6–7, 8–9, 10, 13, 14, 16, 16–17, 26, 42, 49, 50, 54, 55, 57, 65, 67, 68, 70, 82, 90, 95, 109, 111, 113–114, 114, 117, 121, 122, 123, 126, 129, 134, 136, 145, 147–149
Beverley, John, 12, 36
Billig, Michael, 8
Booth, John, 9
boxing, 2, 124–128
Boym, Svetlana, 52, 58
A Brief History of Central America (Pérez-Brignoli), 9, 19n32, 43n4, 46n55, 150n4

Calhoun, Craig, 7
Calle 13, 7
Canjura, Salvador, 16, 111–113, 114, 116–117, 121, 123, 128, 147
cannibalism, 40–41, 42, 48n74, 143
Canto nacional (Cardenal), 36
Cappa, Robert, 133
Cardenal, Ernesto, 12, 15, 23–25, 26, 32, 35–38, 41, 43n4, 46n56, 47n63, 47n69, 52, 58, 77, 97n26, 130, 139n40, 147; *exteriorismo*, 36, 47n61, 77, 96n8
Carías Andino, Tiburcio, 24
La casa de fuego (González), 55–56
"La ceiba" (Alegría), 53–54, 55–56, 57, 59
Cenizas de Izalco (Alegía), 52, 73n29
Central America: A Nation Divided (Woodward), 9, 150n4
Central American-ness, 50, 103, 145–147
Chambers, Erve, 116
Chan Marshall (Chaves), 104–105, 111, 118n18, 119n37, 120n43
Chaves, Luis, 13, 16, 99n60, 101–102, 104–111, 113–117, 118n18, 119n21, 119n37, 120n43, 121, 123, 124–129,

163

164 *Index*

134–136, 137n20, 137n22, 147
Classen, Constance, 91
Clay (Ali)-Liston match, 2
"Coda" (Chaves), 128
consumers, 3, 8, 50, 84, 129, 130, 133
Cortés, Carlos, 103–104
"Cosas raras de Pili, Mili y Lili" (Shade, E.), 133
"Las cosas sencillas" (Reyes), 61
Cosell, Howard, 1, 2, 17n1, 17n3, 137n19
Costa Rica, 9, 10, 12, 13, 19n39, 20n49, 20n53, 25, 26, 50, 97n19, 98n33; CAFTA-DR, 12, 20n50–20n51, 21n54, 117, 118n7; exceptionalism, 12, 25–26, 102–104, 107, 118n9; exiles, 11, 25–26; peace, 11, 26, 42n3, 109; tourism, 106, 107, 114, 115, 118n19–119n20
Cox, Alex, 141–146, 149n2, 150n10, 150n5
"Cuando ellas beben" (González), 55
The Cultural Politics of Emotion (Ahmed), 86

Dalton, Roque, 1, 5, 12, 15, 18n11, 26–33, 36, 37–38, 40, 41, 44n23, 45n30, 52–53, 54, 58, 68, 75n62, 147; death, 18n11, 41, 45n30, 48n79; *committed generation*, 28
Darío, Rubén, 75n58, 79–80
Dawes, Greg, 33, 36, 46n49, 47n63
Day, Graham, 8–9
"Del desempleado H#896440" (Sobalvarro), 77, 81–83, 84
Deleuze, Gilles, 123, 128
Delville, Michel, 79
development. *See* modernization
"Día de la Patria" (Dalton), 31–32
Didion, Joan, 3–5, 17, 17n5, 119n31
disgust, 70, 85–86, 87, 88, 90, 91, 94, 104, 123
displacement, 16, 51–52, 74n46, 116, 123, 124, 136, 146–147
Dividing the Isthmus: Central American Transnational Histories, Literatures, and Cultures (Rodríguez, A. P.), 13
"Dragones de cartón" (Reyes), 62–63, 85

Dunphy, Don, 17n1

El Salvador, 9–10, 12, 19n38, 148; Civil War, 3, 10–11, 25, 29, 39, 40, 44n16, 48n78, 50, 52, 55, 62, 63, 64; Farabundo Martí National Liberation Front (FMLN), 10, 11, 20n53; fear of violence, 3, 5, 17, 17n6, 62
elsewhere, 16, 109, 110, 111, 113, 117, 124
En Cuba (Cardenal), 36
"¿En qué libro guardé tus cabellos Elsa Kuriaki?" (Escudos), 68–70
Escudos, Jacinta, 68–70, 75n65
"Esperando el bus de regreso" (Chaves), 114
El estrecho dudoso (Cardenal), 36
everyday-ness, 16

flagging. *See* nationalism
Foreman, George. *See* Ali, Muhammad
The Future of Nostalgia (Boym), 52

García Márquez, Gabriel, 3, 73n30
Giglioli, Giovanna, 103–104, 119n23
globality, 16, 129, 133, 136, 149
globalization, 9, 13, 14, 15–16, 18n25, 52, 65, 84, 94, 98n28, 104, 107, 109, 110, 117, 128–129, 136, 146–147; CAFTA-DR, 6, 10, 12, 20n40, 20n50, 21n54, 52, 103, 117; cultural identities, 130, 133; immigration, 50, 52; neoliberalism, 12, 14, 50–51, 58, 74n42
glocal, 127, 147
González, Marta Leonor, 16, 49, 55–58, 65–68, 70, 74n39, 85, 92–95, 99n59, 99n60, 111
"El gran despecho" (Dalton), 31
Guatemala, 9–10, 148
Guattari, Felix, 123, 128
Guevara, Che, 26, 130, 138n34

Hall, Carolyn, 9, 19n38–19n39, 43n4
Harris, Ed, 141, 142, 145–146
"Hechos de un buen ciudadano (parte 1)" (Hernández), 38–39, 41, 42, 88
"Hechos de un buen ciudadano (parte 2)" (Hernández), 38–40, 41, 42, 88

"Heredades" (Chaves), 101, 104, 110
here-ness, 5, 9, 51, 70, 111, 146
Hernández-Aguirre, Mario, 28
Hernández, Claudia, 15, 38–41, 42, 48n74, 88–92, 93, 94–95, 104, 112; cannibalism, 40–41
Hernández Martínez, Maximiliano, 24
heroes, 6, 24, 26, 30, 32–33, 35–36, 37, 38, 41, 44n16, 47n69, 77–78, 111, 130, 147; martyrdom, 15, 26, 36, 37, 39, 41, 77
Historia de los espejos (Reyes), 58, 74n41
Historias Polaroid (Chaves), 99n60, 104, 124, 134, 137n20, 137n22
Las historias prohibidas del Pulgarcito (Dalton), 18n15, 28–29, 68
A Historical Atlas of Central America (Hall and Pérez-Brignoli), 9, 19n38–19n39, 43n4
home, 4, 5–7, 10, 12, 13–15, 26, 29, 32, 42, 49, 50–51, 55, 57, 65, 70, 104, 107, 109, 110, 111, 113, 114, 126, 127, 148, 149; cross (traverse), 49, 55, 56, 57, 58, 65, 70, 95, 104–105, 108, 114, 116, 117, 147; disconnection, 67, 68, 90, 106, 108, 109, 114, 134; global, 129; hum (thrum), 8–9, 17; local, 65, 70, 128, 130, 133, 134; markers, 54, 55, 58, 61, 70; virtual, 16, 117, 123, 128, 128–129, 133, 134, 135, 136, 147
homeland, 4, 5–8, 9, 10, 12–14, 16, 25, 26, 35, 41, 58, 59, 61, 66, 67, 68, 70, 82–83, 104, 133–134, 141, 143, 145, 147, 149; as body, 29, 30, 31, 62; as mother, 30; as *patria*, 5–6, 7, 8, 10, 25, 26, 29, 31, 32, 38, 40, 41–42, 54, 82; as place to tour, 16, 49, 81, 110, 111–112, 114, 115–116, 117; as revolutionary goal, 11, 15, 30, 32–33, 68; belonging, 13, 26, 123; citizenship, 8, 14, 23–41, 29, 30, 31–32, 38, 39, 50, 91–92, 107; decay, 70, 82, 87, 94–95, 104, 147; fragmentation, 38, 51, 52, 58, 70, 88, 94, 104, 110; markers, 9, 67, 111, 116, 146; patriotism, 9, 26, 32, 40, 50, 77, 82, 87, 145, 147; post-conflict, 15–17, 26, 63, 65, 91, 94; rootlessness, 117, 133, 147–149; roots, 7, 51, 121, 123, 136, 147–149; scars, 58, 61–62, 65, 70, 146, 147; solidarity, 37, 38, 41, 48n74, 50–51, 92, 94, 107, 109, 119n23, 147
Homenaje a los indios americanos (Cardenal), 36
homesickness, 15–16, 50, 53, 54, 55–56, 71
Honduras, 9, 10, 19n38, 141, 148
"Hora 0" (Cardenal), 23–25, 36, 43n4
Huérfana embravecida (González), 55, 92
Huezo Paredes, Elisa, 64

immigration, 6, 9, 12, 15, 18n16, 25, 49–51, 52, 61, 70, 72n10, 103–104, 149
intellectuals, 10, 26, 129–131, 133, 134, 136, 138n34
Instituto Nacional de Cine Nicaragüense (INCINE), 143, 150n5
"Invierno no" (González), 92–94
Iyer, Pico, 123

Johnson, Lyman, 30, 35, 37

Lake Managua (Xolotlán), 77, 81, 82–83, 88, 91, 96n1, 107
Lara Martínez, Rafael, 29, 45n32
"Salir de 'El Caracas'" (Chaves), 101–102, 104
Liberation Theology, 33, 35
Literature and Politics in the Central American Revolutions (Beverley and Zimmerman), 12
"Lluvia de trópico" (Hernández), 88–92
longing, 15, 52–53, 54, 58, 63, 68, 69, 149
López Guerra, Tino, 77
Luisa en el país de la realidad (Alegría), 53, 54, 73n29–73n30
Lungo, Mario, 88

MacCannell, Dean, 110–111
"Macrocosmos a 90 kilómetros por hora" (Chaves), 114, 123
Malkki, Liisa, 121
"Managua 6:30" (Cardenal), 25
"La máquina de hacer niebla" (Chaves), 121, 134–136
Martel, Roxana, 88

Martín-Barbero, Jesús, 48n74, 123–124, 127–128, 135–136
mass media, 1, 2, 3–4, 8, 9, 12, 16, 62, 84, 117, 123, 124, 125–126, 128, 134, 135, 136, 143–144, 145; television, 1, 17n3, 33, 123, 124, 125–128
Medellín Conference, 33
"Mi ciudad" (Alegría), 54–55
Miguel Mármol:Los sucesos de 1932 (Dalton), 28
misplacement (dislocation), 111, 112–113, 117, 136, 147, 148
modernization, 3, 12, 15, 34, 51, 52, 59–60, 61, 63, 78, 84–85, 97n27–98n28, 102–103, 107, 123, 129, 142, 143, 144, 145, 147
Monsiváis, Carlos, 8, 18n25–19n27, 48n74
monuments, metaphorical, 15, 34, 37, 50, 54, 61, 70
"Moteles, lluvia, trenes, etc." (Chaves), 114

nationalism, 7–8, 45n38, 148; flagging, 8, 31, 67; symbols, 6, 8, 26, 31–32. *See also* homeland; solidarity
Nicaragua, 9, 10, 12, 52, 84, 143; Contra War, 10, 25, 77, 141, 151n17; National Guard, 16, 24, 32, 36, 37, 43n4, 46n55, 96n3; Sandinista National Liberation Front (FSLN), 10, 12, 20n53, 25, 26, 32, 35, 41, 43n12, 43n5, 46n55, 77, 94, 97n27, 130, 131, 139n40, 141, 144, 149n2, 150n5, 151n22; Somoza regime, 10, 16, 24, 26, 32, 35, 37, 42n2, 43n4, 43n5, 46n55, 47n69, 96n3, 151n15. *See also* Lake Managua (Xolotlán); Walker, William
NICA/ragüense (Fleming and Solís), 103
"Nócaut" (Chaves), 137n22
"No hay" (Sobalvarro) 83–84
"No hay poesía" (Sobalvarro), 70–71, 79, 80
nomads, 123, 128, 135, 147
nostalgia, 15, 26, 42, 49, 51–52, 55, 59, 69–70, 82–83, 123, 147, 149; as market, 49, 50, 72n10; as "reflective", 58, 68, 70; souvenirs, 15, 55, 68, 69–70, 108, 109. *See also* longing
nowhere, 113, 127
"El nuevo mundo" (Orantes), 63–65
"El olor de la lástima" (Sobalvarro), 84, 85–88

Omang, Joanne, 3
"Oráculo sobre Managua" (Cardenal), 26, 35–37, 46n56, 47n63, 77
Orantes, Alfonso, 64
Orantes, María Cristina, 63–65
"Los otros" (Chaves), 111
"Los otros" (González), 49, 55, 65–68

El país bajo mi piel, 26
Panama, 9, 12, 19n32
"Los parques" (Reyes), 59–61
"Paseo en la casa de los padres" (González), 56–58, 65
Pérez-Brignoli, Héctor, 9, 19n32, 19n38–19n39, 43n4, 46n55, 150n4
Perra vida: memoria de un recluta del Servicio Militar (Sobalvarro), 77
Pezzullo, Phaedra C., 110
place, 5, 17, 61, 110, 112–113, 116–117, 127, 128, 149; empty, 51, 70, 88, 145; locatability, 113, 147; non-places, 74n46, 116; placeless-ness, 9, 31; place-ness, 111
Pobrecito poeta que era yo (Dalton), 28
"Poema de amor" (Dalton), 29, 68, 75n61–75n62
poetry, 13, 58, 125, 146, 147; as postcards, 13, 59, 60, 61, 107, 117; as snapshots, 93, 108, 110, 111, 114, 119n37, 136, 137n22; intersections with prose, 13, 15, 38, 40, 41, 69, 78, 88, 91, 112, 134, 147; political poetry, 12, 13, 28, 38, 52, 58, 77, 91, 94. *See also* Cardenal, Ernesto
Pope Paul VI, 33
poverty, Central America: indigents, 40, 84–88, 92, 93, 94; necrosis, 85, 86, 87–88, 91, 93
progress. *See* modernization
prose: intersections with poetry, 13, 15, 38, 40, 41, 69, 78, 88, 91, 112, 134, 147; photography, use of, 129, 130,

Index

132–133, 136. *See also* Cardenal, Ernesto
"Protesta pacífica" (Sobalvarro), 94

"Quietud sin paz" (Sobalvarro), 88

Rascally Signs in Sacred Places: The Politics of Culture in Nicaragua (Whisnant), 26
Reifenstahl, Leni, 131
Reguillo, Rosanna, 65, 104
revolutionaries, 1–2, 5, 10, 11, 15, 18n11, 25, 32–33, 37, 41, 43n4, 72n23, 130, 147
Rey, Germán, 127–128
Reyes, Susana, 13, 15, 55, 58–63, 64, 66, 70, 74n48, 85, 111, 147
"Ringside" (Chaves), 124–128
Robinson, William I., 18n16, 18n25, 58, 84
Rodríguez, Ana Patricia, 12–13, 25, 97n20
Rugama, Leonel, 15, 26, 32–41, 58, 77, 147

Salvador (Didion), 3–5, 11, 17, 17n5, 119n31, 141, 146
Sandino, César Augusto, 24, 43n4, 97n26
La santidad de la revolución (Cardenal), 36
Satana, Tura, 135
Shade, Eunice, 129–134, 136
Shade, Raoul, 130
Sobalvarro, Juan, 13, 16, 70–71, 77–88, 90–92, 93, 94–95, 104, 122–123, 129, 136
"Sobreviviente del silencio" (Reyes), 62
Sobrevivo (Alegría), 52
somewhere, 113, 117, 127
Somoza García, Anastasio. *See* Nicaragua
Somoza Debayle, Anastasio. *See* Nicaragua
Sontag, Susan, 132, 133
souvenirs. *See* nostalgia
stench, 77, 82, 84, 85, 87, 88, 90–92, 93, 94–95
Stewart, Kathleen, 51

Stewart, Susan, 69–70
Strummer, Joe, 142

Taberna y otros lugares (Dalton), 5, 28, 29, 31
Taking Their Word: Literature and the Signs of Central America (Arias), 13
"Tal vez 1600-Asas" (Shade, E.), 129–134
"¿Tan rápido llegó el 2002?" (Chaves), 105–111
"Temores" (Dalton), 1, 5, 17, 147
El texto perdido (Shade, E.), 133
there-ness, 4, 5, 51, 70, 146
Thompson, Andrew, 8–9
A Thousand Plateaus: Capitalism and Schizophrenia (Deleuze and Guattari), 128
"La tierra es un satélite de la luna" (Rugama), 26, 32–35, 37, 77
tourism, 82, 102, 106, 110–111, 116, 119n20, 130, 147
tourists, 2, 16, 82, 85, 95, 105, 106, 107–108, 109, 110–111, 114–115, 116–117, 119n29, 121, 123, 147
Toxic Tourism: Rhetoric of Pollution, Travel, and Environmental Justice, 110
"Tres tripping tigres", 115
Turcios, Roberto, 63

Ubico Castañeda, Jorge, 24
Unánime (Sobalvarro), 79, 137n9
Understanding Central America: Global Forces, Rebellion, and Change (Booth, et. al.), 9, 11
"Untitled" (Sobalvarro), 117, 122
Urry, John, 109

"El vaho" (Canjura), 16, 111–113, 114, 116, 123, 147
Vallejo, César, 122, 123
Viroli, Maurizio, 82

Walker (Cox), 141–146
Walker, William: historical figure, 141, 145
Whisnant, David E, 26, 146
Woodward, Ralph Lee, Jr, 9, 150n4
Wurlitzer, Rudy, 141

Yaeger, Patricia, 110
yearning. *See* longing; nostalgia

Zimmerman, Marc, 12, 35–36

About the Author

Yvette Aparicio is associate professor of Spanish and Latin American Studies at Grinnell College. She specializes in contemporary Central American literature and culture. She has published articles and presented papers at national and international conferences on Central and Latin American poetry and narrative.